Warriors, Warlords and Saints

THE ANGLO-SAXON KINGDOM OF MERCIA

John Hunt

Published by West Midlands History Limited
Minerva Mill Innovation Centre, Alcester, Warwickshire, UK.
© 2016 West Midlands History Limited and John Hunt.
© All images are copyright as credited.

ISBN: 0000000

Front cover: Detail of a replica of the Valsgärde 6 helmet from Sweden, dated to approximately 660-710AD.
One of a group of helmets from Sweden sharing decorative features with the Sutton Hoo helmet and the Staffordshire Hoard.
Image by Lindsay Kerr, helm by Grzegorz Kulig.
Back cover: The Lichfield Angel. Used by permission of the Chapter of Lichfield Cathedral.

Caric Press Limited, Merthyr Tydfil, Wales.

Contents

2   Preface

4   Acknowledgements

5   Chapter One   Introduction: Mercia and its People
14   1.1   Place-Names and the Anglo-Saxons

16   Chapter Two   The Origins of Mercia

28   Chapter Three   The Kingdom Builders
38   3.1   Warriors and Warbands
40   3.2   Mercia and the Staffordshire Hoard

42   Chapter Four   Kings, Monks and Saints: the Making of a Christian Kingdom
52   4.1   Mercia and the Saints: Presenting Relics

54   Chapter Five   The Age of Æthelbald and Offa
66   5.1   Coins, Kings and Trade

68   Chapter Six   Court, Church and Country: Mercian Kingship at Work
78   6.1   Offa's Dyke

80   Chapter Seven   Merchants, Markets and the Carolingians
90   7.1   Lundenwic: the Mercian Entrepôt

92   Chapter Eight   Art and Society in Anglo-Saxon Mercia
103   8.1   The Lichfield Gospels (Gospels of Saint Chad)

104   Chapter Nine   The Vineyard of the Lord Devoured by Foxes: a Changing World
114   9.1   Repton and the Vikings

116   Chapter Ten   Mercia, Wessex and the Vikings
126   10.1 *The Anglo-Saxon Chronicle*, Mercian Identity and the *Mercian Register*

128   Chapter Eleven   People and Settlement in Anglo-Saxon Mercia
139   11.1   Manorial Sites – New Directions

141   Chapter Twelve   Magnates, Earls and Earldom: a Tale of Two Families

152   End Notes

153   Glossary

156   Further Reading

160   Index

Preface

What is it about the Anglo-Saxons? In England's rich and varied history, the Anglo-Saxon period remains among the most popular, and seemingly has a particular ability to fire the imagination. In the autumn of 2014, when the Birmingham Museum and Art Gallery opened its Staffordshire Hoard gallery, it attracted some five-thousand visitors a day, recalling those amazing scenes following its discovery in 2009 when people from around the world waited patiently in queues that snaked around the building to see something as 'magnetic' and enticing as Grendel's treasure.

Not only Anglo-Saxon, the hoard generating this enthusiasm is also Mercian; certainly in the sense that it was found in the heartlands of the Anglo-Saxon kingdom of Mercia, and buried sometime around 650 – 670, it takes us straight to one of the most dynamic periods in the rise of the kingdom, the Mercian kings Penda and Wulfhere and their challenge to the power of Northumbria. The hoard reflects the riches that were to be found within seventh-century Mercia, and tells us something about the wealth that kings and the warrior aristocracy might accrue, and where it came from.

Mercia was one of the great Anglo-Saxon kingdoms, a 'great power' in its day, and also one of the most fascinating. Despite the familiarity of names like Offa and Offa's Dyke, and perhaps less so Æthelflæd, 'Lady of the Mercians', or Lady Godiva, linked with Coventry, and the Lady Wulfrun with Wolverhampton, the history of this kingdom has been partially obscured by legend and limited sources. However, in recent years this situation has improved as important discoveries have given scholars the opportunity to re-evaluate Mercia's story. The modern generation of historians and archaeologists have looked again at Mercia, its rise to 'supremacy' and then its decline, and in this they have been stimulated by a series of important archaeological discoveries, among them the mass burials at Repton; Anglo-Saxon settlement sites like Catholme, Yarnton and Raunds; the excavation of cemetery sites like Wasperton; the discovery in Lichfield in 2005 – 2006 of a building unique in fifth- and sixth-century Britain, and in 2003, in the Cathedral, the excavation of what may have been the timber-lined crypt associated with Saint Chad's shrine, and an eighth-century carving now known as the 'Lichfield Angel'; and most recently, excavations that have changed our understanding of Stafford in the eighth and ninth centuries. We are now able to ask questions and explore ideas of a kind that were often denied to past generations, and our understanding of the past matures and is re-shaped.

We can now see more clearly than ever the kingdom of Mercia as a major power with stable foundations and strong traditions, powerful and sophisticated with a rich material culture, and by all measures well able to rival the standing and achievements of the Anglo-Saxon kingdoms of Northumbria, Wessex and East Anglia.

It is not entirely frivolous to suggest that we are now better able to 'feel', 'touch' and 'walk' the history of Mercia than ever before. Recent research has claimed that over a twelve-month period, as many as seventy per-cent of English adults visit heritage sites, and that for many of them the 'sense of place' that this gives them and their communities is of particular importance. Anglo-Saxon England is a part of that heritage, and more specifically, for many, the kingdom of the Mercians has played its part in fashioning people and landscape.

The past and its representation remains as fascinating for people today as it was for the Anglo-Saxons themselves. Indeed, Anglo-Saxon attitudes to history might be described as very modern, or more correctly perhaps, modern views can be very Anglo-Saxon. This book offers the reader not so much a definitive history and narrative of the Mercian kingdom as 'snapshots' of stages in its fascinating story, looking at what we can currently suggest about the emergence, decline and transformation of Mercia; its kings and how they governed; the factors and influences that shaped Mercian affairs, life and landscape; the place and role of the church; and the cultural and material achievements, in many respects the 'legacy', that might be associated with this great kingdom. ✠

Acknowledgements

A book such as this bears the influence of so many people that it is difficult to adequately reflect the indebtedness and gratitude of the author. Perhaps most obviously, but all too often overlooked, it is based on the work of several generations of historians and archaeologists, many of them 'trail blazers' in their specialisms; all historical works inevitably reflect and benefit from the scholarship of others and this book is no different. While some key works have been noted in the 'End Notes' and the 'Further Reading' sections, it has not been possible in a book of this kind to fully reference the wide range of studies upon which it has drawn, or to always explore the alternative interpretations that other historians and archaeologists might offer. However, without their work this book could not have been written.

As for many of us who have the privilege and joy of teaching history and archaeology, I too am indebted to my many students who over the years have both challenged and probed what they were taught, and who have ensured that the effective communication and understanding of the subject is always to the fore.

More specifically, thanks are due to Andy Boucher and Jake Streatfeild-James of 'Headland Archaeology' for information kindly provided on a site that was under excavation at the time of writing.

Thanks are due to the publisher, Mike Gibbs, who shared with the author the view that the time was right to revisit Mercia with a book aimed at a wide readership, and who then encouraged its writing. The publication and editorial team at History West Midlands have guided the project throughout and the book would not have been what it is without their professionalism and intuition. My thanks therefore go to Averil Maskew, Dr Janet Sullivan and especially to Dr Jenni Butterworth for their guidance and support in this process. Finally, I would like to record my particular gratitude to a colleague and friend, Dr Steven Bassett, who kindly read and meticulously commented on earlier drafts of the book. I know that Steven would debate some of what I have written, but he has graciously accommodated this in his advice, saved the author from several pitfalls, and improved the book in the process. Naturally, any errors are the fault of the author alone.

John Hunt

Opposite page: Carved in walrus ivory, this head of a 'T' (tau) cross shows the risen Christ trampling underfoot a lion and a dragon, symbols of sin and death (early eleventh-century, Alcester, Warwickshire).

1

Mercia and its People

INTRODUCTION

Anglo-Saxon England, Mercia and the Modern World

The Anglo-Saxon period lasted longer than the years that have elapsed between the reign of Queen Elizabeth I and ourselves. Unsurprisingly over a period of more than five-hundred years, there was change in all aspects of life. Religious belief and practices; social, political and economic organisation; intellectual and cultural life, and artistic expression and achievement; the physical environment in which people lived, from the ordering of the landscape to the buildings that they constructed and inhabited; and the structure of society itself, were all aspects of Anglo-Saxon life that were transformed in that period between the arrival of the Anglo-Saxons at the end of Roman Britain in the fifth century, and the Norman Conquest in the eleventh century.

Our understanding of these changes is influenced by the interplay of many different sources of information; alongside the range of written accounts and records that have survived, from chronicles and poems to charters and law codes, we have a constantly growing corpus of archaeological material, from the study of artefacts and material culture, to the results of survey and excavation; landscape and place-names, together with buildings that have survived for a thousand years or more all contribute to our interpretation of Anglo-Saxon life and society.

Our fascination with the Anglo-Saxon world perhaps lies partly in its apparent familiarity, but also its distance from modern times. This is not the contradiction that it might at first appear to be. While we are surrounded by the modern use of names like Mercia, these take us back to at least the seventh century, which regional tourism has not been slow to appreciate. This familiarity is also rooted in the fact that there is still much in our daily life and culture that looks back to our Anglo-Saxon forebears, most ubiquitously in the language that we speak and the words and phrases that we use.

This is nowhere truer than in the place-names that we see and use every day. They might be British, Anglo-Saxon or Danish in origin and made up of elements that reveal the names of the individuals or groups who lived there, their ethnicity, and something of the landscape that they inhabited. The dating and mapping of place-names is central to tracing phases of Anglo-Saxon settlement across the country and in assessing the survival of earlier populations; in the western midlands, for example, the Anglo-Saxon settlers found an established British, Welsh-speaking, population whose continued presence was clearly illustrated through settlement names as well as through the names of landscape features and rivers. These were often names that the newcomers themselves gave, reflecting a time when there was some degree of bilingualism among the people of Mercia.

Our very identity, even in a country that has been enriched by centuries of immigration and cultural assimilation, returns to a 'baseline' that we call 'English', one that is constantly developing as has always been the case, but which is derived from the name 'Angle', one of the Germanic peoples who invaded and settled post-Roman Britain. They were

"…there is still much in our daily life and culture that looks back to our Anglo-Saxon forebears, most ubiquitously in the language that we speak and the words and phrases that we use."

The incursion of Angles and Saxons into Britain; river valleys provided the key routes inland.

the principal Germanic folk within what was to become Mercia, moving down the Trent valley and inland from East Anglia into the midlands of England. Our literary heritage looks back to the Anglo-Saxon past, with riddles and poetry, and engrossing epics such as *Beowulf* and the *Battle of Maldon*, aspects of which have been represented to us by modern narrators and film-makers, and indirectly through the engaging imagination of authors such as J.R.R.Tolkien. Stories of heroic deeds, warrior societies, demons and dark forces are as popular now as they were to the Anglo-Saxons.

A love of landscape and of 'place' is also a trait that many people today share with early medieval society. The Anglo-Saxon landscape had 'spiritual' qualities

about it, and Anglo-Saxon life was rooted in it. For most people, the landscape was the backdrop to their daily lives, and their use and intimate knowledge of it, and how it developed in their custody, can still be reconstructed and to some extent seen. Field systems, settlement patterns, many of our towns, monuments like Offa's Dyke, and the administrative boundaries that we still use, like shires, dioceses and parishes, all have their origins in the Anglo-Saxon past.

The religious and cultural heritage of England that resides in its Christian identity also has its principal origin in the Anglo-Saxon period, when with the Church came writing and the book. Upon the piety and faith of early medieval communities was built a stunning artistic and cultural achievement, still familiar from intricate metalworking, stone carving in churches and on cross-shafts, manuscript painting, and the construction of churches built in the Mercian countryside more than a thousand years ago, all of which we can still see and visit.

An Overview

The Mercian kingdom sprang ultimately from the incursion into midland England of Germanic settlers from around the late-fifth and sixth centuries AD following the collapse in the early fifth century of Britain's position as a province within the Roman Empire, moving into the region from eastern England and via the Trent valley. In the case of the Mercian settlement these incomers were primarily Angles, a folk whose traditional homelands lay in northern Germany, around Schleswig-Holstein, but as recent genetic studies of the United Kingdom population have now underscored, these migrants mixed and intermarried with the British population to a significant extent, giving rise to an Anglo-British population whose Germanic ancestry, based on genome-wide or common genetic variation data, most likely fell within the range of ten to forty per cent. In short, as the archaeology of the region has long suggested, and as discussed in the next chapter,

Cross-shaft fragment depicting a great Mercian beast entangled in interlace, symbolising sin (early ninth-century, St Oswald's, Gloucester).

Mercia was a fusion of people and influences in which the part played by the indigenous population should not be understated. Indeed, it is all the more remarkable that in such a demographic mix it was an essentially English culture and 'Englishness' that emerged as dominant, albeit one that was influenced through the processes of assimilation. That it was not a simple matter of imposition is a point now well made by the genome data. By the early seventh century an early Mercian kingdom was emerging as a distinctive political territory, whose heartlands lay around the upper reaches of the Trent valley, where the principal sites would come to include Tamworth, a major royal estate; Lichfield, the bishopric associated with the cult of Saint Chad; and Repton, a monastery which was endowed by the Mercian royal family and became the mausoleum for several of its kin.

During the course of the seventh century Mercia would develop as the dominant kingdom of midland England, whose kings asserted its independence from its powerful neighbours and extended their authority into adjacent territories, at each point creating a larger and more complex kingdom. The Mercian

Defining Mercia: the topography of the midland kingdom.

kingdom expanded westwards to dominate what is now Herefordshire, Shropshire and Cheshire, while to the south the Thames valley represented a natural early frontier zone. Similarly, Mercian expansion reached eastwards across those lands that are now considered as forming the East Midlands: Nottinghamshire, Leicestershire, Northamptonshire and Bedfordshire, towards the Fens and the powerful East Anglian kingdom. To the north, Mercian expansion looked towards the River Humber, another natural boundary, and one which with its associated marshlands and the difficult terrain of the time, formed a major landscape feature and barrier across north-eastern England. It was quite natural for contemporaries to think of England as comprising those people, whatever their other associations, who lived to the north of the Humber, the Northumbrians, and those to the south, the Southumbrians. Thus, Mercian growth would push across Derbyshire and into Lincolnshire. Collectively, these changes would totally reshape the political geography and the 'landscape of power' not only of the midland region, but also of Anglo-Saxon England.

In addition to defining the Mercian kingdom and its core midland territories, the seventh century would see the Mercian kings seeking at various points to dominate their Northumbrian, West Saxon and East Anglian counterparts, while also extending their influence and then authority into south-eastern

"The Anglo-Saxon landscape had 'spiritual' qualities about it, and Anglo-Saxon life was rooted in it. For most people, the landscape was the backdrop to their daily lives, and their use and intimate knowledge of it, and how it developed in their custody, can still be reconstructed and to some extent seen."

England. These were developments that took place over the century as a whole, and ran on into the eighth century; what had been won had to be defended, consolidated and in many cases, formally and structurally incorporated into a reshaped Mercian kingdom. The growth and increasing complexity of the Mercian realm, and of Mercian society, made ever more demands of Mercian kingship and governance, and consequently over this period the infrastructure of power, and of the kingdom itself, developed. The reign of King Offa (757-796) has commonly been regarded as the highpoint in Mercian fortunes, when Mercian power seemed unassailable, the kingdom was culturally sophisticated and accomplished, and some have seen in Offa a 'template' for the possibility of a unified English kingdom well before this was pursued by the West Saxon kings. However, as the following chapters will show, Offa stood on the shoulders of his predecessor, King Æthelbald, and was followed by the very competent king, Coenwulf.

However, from the second quarter of the ninth century there was a turn in Mercian fortunes, as a resurgent West Saxon kingdom ushered in a new complexion for the relationship between Wessex and Mercia, one which arguably was more equable and based on a partnership of shared interests. Yet this was also a period of dynastic tension within Mercia, and Mercian power, while still considerable, was not what it had been, and certainly failed to withstand the arrival of the Vikings in the second half of the century. These developments set in motion the demise of the Mercian kingdom, although the detail of these events may be hotly debated as from this time onwards our perception of these years, and of the century which follows, is heavily influenced by the West Saxon perspective as preserved in their great literary creation, the Anglo-Saxon Chronicle. While there is scope to debate the extent to which Mercia and its rulers were dependent upon Wessex, and particularly whether or not they remained independent of the West Saxon kings Alfred and his son, Edward the Elder, it was the case that by 925 the latter had extended his realm to include Mercia, and while a Mercian sense of identity would persist, the kingdom did not reassert itself.

In the chapters that follow, the rise of the Mercian kingdom, its various transformations and their implications, and then the events surrounding its disappearance as an independent Anglo-Saxon kingdom, will be charted. But this will not be where the story of Mercia is brought to a close. Having been partitioned by Scandinavian settlement in the wake of the Viking conquests, the recovery and assimilation of the east Mercian area under Danish occupation was a prominent task, while the changed political geography that Edward the Elder created also called for internal reorganisation within the former Mercian kingdom, not least the establishment in the tenth century of shires across Mercia. But

Mercia did not lose its distinctiveness and in the later chapters of this book the role played by the great aristocratic families of the region in the tenth and eleventh centuries will be examined and followed through to the Norman Conquest of 1066. On the eve of the Conquest the earls of Mercia were among the most powerful and influential of the great noble houses of late Anglo-Saxon England, and the geography of their authority, while more circumscribed and less extensive than that of the former Mercian kingdom, nonetheless had some resonance with it. However, in 1071 the last earl of Mercia was killed and the earldom of Mercia ceased to exist.

Themes in Mercian History and Society

What kind of society will be found within the pages of this book? What can we see of Mercia and its people behind the narrative of these events in English history? Dynamic but violent; sometimes brutish and discriminatory; a warrior elite; religious and personally pious; wealthy and entrepreneurial; accomplished, creative, scholarly, cultured and artistic are all words, among many others, that might be used of Anglo-Saxon Mercian society at some point and they are reflected in this book. It was an increasingly complex and sophisticated society, and one which inevitably witnessed considerable change during the five-hundred years or so that this account covers.

There is much in this book about kings and their deeds, as these represented the scaffolding around which kingdoms were built or fell, and could be critical in setting the tone and opportunity for the growth and prosperity of a society. They also preoccupied many of the early written sources to which we turn to help build our picture of Mercia, as it was through such events of course that a kingdom was made 'visible' in these sources, rather differently

from the generally less-partisan archaeological evidence. But kingship, and the institutions associated with it, was something that grew in Mercia, as in the other Anglo-Saxon kingdoms, over time, partly in response to the growth of the kingdom and its increasing complexity, but also as the influence of the Roman Church was increasingly felt, with its favoured models of kingship and an increased awareness of other Christian kings; and also as the role of lordship in society itself developed and prompted interactions between the interests of aristocratic kindreds and the kingdom. So in this book not only kings and their deeds, but also the nature of kingship and how it worked in Mercia are essential themes.

But Mercian history is not, and should not be, just about kings. This book is also about the wider Mercian experience, that of Mercian society more broadly. At the heart of Anglo-Saxon society was the family and kin, the basic social and economic unit. Although there was not a caste system within Anglo-Saxon society, it was one that was familiar with hierarchy from an early point; however, this is generally difficult to detect in the archaeology of the earlier period, suggesting that the separation between lords and the rest of society was something that grew gradually. Even so, this separation became emphatic with a strengthening of seigneurial rights and controls, and by the ninth century in Mercia, men and their families may well be tied to their lords and the estates on which they lived. These characteristics in Mercian society came to be reflected in the landscape, the nature of rural settlements, and the rise of manorial society.

It was a society that was essentially rural and agrarian in nature, that lived by growing crops and raising stock. Here too, however, there was change over time, as the nature of rural settlement changed,

11

AOGOBTU MEHSEM LEO FEBUIDUS IGHE P UAIT.
AGUSTUS HABEI DIES · XXX · LUHA · XXIX:

Harvest time (c.1025-1050) reflects a society that was essentially rural and agrarian, that lived by growing crops and raising stock.

how it looked, and its relationship with the countryside. A discussion of these changes from the late-seventh and eighth centuries is a critical part of how the Mercian countryside and its people responded to changing circumstances, as estates were reorganised, settlement forms changed, and there was an intensification of agricultural production. But mercantile opportunity was always present and by the eighth century Mercia had a sophisticated coinage and operated a coin economy. It was part of an international trading network through the great town and trading port of London, behind which lay a network of manufacturing and trading places across the kingdom, and in which the salt production of Droitwich was perhaps of particular importance.

It was a wealthy society, certainly among the elite, an observation immediately borne out by the character of the Staffordshire Hoard found in 2009, a find that takes us straight to the great poem *Beowulf*, the Anglo-Saxon love of gold, and the sense of a heroic warrior society. This wealth, rooted ultimately in trade and the land, but supplemented by the plunder of warfare, was evident in the development of the Mercian state, but it is often most obvious to the modern viewer when displayed in the exquisite products of the artists and craftsmen of the day, such as the metalworkers producing sword fittings, strap-ends, pins, rings, brooches and the like. Here too change followed, not only in the emergence of new and distinctive artistic styles, but also in the move away from the use of gold to silver, often silver-gilt.

Inescapable in this book is the important and central role played in Mercian affairs and culture by the church, particularly by the Roman Church. Despite the problematic relationships that Mercian kings often faced with the church and churchmen, it was a part of the very fabric and lifeblood of early medieval societies, as the roots and branches of secular and ecclesiastical power were inextricably intertwined. The power of the saints, in life and death, was very real and frequently experienced, as we see with the influence of men like Boniface and Guthlac. Members of Mercian royal kindreds joined their ranks, and were often enthusiastic patrons of monasteries, although their enthusiasm was often as much pragmatic as it was pious. Not only were the church and its personnel an integral strand of kingdom, society, economy and the exercise of power, they also provided the bedrock upon which much of Anglo-Saxon England's cultural and artistic achievements were built, some of which were among the most accomplished in the history of medieval European art.

Mercia can claim a rich cultural history. This artistic record may be seen from the earliest stages of the Mercian settlement in the furnishings of pagan Anglo-Saxon cemeteries, although this material has been surpassed by the incredible artistry of items in the Staffordshire Hoard. However, the most substantial and coherent corpus of material that reflects Mercia's cultural milieu, and its accomplishments, are those related to the Christian faith and church, all the more fascinating not only for their artistic accomplishments, but also for the additional

Courtesy John Hunt

Delicately carved panel depicting an apostle (late eighth-century, Castor) .

dimensions that some bring through their symbolism, sense of identity and deployment on behalf of both secular and ecclesiastical authority. Mercian art indeed offers an eloquent insight into the society that produced it and used it.

In what follows this writer has attempted to interweave written sources, art, archaeology and landscape in revealing the story of Mercia, but in an introductory book of this kind there is inevitably a greater emphasis upon what presents a coherent narrative of this midlands kingdom. But the reader will quickly recognise that archaeology is no 'handmaiden' to the documents in understanding Mercia; not only is its testimony integral to the whole story, this book takes up themes such as the pagan cemeteries, the changing landscape and the development of burhs which would be irretrievable without it.

The reader should also be aware that while it is the writer's intention to offer a clear, coherent and interesting account of Mercian history, there is much left unsaid. Many themes might be discussed at greater length, and the debates among historians considered more fully, but this book will have done its job if the reader finds what follows interesting and engaging, has a better understanding of Mercia, and is perhaps prompted to pursue some aspects of the Mercian story in other ways. ✠

Place-Names and the Anglo-Saxons

Hanbury in Worcestershire: the place-name captures the essence of its location, a fortified hill top.

A place-name can often be the starting-point for investigating the history of a settlement, capable of saying something about who the place was associated with, their ethnicity, the date at which the place-name was coined, and its landscape setting. The mixture of languages found in English place-names reveals the successive incursions of peoples into England, and may be used to chart their progress and contribute to our understanding of their relationship with the populations already present and the landscape that they occupied.

On the eve of the Anglo-Saxon settlement, the principal language across the former Roman province was 'Celtic', often referred to as 'British' or 'Welsh', of which modern Cornish and Welsh are descendants. Latin was also used in Britain, both inherited from Roman Britain and from the seventh century used by the Anglo-Saxons for administrative purposes, both languages being represented in the place-name stock of Mercia. Anglo-Saxon, or 'Old English', eventually displaced the prevalence of 'Welsh', although the latter was still represented in the names of many settlements and topographical features – for instance, river-names, such as the Avon and the Lugg – the density of whose survival progressively increases moving westwards. The majority of the place-names still used in England, and in Mercia, were coined in the Old English language, but the Danish invasions of the ninth and tenth centuries introduced a further linguistic strand, namely Old Norse, brought by Norwegian and

Danish settlers. Their place-names are particularly evident in eastern England north of the Thames, and in the north-west, and while rare in western Mercia they are prominent in eastern Mercia. The Norman Conquest, in turn, promoted the influence of Norman French on place-names and language, but it did not come to dominate in the way that English did many centuries earlier.

Place-names are made up of 'elements', like Hanbury in Worcestershire, comprised of *han* and *bury*. A name may be of one language, or a combination of two, as when Danish settlers commonly combined English and Scandinavian elements. Hanbury is entirely Old English, but before its meaning can be determined, the earliest form of the word must be established; in this case, the forms *Heanburh* and *Heanbyrg* were used in eighth- and ninth-century charters respectively. For many places, the form found in Domesday Book is often the earliest recoverable spelling, which at Hanbury appeared as *Hambyrie*. The place-name

means 'high burg', 'high fort' or high fortified place, incorporating a reference to the presence here of an Iron Age hill-fort, a hill top that by the seventh century became the centre of a royal estate and the site of a minster church.

Place-names fall into two main groups. They may be topographical in nature, descriptive of their location but without reference to a habitation, perhaps using features such as a hill or a ford, like Clifford in Herefordshire where the first element, Old English *clif*, describes an escarpment, and the second, a fording place, as at Oxford and Hereford. The commonest topographical element in English place-names is *leah* (ley), representative of 'wood pasture'. The second main group of place-names are habitative, containing a word for a settlement, such as *ham*, *tun*, *cot* and so on. As in the case of Hanbury, the combination of elements generally has specific meanings or may utilise personal names; the place-name Bretforton describes a *tun* at Bretford where the ford was

provided with planks while Wolverley refers to the *leah* of Wulfweard's people. Names might change. Wolverhampton was originally *hēatūn* or *heantune*, meaning 'high tun', but the place-name acquired a prefix after the estate was given to the lady Wulfrun in the tenth century.

It was once assumed that habitative names were earlier than the topographical type but it is now recognised that topographical names occur among both the very earliest and the latest place-name forms (see End Notes, EN1), while between these extremes there was a long period in which the prevailing fashion was for names in *tun* and *leah*.

Place-names studied against the backdrop of terrain and soil quality have contributed immensely to our understanding of the Anglo-Saxon settlement, and, particularly together with charters and their estate boundaries, to our knowledge of what the Anglo-Saxon landscape looked like, and how it developed. ✠

"A place-name can often be the starting-point for investigating the history of a settlement, capable of saying something about who the place was associated with, their ethnicity, the date at which the place-name was coined, and its landscape setting."

2

The Origins of Mercia

The description of the Anglo-Saxon period as a 'Dark Age' is now largely discarded but if ever there was a time that seemingly justified it, surely it was the passage of events that surrounded the transition from Roman Britain to Anglo-Saxon England. It was this obscure period which saw the incursion and settlement of the Anglo-Saxons and the foundation of their kingdoms, including Mercia.

The means by which these momentous changes took place remain a matter for debate among historians and archaeologists. Some favour a 'migration thesis' and variants of it, essentially arguing for the large-scale immigration into Britain of Anglo-Saxon settlers who displaced British communities. Others place more emphasis on smaller numbers and invasion rather than migration, often looking particularly at the impact that elites might have on local society. There is much scope for variation in thinking between these two basic concepts. Inevitably, central to these critical events and how we understand them was the nature of the relationship between the British population and the new arrivals. These key questions are at the heart of modern research and debate and there is now an increasing realisation that many of these are best explored through localised studies as the experience of communities, even of neighbouring communities, might differ.

The End of Roman Britain

Traditionally, English history begins this period of transition with a 'break from Rome' when in 410 the Emperor Honorius instructed the '*civitates*' or cities of Britain to look to their own defence. As is so often the case, such precise dates and events can mislead.

Even before the opening of the fifth century, the Roman province had been denuded of its forces, largely to support the imperial pretensions of Britain's governors. By the early fifth century it is likely that the bulk of the Roman forces that were prepared to leave had already gone, to be followed by the remaining provincial administrators, both civilian and military. The closing phases of the western Roman Empire were marked by the disruption and uncertainty that followed in the wake of a movement of peoples, often referred to as the 'barbarian migrations', which broke through the frontiers of the empire. The hard-pressed Empire now found that for the time being the defence of Britain was beyond its capacity and therefore advised the towns and cities to look to their own resources. That these instructions were directed to the communities themselves suggests that any centralised provincial administration was already either absent or ineffective and that authority in Britain was fragmenting.

What followed has been much debated and has given rise to semi-mythical accounts that have shaped how our early history has been imagined. Some have argued for the persistence into the fifth century of a provincial authority, variously associated with Vortigern, Ambrosius Aurelianus and even Arthur. More probable however was a political fragmentation that led to the creation of a patchwork of territories and a sense of identity that was largely underpinned by the '*territoria*' or districts associated with late-Roman towns; and with pre-Roman tribal lands, the importance of which had never been lost. The territory of the Hwicce, for instance, whose distinctiveness and autonomy seem to have lasted well into the eighth century, was formed out of the lands in the lower Severn and Avon valleys occupied by the Late Iron Age tribe, the Dobunni. The diocese of

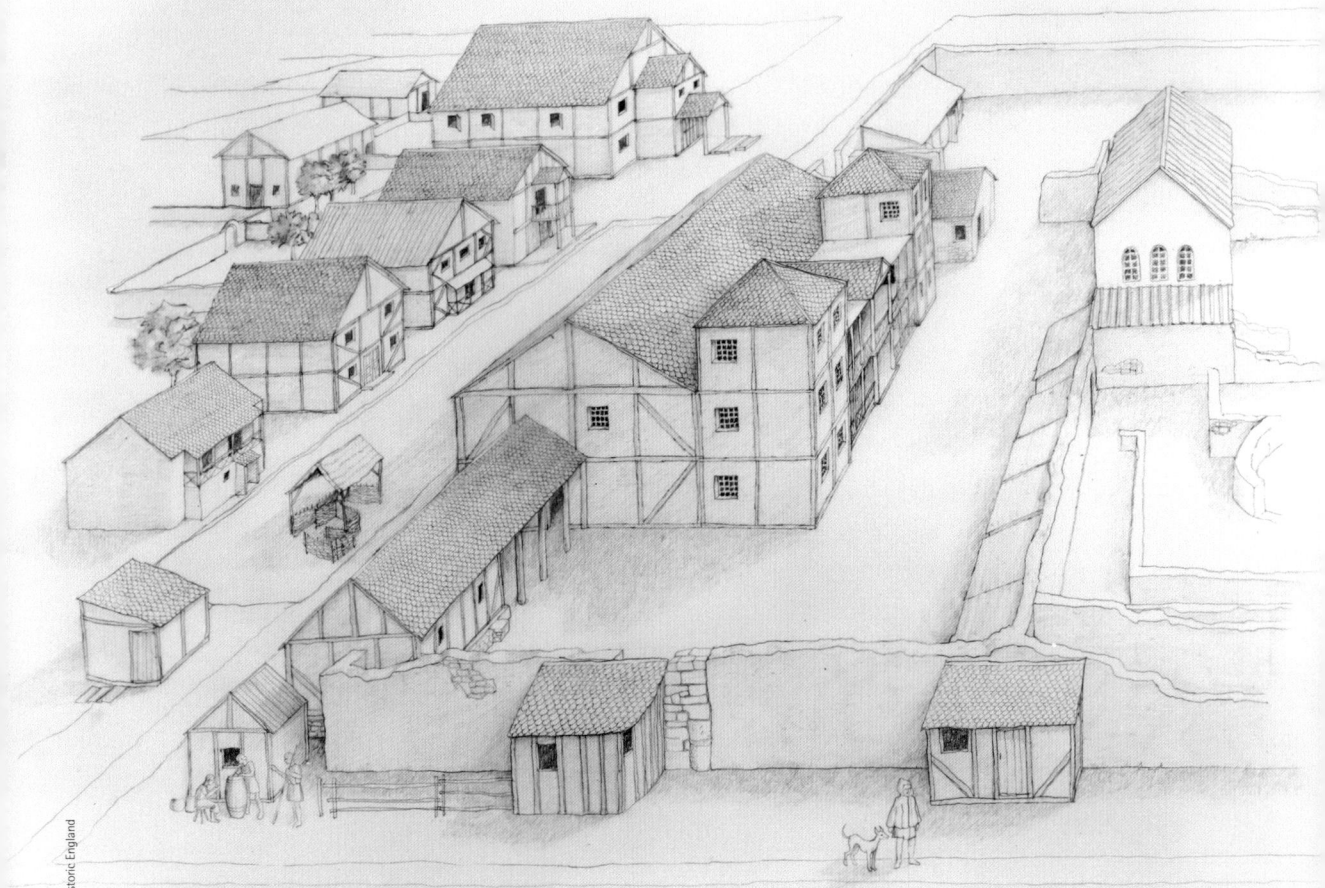

Timber-framed buildings show the continuation of organised life in Wroxeter in the late sixth century.

Worcester, established in the late seventh century, largely reflects the extent of this British region.

Change was inevitable following the departure of Roman authority in the province, but it should not be presumed that this necessarily precipitated chaos. Sustainable political and economic systems were present and excavations like those at Wroxeter in Shropshire have demonstrated the potential for organised life to continue in some Roman towns throughout the fifth and sixth centuries. However, important as towns were in Roman Britain, they should not overshadow the importance and resilience of rural communities and their economy in maintaining a coherent post-Roman society. However fragmented political life might have become, farming continued largely uninterrupted, albeit on a reduced scale now that the demands of Empire had been removed. Across midland England many Romano-British settlements and territories of varying size and importance may have fallen into such a pattern.

Although we are cautious of our documentary sources for this early period, the most probable post-Roman political geography was characterised by a multiplicity of 'kings', such as the three that the Anglo-Saxon Chronicle associated with Gloucester,

Cirencester and Bath in the late sixth century. This patchwork was made all the more 'colourful' by the arrival of the Anglo-Saxons, who may not have been seen as a necessarily threatening presence by all British communities, particularly those that were ambitious and aggressive, or those that feared their neighbours. Similar later episodes of 'acceptable intrusion' may be associated, for instance, with the Vikings in Ireland and elsewhere.

The *'Adventus Saxonum'*

Traditionally the arrival of the Anglo-Saxons, the *'Adventus Saxonum'*, has been represented as a single event, in which a British leader, Vortigern, invited into Britain a group of Anglo-Saxons to serve as mercenaries, led by Hengest and Horsa. This whole episode has the character of an 'origin myth' that, in the absence of alternative explanations, has simply passed into the fabric of English history through the polemical writings of Gildas in the sixth century and the attempts of Bede, writing his *History of the English Church and People (Historia ecclesiastica gentis Anglorum)* in the eighth century, to make sense of the sources available to him. Hengest and Horsa are now dismissed as semi-mythical characters, and more fundamentally, the certainty once attached to the archaeology of Germanic 'federate' or mercenary settlement, has faded. Nonetheless, while the details are most probably irrecoverable, the notion of Anglo-Saxon groups being initially drawn into Britain to

reinforce depleted military power remains plausible and consistent with late-Roman practice elsewhere in the Empire, from which Britain was technically estranged rather than divorced. The Anglo-Saxons were coming into Britain throughout the fifth century, perhaps in a mixture of controlled and uncontrolled settlement, for the most part unrecorded, the newcomers gradually gaining the initiative in many areas.

The Settlement of Central England

The very name 'Mercia' is derived from the Old English word '*Mierce*' which means 'boundary folk' and would seem to suggest that the Mercians were in some way at the fringes of the main Anglo-Saxon settlements, most probably recalling the western boundaries of English penetration during the pagan period, the area around the upper reaches of the Trent river system forming the Mercian heartland.

In the absence of surviving traditions for Mercian origins, some historians have looked cautiously to English post-Conquest chroniclers for help, such as the twelfth-century *Historia Anglorum* of Henry of Huntingdon and the thirteenth-century *Flores Historiarum* of Roger of Wendover and Matthew Paris. What emerges from these accounts is the suggestion of multiple settlements in Mercia that sprang from East Anglia, or from a migration that also affected East Anglia during the sixth century, impressions that are fairly consistent with

"Change was inevitable following the departure of Roman authority in the province, but it should not be presumed that this necessarily precipitated chaos. Sustainable political and economic systems were present and excavations like those at Wroxeter in Shropshire have demonstrated the potential for organised life to continue in some Roman towns throughout the fifth and sixth centuries."

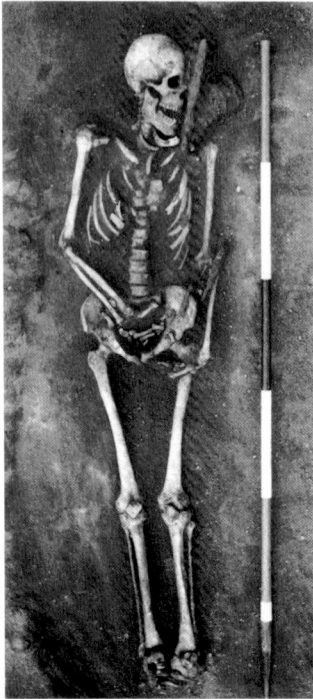

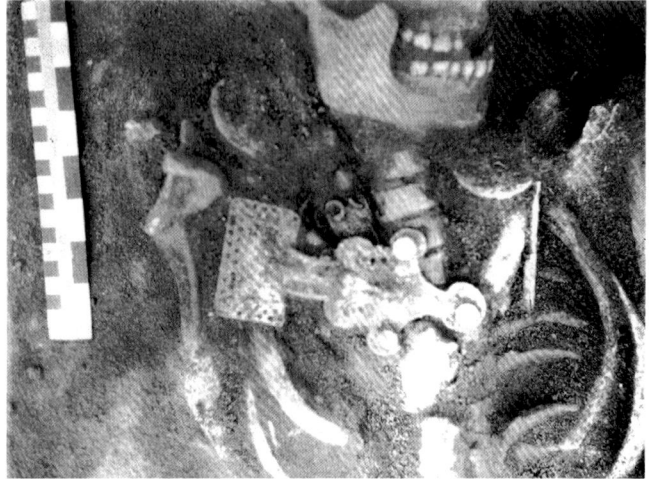

Inhumation burials from Worcestershire cemetery Beckford A, Grave 8 and brooches and beads from Grave 11, dating from the late-fifth to the mid-sixth century.

the archaeological evidence. Excavations at some cemetery sites in the Avon valley have confirmed from brooch types early links with East Anglia, although changes in favour of Wessex and the upper Thames valley followed during the sixth century.

Our understanding of the Anglo-Saxon incursion into the English midlands has traditionally been shaped by the testimony of archaeology, particularly from cemeteries. The deposition of Anglo-Saxon grave goods is presumed to reflect Germanic settlement from the fifth century, with the earlier material tending to be found towards the east; the area around the confluence of the rivers Soar and Wreake in Leicestershire saw settlement by the mid-fifth century, and the Avon valley of Warwickshire by the late-fifth century, but most west midlands cemeteries are generally later, dating to the sixth and early seventh centuries. However, to directly equate all grave furnishings with Germanic migrant

settlement risks considerable overstatement; while some certainly represented the arrival of incoming Anglo-Saxon settlers, it is possible that much usage may have been the result of spreading cultural influence rather than actual settlement, the British population choosing to adopt these new fashions, perhaps as they aligned themselves to the reshaped polities in the region.

Mercian Cemeteries

In the Mercian heartlands, pagan Anglo-Saxon burials tend to be concentrated in the south-eastern part of the region, that is, south-eastern Warwickshire and south Worcestershire. There are also Anglo-Saxon burials in the Trent valley, particularly in south-east Staffordshire, while in the Peak District there is a distinctive group of barrow burials. The largest of these cemeteries occur in Warwickshire, at Bidford-on-Avon and Wasperton, each with more than two-hundred burials, followed

Anglo-Saxon cemeteries and some post-Roman folk groups in western Mercia: invasion or integration?

by Alveston Manor and Baginton in Warwickshire, and Beckford A and B in Worcestershire, each with more than a hundred burials.

Anglo-Saxon burial practices embraced urned-cremation and inhumation, in some instances reusing the burial places of earlier people, as in the Peak District; at Wasperton; and in Beckford Cemetery A where the excavators suggested that the siting of both the Beckford cemeteries was influenced by nearby prehistoric barrows visible at the time of the burials, attracting the Anglo-Saxons to the site.

In the early Anglo-Saxon period most of our artefactual evidence comes from cemeteries, so we are effectively studying early English society through their dead and what they took with them to the grave. Until the impact of Christianity on the arts, grave goods represent the most significant corpus of artistic material in England, generally in the form of brooches and metal fittings, although ceramic 'decoration' also survives. It is also through the study of skeletal material that questions such as stature, diet, health and disease in early populations

The Baginton hanging bowl is a high-status object that displays late Celtic art in its use of running scroll and red enamel.

can be approached, while isotope analysis yields pointers to place of childhood home.

With some thirty-six recorded burial sites, Warwickshire has the largest number of Anglo-Saxon cemeteries and burials in the Mercian region, many clustered around the Avon valley. Among the early discoveries was Longbridge Park near Warwick, a cemetery of late-sixth or early-seventh century date found in 1875. It comprised both male and female inhumations, the former including several warrior graves with accompanying weapons, including some with swords, at least one in a wooden scabbard with probable traces of ornamentation. Other finds included wooden and bronze buckets with a glass vessel and textile fragment; and a variety of brooch types, including saucer brooches, one pair with a circular garnet setting and zoomorphic decoration (stylised animal forms), and a particularly large cruciform brooch

from a wealthy female grave, in which there was also a silver bracelet. Rare for Warwickshire was the discovery of two bracteates (repoussé single-sided disc pendants), one of gold, derived ultimately from Roman coins or medallions.

Of similar date, the cemetery at Baginton, comprising male and female inhumation and cremation burials, with some indications of clustering between the two rites, was first discovered between 1933 and 1934. An outstanding item from the site is a fine hanging bowl, of Celtic origins. The four escutcheons of openwork design are cast in one piece with hooks, using running scroll and, originally, red enamel. Other fragmentary bronze bowls, used for cremations, were also found.

There were between sixty-seven and seventy-five cremation urns, decorated and undecorated, one carrying the rune '*gyfu*' or 'gift'. Bone analysis

"Our understanding of the Anglo-Saxon incursion into the English midlands has traditionally been shaped by the testimony of archaeology, particularly from cemeteries".

has shown the inclusion of animal bone as well as human bone, and site finds are said to have included a horse's bit and fragments of horse trappings. On the basis of surviving shield bosses and spearheads there were a minimum of twenty-seven inhumations. The extensive range of metalwork included forty-eight brooches, among them cruciform, annular, penannular, disc and saucer brooches, and one of the square-headed brooches appears to have been produced from the same mould as a brooch found at Bidford.

It was the remains of a bucket carrying triangular and zoomorphic bronze ornament which suggested in 1860 the presence of a cemetery at Bidford-on-Avon. This mixed cemetery of inhumations and cremations, some with weapons, bronze bowls and personal jewellery, has also been excavated, finds including saucer brooches decorated with running spirals, stars and zoomorphic ornament; zoomorphic-decorated applied brooches; and disc brooches carrying ring and dot ornament.

Although Anglo-Saxon burials were regularly furnished, often with very distinctive artefacts, we have come to recognise that deductions drawn from the study of grave goods must be approached with increased caution; for instance, grave goods cannot be regarded as a reliable indicator of ethnicity, or even of the date of a burial, particularly as distinguished or cherished objects may have passed through several generations of a family before their deposition. Furthermore, the possibility of acculturation, where one culturally distinct community might adopt the cultural traits and therefore the cultural appearance of another, has already been highlighted. Do we observe the expansion of a people, or of their culture?

So what does recent research on the Mercian cemeteries suggest about the nature of the Anglo-Saxon settlement in midland England? In particular, what can be recovered regarding the relationship between the Romano-British population and the newcomers? Those who think in terms of invasion and the intrusion of Anglo-Saxon authority into the region may look to the excavations at Alveston Manor in Warwickshire, a cemetery dating from the early sixth to the early seventh centuries, where the high proportion of male burials with weapons has been taken to indicate the presence of a warrior and social elite. However, at the Stretton-on-Fosse and Wasperton cemeteries, excavations have revealed both late-Roman and Anglo-Saxon burials, offering an opportunity to look more closely at questions of relationship between the two communities.

At Stretton-on-Fosse, a late Roman cemetery continued in use into the fifth and perhaps early sixth centuries; but from around 480, Anglo-Saxons were also

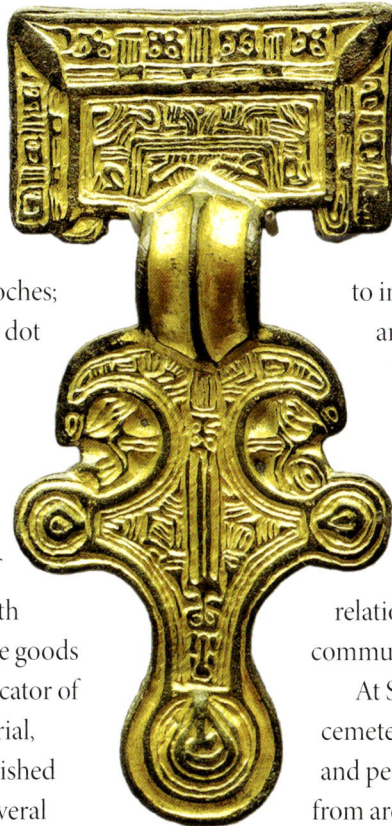

By kind permission of Warwickshire Museum

Gilded copper-alloy great square-headed brooch, decorated with stylised zoomorphic design, from a woman's burial (inhumation 65) at Wasperton, Warwickshire.

present at Stretton, burying their dead on an immediately adjacent site. Traits in the skeletal material have suggested a lengthy period of coexistence followed by a merger of the two communities through intermarriage. The presence of British features in the Anglo-Saxon burials, among them British textiles, graves lined with charcoal, slabbed cist graves and the practice of decapitation, all lend further weight to this proposed scenario.

The same broad thesis emerges from Wasperton, although the dating differs. This cemetery was established in the fourth century around a series of family plots for a cosmopolitan society of diverse origins. In the late fifth century, however, a group of cremations were introduced into the cemetery, within their own fenced space, and later some inhumations, reflecting the arrival of incomers. By the sixth century the whole cemetery was characterised by burials furnished in the Anglo-Saxon manner; as at Stretton, the initial cultural linkages with East Anglia gave way by the mid-sixth century to those with the Thames valley, supporting the notion that this change was widespread across the lower part of the Avon valley. Wasperton does not reflect the presence of a warrior elite in the way envisaged elsewhere and there is no reason to conjecture that Wasperton reflects a community dominated or 'taken over' by Germanic-speaking incomers. The Anglo-Saxon incomers were here simply one element on a wider canvas; integration and acculturation seem to be the defining mechanisms, rather than assertive

intrusion and a 'power grab' by a ruling elite.

In the case of Beckford, dating from the late fifth to the mid-sixth centuries, yet another scenario may be suggested, with an isolated and inbred community on the very edge of Anglo-Saxon settlement, having relatively little contact with other Anglo-Saxon communities although they did have some connections that ran into the upper Thames valley and towards Wessex.

Looking north to south-east Staffordshire, there is an important and relatively rare site for Mercia, the early medieval rural settlement at Catholme, situated on the gravels of the Trent valley adjacent to the Anglo-Saxon cemetery at Wychnor. The settlement was in use for around three-hundred years from about the early seventh century; if the earliest phases pre-date c.600 then it is probable that the population of Catholme at that time was largely, if not entirely, British. However, change came to this community. The buildings being erected here were consistent with Germanic practice on the Continent. Therefore, Anglo-Saxon architectural forms were in use, while the adjacent cemetery had burials that incorporated Germanic features, although both incursion and acculturation might have played their part here. Although it cannot be demonstrated with certainty, it seems probable that the British population remained at least a constituency within the Catholme community, and it has been suggested that this was predominantly the case but that they had become archaeologically invisible by adopting Anglo-Saxon cultural trappings, as argued for many cemeteries.

"…the overwhelming impression is that early Mercia is best imagined as an Anglo-British society, albeit one where Germanic cultural traits were increasingly assimilated until in time the customs associated with Christianity became the overriding influence."

The scenario therefore is a diverse one and what might be suggested at one place was not necessarily replicated in all of its details elsewhere. The picture that emerges is one of Germanic incomers into central England from the late fifth century, spreading gradually further westwards during the sixth and early seventh centuries. However, the nature of their relationship with the British in these early phases seemingly varied from place to place, and was itself subject to change over successive generations. The excavated remains of some communities suggest integration while elsewhere the Anglo-Saxon settlers seem to have remained apart from the British, at least in so far as their cemeteries can reflect this. In some cases the Germanic settlers appear to have represented an elite, presumably with local authority, but this was not necessarily always the case. Precise details generally elude us. For example, it has been suggested that a block of land across the headwaters of the River Alne in Warwickshire, associated with the Stoppingas folk, may represent land settled by an early Anglo-Saxon community, but nothing is revealed of the context in which this came about.

Nonetheless, the overwhelming impression is that early Mercia is best imagined as an Anglo-British society, albeit one where Germanic cultural traits were increasingly assimilated until in time the customs associated with Christianity became the overriding influence. It is clearly difficult to sustain any notion of central England being swamped by a mass Germanic migration; evidence for a sizeable and continuing British population is readily available, not least in place-name evidence and later Anglo-Saxon law codes, while recent DNA studies in England have reversed former arguments favouring the dominance of those with Germanic or Scandinavian blood, noting that there has

actually been little genetic change since the Neolithic period. Some archaeologists still eschew 'multi-cultural models' for the period, suspecting that such concepts simply would not reflect the mentalité of the times, arguing instead for thorough Anglicisation and an intolerance of diversity. However, in the early phases that laid the foundations of Anglo-Saxon Mercia, it is difficult to avoid the conclusion that such accommodations were being reached in some communities. While some Germanic settlers do appear to have established local domination, military, social and presumably political, not all sixth-century Anglo-Saxon cemeteries represented regional elites.

Such dynamics underpin the origins of Mercia but leave unresolved the precise means by which it was shaped to emerge as a part of the geo-political makeup of early medieval England, in the wake of which the midland region would acquire a cultural uniformity that it had not previously experienced.

The *Tribal Hidage*

An impression of the geo-political landscape that formed in central England, arguably reflecting the folk of early Mercia, may be gained from a document known as the *Tribal Hidage* (Harleian MS 3271 fol 6v), one of the most tantalising of documents associated with the history of Mercia. Essentially a list, and without parallel in its time in England, it survives as a copy in an eleventh-century manuscript, but most probably dates to the second half of the seventh century.

In this probable tribute list we see something of the 'jigsaw' of peoples who would eventually be absorbed into the kingdom of Mercia at its greatest extent. Alongside a sense of identity that embraced communities as readily as territories, we can perceive, through these 'successors', something of the region in

Myrcna landes ys þrittig þusend hyda þes mon ærest myrcna hæt þocen þætna is þrittig þusend hida. Weocen sæt þa Westerna eahtaþels hund hyda. Elmed sætna syx hund hyda. Lindes farona syfan þusend hyda mid hæþ feld lande. Suþ gyrwa syx hund hyda. Norþ gyrwa syx hund hyda. East wixna þriu hund hyda. West wixna syx hund hyda. Spalda syx hund hyda. wigesta nygan hund hyda. Herefinna twelf hyda. Sweord ora þriu hund hyda. Gifla þriu hund hyda. Hicca þriu hund hyda. Wiht gara syx hund hyda. Nox gaga fif þusend hyda. Oht gaga twa þusend hyda. þæt is syx þritig þusend hyda jan hund hyda. Hwinca syfan þusend hyda. Cilternsætna feower syx þusend hyda. Hendrica þriu þusend hyda. Unecung ga twelf hund hyda. Aro sætna syx hund hyda. Færpinga þreo hund hyda. Bilmiga syx hund hyda. Widerigga twa þusend hyda. East willa syx hund hyda. West willa syx hund hyda. East engle þrittig þusend hyda. East sexena syofon þusend hyda. Cantwarena fiftene þusend hyda. Suþ sexena syofan þusend hyda. West sexena hund þusend hyda. Dic tallestra þusend stra feorewrtig þusend hyda. Twa þusend hyda.

Victoria ægyptiorum. Inuidia iudeorum. Sapientia grecorum. Crudelitas pictorum. Calliditas uelforatitudo romanorum. Lasitas longabardorum. Gula gallorum. Superbia uelferocitas francorum. Ira brittanorum. Stultitia saxonum uel anglorum. Libido ibernorum;

The *Tribal Hidage*, probably a tribute list compiled in the second half of the seventh century, is now preserved as a copy in this eleventh-century manuscript.

the sixth and seventh centuries. The groups of folk listed ranged considerably in size. They may themselves reflect transformations from earlier patterns and it has been suggested that those groups with '-*saete*' names may have been of British origin, presenting a variegated pattern reflected too in Anglo-Saxon charters and the testimony of Bede.

In the list, each of the thirty-five groups recorded south of the River Humber is accompanied by an assessment in hides. Defined by Bede as the amount of land required to support a household, the 'hide' became the Anglo-Saxon unit of assessment against which burdens, requirements and payments were assessed, implicitly reflecting the organisation that was emerging by the seventh century to give coherence to overlordship.

Kingdoms are present but it is a list that is expressed more in terms of people than of land – communities rather than territories. Opening with 'the area first called Mercia', assessed at 30,000 hides, the list ranges from the West Saxon kingdom of 100,000 hides to such as the Wreocensæte and Hwicce with 7,000 hides, the Arosæte at 600 hides and the Gifla with 300 hides. It is questionable whether these represent 'real' assessments, or were notional ones based on negotiation, and while many of these peoples are problematic to locate, we see a relatively small, early version of Mercia surrounded by an assortment of satellite provinces that provided a 'buffer' to her main rivals.

While very probably a Mercian document created to administer tribute collection following the expansionist policy of Wulfhere, it has also been interpreted as a Northumbrian list to collect tribute from Mercian territories, required by Oswald, or by his successors Oswiu and Ecgfrith, all of whom enjoyed brief periods of domination over the rest of England. In either case, its insight into the peoples and 'political geography' of England south of the Humber is invaluable.

Thus, patterns of political authority in midland England, and how they were shaped, among them kingdoms, cannot be charted in detail. However, within the context of an Anglo-British population, we may postulate the existence of competing elites within communities, both English and British, who allied with or opposed each other according to local circumstances. It is probable that there was a 'take-over' and transfer of pre-existing territories in Mercia, as well perhaps as some disintegration and the creation of new entities.

Integral to this process was the acceptance by British communities of Anglo-Saxon culture, following a period of coexistence that suggests opportunities for familiarisation, accommodation and redefinition, reducing any sense of intrusion. What prompted this? The progress of acculturation obscures the processes of 'power transfer' but the crucial factor was probably the adoption of Christianity by the Anglo-Saxons, a process in which the British population was particularly influential (EN 2). Christian rulers, even Anglo-Saxon ones, might have been easier for the British population to accept when the changing balance of power in the region urged it, and this paved the way towards sustainable kingdom building. A series of local scenarios were therefore in play until the expansion of the authority of the Mercian royal family, the *Iclingas*, or the kin of Icel, began to significantly reshape the political geography of central England from the late sixth century. The kingdom building of the seventh century saw the extension of this Anglian dynasty's authority across an Anglo-British population, encompassing British and English rulers alike. ✠

3

The Kingdom Builders

The seventh century has often been characterised as a 'heroic age', a society that we can still see partially reflected through great Old English poems like *Beowulf*, set two centuries earlier. It was certainly an age of warlords and saints, and both played their part in forging the Mercian kingdom and its struggle for supremacy over its neighbours, vying in particular with the Northumbrian and West Saxon kingdoms.

Mercia in the seventh century was forged through warfare and the campaigns of its warrior kings, pre-eminent among whom was Penda. The genealogy of the Mercian royal kin, the *Iclingas*, traced itself back to Icel, and subsequently to Woden, but it was Penda and his brothers, the sons of Pybba, who represented the 'historical threshold' of this lineage, as kings of Mercia into the early ninth century claimed descent from either Penda or from one of his brothers, Eowa and Coenwealh. The figure of Penda dominated the history of seventh-century Mercia, bestriding 'the political stage like a Colossus' (EN 3).

Post-Conquest annals associate the foundation of the Mercian kingdom with Creoda in the late sixth century. Bede, whose *Ecclesiastical History* is by far our most important source for the age, refers to Cearl as the first Mercian king, but his name does not appear in the surviving Mercian genealogies. Whatever role they might have played in laying the foundations for a Mercian dynasty is unknown, although a concentration of place-names in the south-west midlands formed using the personal names of Pybba, Penda and also Creoda may reflect a dynastic tradition if not historicity and recall the popularity and achievements of the *Iclingas* in the area.

The Genesis of Mercian Supremacy

At the start of the seventh century the Mercian rulers faced several inter-connected challenges. From their heartland they looked out upon a patchwork of Anglo-British provinces and territories across midland England whose adherence had to be made secure, and with it the standing and authority of the Mercian royal kin itself. There is no reason to suppose that at this point the claims of Penda and his predecessors to power were any more compelling than those of other local dynasties.

Perhaps even more daunting was the dominance of the Northumbrian kingdom. Bede offers a list of seven kings, in Old English '*bretwaldas*', who held sway over the provinces south of the Humber, the fifth of whom was Edwin, the Deiran king of Northumbria, who Bede tells us was married to a daughter of Cearl. With the help of Raedwald of East Anglia, Edwin's precursor on Bede's list, Edwin returned from exile to take power in Northumbria in 616 and had become sufficiently threatening by 626 for the West Saxon king to attempt, unsuccessfully, his assassination. Apart from the most powerful, most kings probably accepted the authority of their greater neighbours, and the plot of Cwichelm of Wessex against Edwin and the latter's subsequent campaign against Wessex suggests that the intervening Mercian lands recognised Northumbrian overlordship. This was a constraint that an ambitious Mercian dynasty would have to address, and in doing so it became evident that the most natural and effective response was to build instead a Mercian overlordship.

Opposite: A battle scene in an Old English Hexateuch (the first six books of the Old Testament) of the second quarter of the eleventh century, this detail from Genesis.

Kings of Mercia and the *Iclingas*, the Mercian royal kin

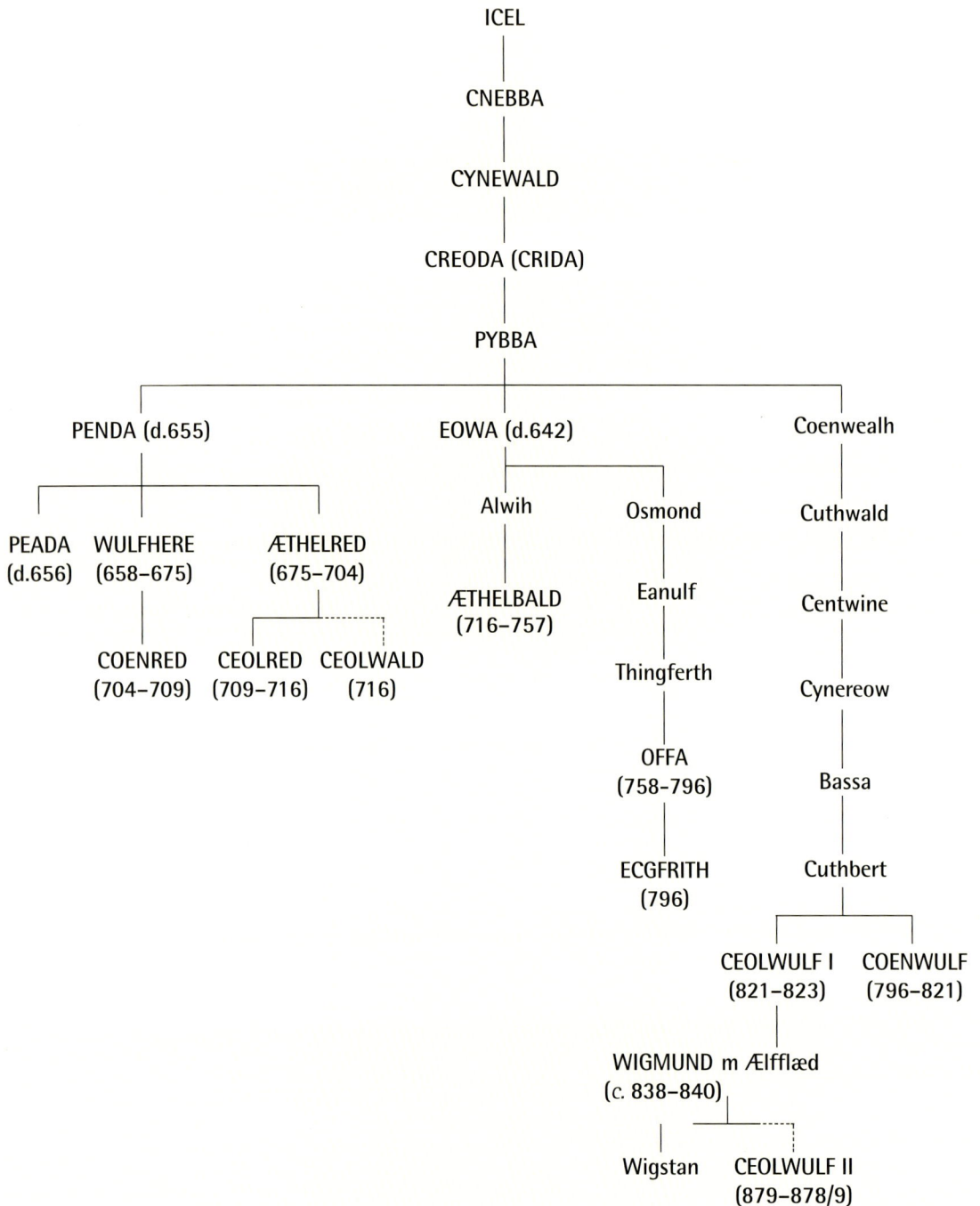

ICEL

CNEBBA

CYNEWALD

CREODA (CRIDA)

PYBBA

PENDA (d.655)   EOWA (d.642)   Coenwealh

PEADA   WULFHERE   ÆTHELRED   Alwih   Osmond   Cuthwald
(d.656)   (658–675)   (675–704)

ÆTHELBALD   Eanulf   Centwine
(716–757)

COENRED   CEOLRED   CEOLWALD   Thingferth   Cynereow
(704–709) (709–716)   (716)

OFFA   Bassa
(758-796)

ECGFRITH   Cuthbert
(796)

CEOLWULF I   COENWULF
(821–823)   (796–821)

WIGMUND m Ælfflæd
(c. 838–840)

Wigstan   CEOLWULF II
(879–878/9)

It was also in 626, or thereabouts, that Penda came to the Mercian throne. Bede, who had little regard for Penda other than as a maker of Christian martyrs, nonetheless described him as 'a man of the royal stock of the Mercians, exceptionally gifted as a warrior'. It was Penda's prowess in war that cut the pathway to Mercian power.

Penda the Warlord

In Penda's world, warfare was the only credible option available to him, and it was to Mercia's good fortune that for some thirty years he proved to be, in Nicholas Brooks' words, 'a war leader of genius'. At his first appearance in the historical record around 628, at Cirencester, he is seen successfully rebutting West Saxon influence in the south-west midlands, as a consequence of which the province of the Hwicce was brought under Mercian overlordship. Still a young man building his reputation and his fortunes, he entered at a critical moment into an alliance as a junior client with the great British warlord, Cadwallon of Gwynedd. Alarmed at Northumbrian expansion against the northern British, Cadwallon saw that the loss of East Anglian support made Edwin of Northumbria more vulnerable than had previously been the case. Cadwallon built an Anglo-British alliance to challenge Northumbria and in 633 met Edwin in battle at Hatfield Chase, near Doncaster, where Edwin was killed and his army destroyed. For Bede, these events were all the more terrible because Cadwallon, a Christian king, had allied himself with the idol-worshipping Penda and the Mercians. The defeat of Edwin had profound repercussions, throwing Northumbria into confusion. The land was ravaged and Edwin's queen, with Bishop Paulinus, fled, while Penda, who had now given the Northumbrians cause to remember him, returned south with one of Edwin's sons as a hostage.

Northumbrian recovery came under Oswald, who in 634 killed Cadwallon at the battle of Heavenfield near Hexham. This undoubtedly made Penda's position less secure and he may have sought to ingratiate himself with Oswald by killing Edwin's son, Osfrith, but his attentions were increasingly focused on East Anglia, culminating in a campaign in 635 in which he slew King Ecgric and ex-king Sigeberht, forced out of his monastic retirement at Bury St Edmunds in order to lead the army. However, the establishment of Mercian authority in East Anglia constituted a threat to Oswald, who may have consequently supported Anna in his bid for the East Anglian throne.

Mercian fortunes were fluctuating at this point. Oswald's reach ran deep into the upper Thames valley where around 635/40 he stood sponsor to the West Saxon king Cynegils at his baptism, an influence which Penda may have tried to offset by

"Warfare was not a 'last resort' for early kings like Penda. It was part of the very fabric of elite Anglo-Saxon society, and a vital 'tool' in the power-politics of the day. With it came reputation and fame, plunder and tribute; success in war dominated the defeated, encouraged the submission and loyalty of others, and attracted more warriors to the retinue."

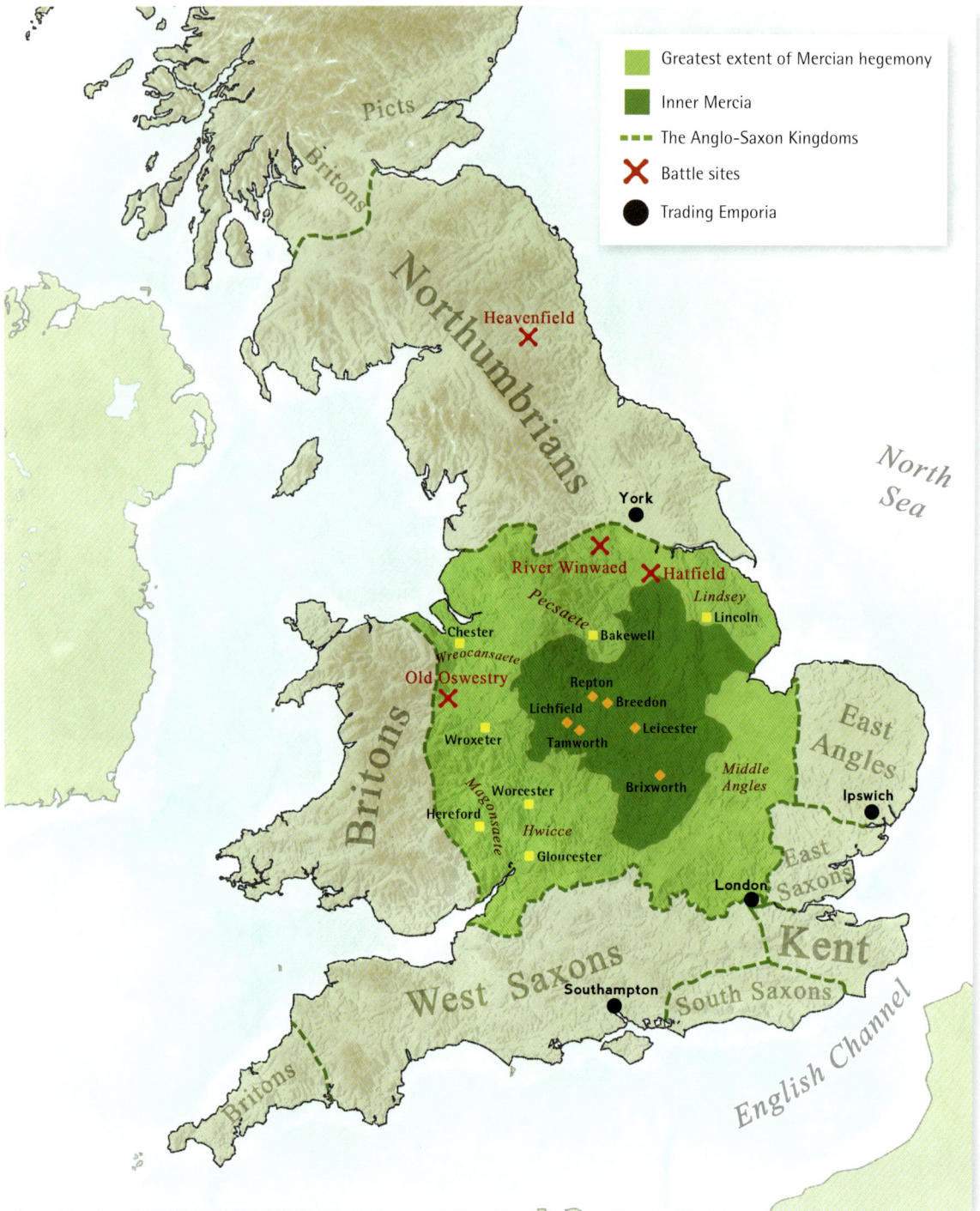

The 'political geography' of midland England in the seventh century; the Mercian heartland and subordinate 'satellite' provinces.

marrying his sister to Cynegil's son, Cenwealh. It has been suggested that Penda's brother, Eowa, may have been a client of the Northumbrian king, ruling at least part of Mercia. While client status and the question of Penda ruling jointly with his brother are debatable, a resurgence of Northumbrian overlordship in Mercia seems very probable.

However, Oswald's position was not secure and his vulnerability south of the Humber led him to campaign into Mercia. Penda again looked to his British allies for support, among them Cynddylan ap Cyndrwyn, prince of Powys. At the battle of Maserfelth in 642, traditionally but not certainly associated with Old Oswestry in Shropshire, Penda defeated and killed Oswald. Eowa, Penda's brother, also died there, possibly fighting in support of his Northumbrian overlord, but whatever the truth of this, the outcome of this battle, with disarray north of the Humber, was to leave Penda as sole king of Mercia, with an enhanced reputation and standing among the Northumbrians and the Welsh.

Success brought little respite, and it is doubtful that it was either expected or necessarily wanted. In 649 and 652 Penda returned to East Anglia, expelling Anna, and a few years later, in 654 or 655, he killed the East Anglian king and put Anna's brother, Æthelhere in his place. Meanwhile, when Cenwealh, king of the upper Thames valley Saxons repudiated his wife, Penda's sister, the Mercian king drove him into exile and around 650 brought the upper Thames valley under Mercian influence.

Midland hegemony had been achieved through a series of expansionist campaigns, in several directions, almost simultaneously. Warfare was not a 'last resort' for early kings like Penda. It was part of the very fabric of elite Anglo-Saxon society, and a vital 'tool' in the power-politics of the day. With it came reputation and fame, plunder and tribute;

success in war dominated the defeated, encouraged the submission and loyalty of others, and attracted more warriors to the retinue. Furthermore, as Penda's last campaign clearly demonstrates, tributaries put their own military power at the disposal of their overlords.

Mercian 'Statecraft'

But while warfare underpinned it, this was not the only means by which Penda promoted Mercian authority, and in this we see another face of seventh-century kingship and 'statecraft'. The fragmented political geography of the midland region, at least partially reflected in the *Tribal Hidage*, called for a response that went beyond military suppression. If these territories were to be at the heart of Mercian power, more reliable bonds had to be promoted.

Penda's influence and authority in the south-eastern midlands were revealed when in around 653 he made his son, Peada, the '*princeps*' or ruler of the Middle Angles. There had not previously been such an eastern midlands kingdom and his actions might be seen as both providing his son with an opportunity to develop his own skills of kingship while at the same time strengthening the control of the Mercian royal kin by interposing a local king. Penda appears to have done something similar with the territory of the Magonsaete to the west, the area later defined by the medieval diocese of Hereford, where Merewalh, Penda's son or son-in-law, was established as king. The territory of the Hwicce to the south-west was also closely dependent upon Mercia.

Penda was effectively creating a series of dependent 'buffer' provinces around the Mercian heartland. These were also bound by a tributary relationship, where the superiority of one king was acknowledged through the render of tribute by others. Such relationships were at the heart of overlordship and Penda, like his contemporaries, used them, and indeed had experience of both 'sides' in such arrangements. Such relationships were liable to fluctuate, but at various times Penda was able to impose tributary status on the East Anglian kingdom, on the West Saxons, on Lindsey, and perhaps on Deira, and it has been suggested that Gwynedd too might have been embraced by his 'imperium'. The frequency of warfare in Penda's reign reveals that this situation was rarely stable, but it clearly shows Penda's ambition to dominate the patchwork of territories, provinces and kingdoms that characterised England, rather than to weld them together into a single massive kingdom under his rule.

Penda also drew upon a range of more subtle mechanisms to underpin his power. The marriages of his children and kin were a means of attempting to consolidate his influence, and he undoubtedly was aware of the importance of gift-giving and royal generosity in creating bonds. Hostage-taking too, in which Penda participated, was a common means of encouraging compliance.

Penda's Kingship

Penda's kingship was personal, sophisticated and effective, balancing coercion with bonds based on kinship, respect and friendship; taking tribute but showing generosity; inspiring fear, but offering protection. Such reciprocal relationships and ritual underpinned early kingship. There is no reason to suppose that Penda's court was any less impressive than that which Bede describes in the Northumbrian kingdom, albeit at this time without the Christian overtones. Indeed, as the historian Damian Tyler has observed, it is likely that Penda's court was cosmopolitan and tolerant in nature, where British and Anglo-Saxons, and Christians and non-Christians readily mixed. Ultimately, however, Mercian expansion by the end of the seventh century was achieved at the expense of the British kingdoms, particularly of Powys, so that former allies would become enemies.

Past generations of historians, no doubt influenced by Bede, seem to have overlooked the sophistication and achievement of Penda's reign, distracted particularly by the fact that he remained a pagan until his death, an impediment to the progress of the Roman church and Christian kingship. Such a perspective is, however, rather partisan. Penda's decision not to accept Christianity might reflect personal devotion and a sense that the traditional gods, closely associated with war, had served him well. But there may also have been a political calculation in that to accept baptism overseen by a Northumbrian royal sponsor, as might well have been the case, would have implied a dependence that he could not afford to acknowledge in his struggle for supremacy. And despite his commitment to the old gods, Penda was clearly pragmatic and tolerant in his dealings with Christians. The population at the heart of his territories undoubtedly included Christian communities, while his overlordship and range of allies clearly embraced Christian warlords.

"Penda's kingship was personal, sophisticated and effective, balancing coercion with bonds based on kinship, respect and friendship; taking tribute but showing generosity; inspiring fear, but offering protection."

Furthermore, Penda's son, Peada, was converted to Christianity and even Bede observed that Penda 'did not forbid the preaching of the Word, even in his own Mercian kingdom'. Penda was not a militant anti-Christian, but in the new polity that was his world, most of his enemies happened to be Christian.

The Fall of Penda

The Northumbrian kingdom, now ruled by Oswiu, was clearly still perceived as a threat and Penda resolved to address this by dealing the Northumbrian kingdom a punitive blow; to do so he brought together an impressive army from among his allies and client kings. Bede speaks of Penda leading an army of 'thirty battle-hardened legions under famous commanders', that is, the warbands of men like Æthelhere of East Anglia, Œthelwald of Deira and Cadafael ap Cynfedw, king of Gwynedd. Such a broad coalition reflected the wide-ranging overlordship that Penda had created by the mid-seventh century, and although the motivations of its members were undoubtedly mixed, it was essentially a testimony to Penda's personality and the personal nature of his power.

In 655 Penda led his army deep into the Northumbrian kingdom, reaching as far north as Stirling and forcing Oswiu to deliver to him his son as a hostage and 'all the riches that he had in the city' which he then distributed among his allies – Penda's generosity and 'good lordship' in action! In this Oswiu was acting pragmatically but also inherently acknowledging the overlordship of Penda. However, like Penda at an earlier point in his career, he evidently determined that his best course of action was to bid for his own overlordship, and he did so quickly. While they were returning south, Oswiu caught up with the Mercians at the River Winwaed near Leeds and defeated them, killing Penda. Some of Penda's allies had already departed before the battle and Bede tells us that the river, in flood through the autumn rains, claimed more lives than the battle itself. Mercian supremacy, essentially the personal creation of one man, now lay in ruins and Northumbria was again dominant in Mercia.

Some sense of the 'watershed' that Oswiu thought these events marked is conveyed by his foundation of twelve monasteries, each endowed with ten hides of land, in thanks for his victory over Penda. He was now to rule Mercia for three years, appointing its bishops and governors, but also allowing Peada, who was murdered within a year, to rule the southern Mercians. However, in 658 Mercian noblemen rebelled and put Wulfhere, the son of Penda, on the throne. It seems probable that he had spent the years of Oswiu's dominance in hiding.

King Wulfhere

Unlike his father, Wulfhere (658-75) was a Christian king who oversaw the conversion of Mercia, but he also built on the gains that his father had made as he sought to restore Mercian fortunes. From his reign onwards, historians are also able to turn to the evidence of Anglo-Saxon charters in reconstructing Mercian society and affairs.

Like his father, he looked to warfare and relationships, but he also had the added opportunities that Christian kingship brought, as when before 661 he stood sponsor in his court to the baptism of the South Saxon king, Æthelwealh, who was married to a Hwiccian princess. He began developing an extensive network of Mercian royal religious patronage, enhancing royal authority and presence within local society, beneficiaries including the minster at Much Wenlock and the territory of the Hwicce. And in later centuries the

The Sutton Hoo 'Great Buckle', decorated with animal interlace, recalls the wealth and 'ambience' of early Anglo-Saxon kingship.

monastery at Peterborough claimed a tradition of Wulfhere as a benefactor. The management of the satellite provinces remained central to Mercian interests.

He was also clearly successful in reasserting Mercian influence over some of the southern kingdoms, particularly in south-eastern England, and was married to a Kentish princess. He campaigned against the West Saxons and was able to dispose of the Isle of Wight and lands on the mainland that fell within their orbit; that these were passed to the South Saxons demonstrated his standing there too. His authority was accepted in Surrey, where he approved land grants made by his sub-king, Frithuwold, to Chertsey minster, witnessed by a further three sub-kings.

Bede tells us that Wulfhere was acknowledged as overlord among the East Saxons where his success in gaining control of the East Saxon territories around London, whose bishopric he was able to sell, was critical. Wulfhere made London a Mercian town, an association that lasted into the ninth century. This was to have far-reaching consequences for Mercian kings whose access to

wealth was thus expanded. In the early English kingdoms trade was an important source of wealth, England being firmly embedded in trade networks that reached out across Europe and Scandinavia. Fundamental was an '*entrepôt*' and now London served Mercia in the same ways that *Hamwih* (Southampton) served Wessex, *Eoforwic* (York) served Northumbria and *Gipeswic* (Ipswich) served East Anglia.

However, as for his father, Northumbria was to prove his nemesis. The author of the early eighth-century *Life of Wilfrid* observed that 'King Wulfhere of Mercia, a man of proud and insatiable will, stirred up all the southern nations against our own (*i.e. Northumbria*), intent not merely on war but meaning even to enslave us to him as tributaries'. However, Wulfhere's campaign of 674 failed, defeated by King Ecgfrith, and Mercia itself was put under tribute. Wulfhere died a little later.

Æthelred, King and Saint

Wulfhere was succeeded by his brother, Æthelred (675-704), who sought to follow in the footsteps of his predecessors. In 676 Bede tells us that he 'ravaged Kent with his wicked soldiery, profaning churches and monasteries without fear of God or respect to religion', and in 679 Northumbrian authority south of the Humber was curbed when Æthelred defeated Ecgfrith in battle near the River Trent, as a result of which Lindsey was recovered permanently as a Mercian province. Bede adds that Theodore, archbishop of Canterbury, intervened after the battle to negotiate peace between the two kings.

While stability might have been achieved on the northern frontiers, Mercian authority among the southern English was now less emphatic than it had been previously. The world had changed with the rise of a powerful West Saxon kingdom that challenged Mercian ambitions. In 704 Æthelred abdicated his throne and retired to the monastery of Bardney in Lindsey, where he died twelve years later as its abbot. Even in these closing acts of his reign 'Mercian statecraft' shines through. He retired not to a Mercian monastery, but to one in a province that he had detached from Northumbria, and where both he, and his Northumbrian wife, Osthryth, came to be revered as saints. The promotion of Mercian royal saints' cults was integral to consolidating Mercian royal authority and identity across the satellite provinces and in this Æthelred's own death was to play its part.

Kingdom Building

Penda and his sons transformed the geography of power in the midland region and in doing so they began building a kingdom and laid the foundations for the Mercian supremacy of the eighth century.

Despite short interruptions, Mercian dominance of midland England had been demonstrated and sustained. Critical in this had been the building of working relationships with neighbouring territories and polities to north, east, west and south, binding some to the Mercian royal house not only through tribute but also by setting members of the royal kin over them. A miscellany of peoples and communities were realigning themselves afresh with Mercian interests.

It was Penda's sons in particular who fostered an environment in which local hegemony might begin developing towards kingdom building. It was not simply a matter of imposition as it required that the numerically superior British population should conclude that their interests were best served by opting for an 'Anglo-Saxon future'. This came in the late seventh century. Penda's defeat at Winwaed marked the end of any sense of security that the midlands British might have felt through their neighbours in Gwynedd and Powys, while the resurgence of Mercia under Wulfhere and Æthelred demonstrated where credible protection might now be found. The Hwicce and the Magonsæte entered into a client status, and even some of the men of Powys, the Wreocensæte, came to accept Mercian authority. That Wulfhere and his successors offered Christian kingship brought a positive encouragement and a potential for sustainability that Penda had not. Furthermore, since Wulfhere had accepted Roman Christianity, this brought with it an English identity that the people of British descent gradually absorbed, further strengthening these foundations. ✠

"Penda and his sons transformed the geography of power in the midland region and in doing so they began building a kingdom and laid the foundations for the Mercian supremacy of the eighth century."

Warriors and Warbands

Warriors and warbands were the basis of power for seventh-century kings and it was this elite world that we see depicted in the 'fyttes' of *Beowulf*, the king living in the company of noble warriors who served him and shared the hospitality and succour of his hall. A king's fortunes rested on his ability to attract to his hearth the most proficient and best-equipped of warriors, and then to retain their loyalty through his 'good lordship', his ability and willingness to offer generous reward.

Guthlac leaves his Mercian warrior band to enter the monastic life at Repton (manuscript illumination of c.1175–1225).

38

Warrior society produced a steady stream of young men seeking opportunity and profitable service. Around 690 Guthlac, the son of a Mercian nobleman and then aged about fifteen, remembering 'the valiant deeds of heroes of old', gathered a band of 'companions from various races' and won fame through military adventures, amassing 'immense booty'. When Beowulf and his band arrived at the court of King Hrothgar, they came not as exiles but in search of adventure, while an Old English 'wisdom poem' declared –

> *Good comrades must encourage a young nobleman to war-making and to ring-giving. In a warrior belongs courage; the sword must experience battle, blade opposing helmet… a good man belongs in his native land, forging his reputation.*

Such men, whether they came as individual warriors or as leaders of their own warbands, were crucial to royal ambition. Kings were able to call upon all freemen to meet military obligations, but it was their retinue of young warriors, together with the companions of the nobles close to them, who made these armies potent forces. These were the most battle-seasoned and best-equipped of the king's men, with sword, helmet and a shirt of mail. They were expected to stand their ground in the thick of battle, and if captured, might expect to be executed or sold into slavery. Such battle-hardened warriors were probably a relatively small group of men, and so this was a sure way of undermining, at least temporarily, the threat of an enemy. The loss or movement of warriors from one kingdom to another had profound consequences for the military effectiveness of the kings concerned.

Ambitious warriors were clearly attracted into the companies of kings renowned for their fame and success, like King Hrothgar in the poem *Beowulf*, but the vital part played by royal generosity in maintaining the cohesion of these retinues is also much in evidence. *Beowulf* is imbued with the significance and symbolism attached to gold, and to the giving and receipt of it; the social and emotional significance of giving gold, and of wearing it, ran deep in early Anglo-Saxon society. The poem conveys the ethos of companionship in the service of the lord who was a 'dealer of wound gold', a 'ring-bestower' and 'distributor of rings'; and 'the gracious lord who granted us arms'. The gift of fine weapons, particularly swords, brought an added frisson for the warrior, as it enhanced the honour of the recipient and reflected the esteem in which he was held by his lord.

Kings prospered because they were able to attract and maintain noble and well-equipped warriors but as Patrick Wormald remarked: 'Royal power is like a snowball; while it moves it grows, but when it stops it melts'. Constant generosity required constant campaigning but eventually this would become more difficult to sustain and the opportunities fewer. But this is how the foundations of kingdoms were laid and maintained, and this is the context in which the immense moveable wealth associated with such riches as the Sutton Hoo ship burial or the Staffordshire Hoard can be best understood. ✠

"Kings prospered because they were able to attract and maintain noble and well-equipped warriors but as Patrick Wormald remarked: 'Royal power is like a snowball; while it moves it grows, but when it stops it melts.'"

Mercia and the Staffordshire Hoard

In July 2009 one of the most remarkable discoveries in British archaeology was made by a metal detectorist in a field at Hammerwich, not far from the Watling Street in south Staffordshire. What has become known as the 'Staffordshire Hoard' is the largest find of gold and silver yet made in England, comprising almost 4,000 pieces and five kilograms of gold.

The wealth represented by the hoard immediately prompted comparisons with the famous Anglo-Saxon boat burial at Sutton Hoo in Suffolk, but wealth and artistic comparisons aside, the two are very different. While Sutton Hoo was a carefully laid out burial, no doubt accompanied by considerable ritual, the Hammerwich find has the appearance of a hasty deposit, 'in extremis', in an isolated spot; neither burial nor obvious ritual has been detected.

In its character the hoard material is masculine, military and elite, capturing the essence of Anglo-Saxon warrior society. The assemblage is dominated by pommel caps, hilt plates and fittings from swords, seaxes and other equipment. There was also at least one helmet, and if some of the die-impressed foils currently linked with the helmet prove to have possible associations with flasks and drinking cups, then the ethos of the mead hall would be even more emphatic.

The assemblage is astonishingly rich, visually stunning and full of symbolism. The magical quality of gold was emphasised by a metallurgical process that added lustre, while the gold filigree and cloisonné work, using glass and garnets, is among the finest known from Anglo-Saxon England. The hoard included several Christian objects, most notably an animal and garnet decorated processional cross, among the earliest found in Europe, and an inscribed cross, both of which may well have been no stranger to the battlefield.

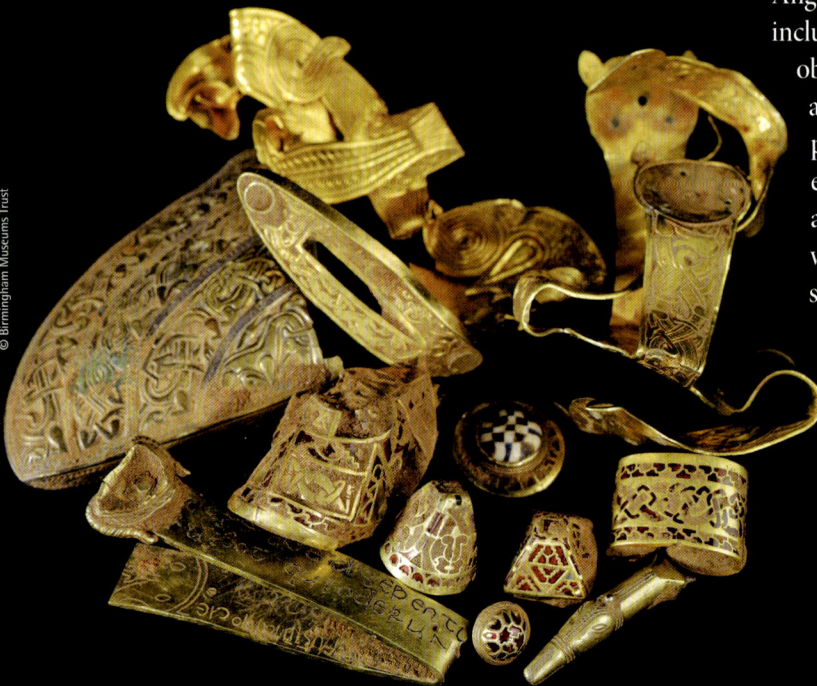

© Birmingham Museums Trust

Reflecting a warrior elite, the Staffordshire Hoard is made up of 'hack metal', perhaps the spoils of war, intended to be melted down for reuse.

"The assemblage is astonishingly rich, visually stunning and full of symbolism."

All of the hoard objects were distorted and torn, damage that had been inflicted before their burial. While the hoard included items of an early date, perhaps ancestral heirlooms, the stylistic analysis of the hoard suggests that it was buried between AD 650 and 670.

Although research on the hoard is still in progress, it is already clear that it will have a significant impact upon our understanding of seventh-century England. The geographical and cultural range of the assemblage is remarkable. Pagan and Christian, with links to East Anglia, Kent, Germany and Scandinavia, drawing upon influences from the Germanic and the late Roman or Byzantine world. The 'flux' of the earlier 'Migration Period' still has a cultural resonance here.

What does the hoard tell us about Mercia in this period? It allows us to visualise the rich and varied, indeed cosmopolitan, artistic and cultural environment that Mercia was part of; a world characterised by links rather than barriers! The hoard is assumed to be royal, and Mercian, albeit on the basis of limited evidence, and while some of it might have been made in Mercia, much of it was not. Thus it is reasonably seen as the loot of victorious campaigns, whether as battlefield booty or exacted tribute. If there was any doubt as to the resources that

Mercian kings in the seventh century might muster, how they might enhance them, and the world they moved in, this discovery provided direct artefactual evidence for it. The character and condition of the hoard objects suggests that by the time of their burial they had become 'hack metal', ready to be picked apart and melted down for the manufacture of new pieces. With failing gold supplies, such collections would have become increasingly important in sustaining court craftsmen, particularly goldsmiths.

More broadly, the hoard has brought new objects to light, such as new sword pommel forms, and added immensely to our art-historical 'data base' for the period. Questions are raised about the extent to which the skills of eighth-century Mercian metalworkers should now be sought in the preceding century, and on the relationship between the art of metalworkers and manuscript illuminators in manuscripts such as the *Book of Durrow*.

But the matter of how it was brought together is not certain. The diversity and range of the assemblage is striking, suggesting that it was brought together over a period of time from many sources. This may indeed be so, and while a Mercian king might have been the prime mover in

this, it is also possible that it was acquired at a time when these characteristics were already established. But it perhaps has more to say about the links, cultural associations and family histories of their previous owners, all brought together in an ultimately doomed campaign.

The significant stylistic links with East Anglia (and thence Scandinavia) naturally draw attention to Penda's campaigns there between 635 and 655, while the Kentish associations might recall Wulfhere's campaign in south-east England or Æthelred's devastation of Kent in 676. It is a matter of speculation, but the presence of the East Anglian objects, and the absence of specifically Celtic or Welsh items, arguably strengthens the case for Mercian associations.

It is, of course, naïve to think that all archaeological finds can be placed within the context of known and recorded history. However, to conclude with further speculation, the deposition of the hoard might find a context in the retreat of the Mercians following Penda's death in 655; following the defeat of Wulfhere in 674; or possibly with the Northumbrians, burying what they had seized when Wulfhere retook Mercia in 658. ✠

4

Kings, Monks and Saints

THE MAKING OF A CHRISTIAN KINGDOM

A defining feature of England and its culture was its Christian character and the making of the Anglo-Saxon kingdoms was closely interleaved with the making of the English Church. The 'building blocks' of the Christian kingdom of Mercia included the evangelisation and the engagement of its kings and elite society with the Roman Church; the shaping of ecclesiastical organisation and the establishment of monasteries; the cult of saints; and a distinctive literary and artistic culture.

However, Christianity was not new to the province of Britain when Saint Augustine arrived in 597; it was already present in the midland region before the Anglo-Saxon incursions and there can be no doubt that Christian communities were an integral part of Mercia's Anglo-British population in the sixth and seventh centuries.

Late Roman Christianity and the British Church

Christianity, present in Roman Britain since the third century, by the fourth century had a system of bishops and dioceses serving some thriving Christian communities. Archaeological evidence, like the Water Newton hoard and the Hinton St Mary mosaic, suggests a marked Christian presence in East Anglia, and in the south-eastern third of Roman Britain, extending towards the villa estates of Dorset and up towards Gloucester and Cirencester; and northwards along the eastern flank of the Pennines. The presence of Christian communities in the western midlands is suggested by place-names incorporating the element 'eccles', like Eccleshall and Exhall, from 'ecclesia' meaning church or Christian

community, found in Staffordshire, Warwickshire and Herefordshire, while Christian communities also occurred at the western margins of the region. At some places, such as Gloucester, Worcester, Wroxeter and Lichfield-Wall, later bishoprics or churches seemingly followed on sites with established Christian associations.

While problematic, the argument that these post-Roman Christian communities had their roots in the late-Roman Church is credible, as is the case for a working British Church in the region when the Anglo-Saxons arrived. Visiting missionaries played their part, as perhaps in the conversion of King Merewalh of the Magonsæte around 660, but the suggestion that much was owed in the west midlands to assimilation with the existing British Christians is very persuasive, if unprovable.

The Roman Mission and the Synod of Whitby

Despite the activity of the British Church, unsurprisingly for Bede the key event in establishing an English Church was the mission sent by Pope Gregory the Great. In 597 Augustine arrived at Thanet with forty companions, meeting King Æthelberht of Kent within a few days; it was agreed that the mission might stay in England and receive land in Canterbury upon which to establish itself.

Bede's narrative follows the fortunes of the mission; the journey north of Paulinus to the Northumbrian court of King Edwin, where in 627 while at the royal residence of *Ad Gefrin* (Yeavering) he was 'constantly occupied in instructing and baptising'. However, there were reverses as well as successes and the primacy that came to be accorded

Previous page: This gold and garnet pectoral cross (Staffordshire Hoard), decorated with filigree scrollwork, may have contained a relic or token.

"A defining feature of England and its culture was its Christian character and the making of the Anglo-Saxon kingdoms was closely interleaved with the making of the English Church."

to the Roman Church in Anglo-Saxon England can hardly have been regarded as inevitable in the early seventh century, with 'backsliding' converts and a flourishing Celtic tradition.

A defining moment in the fortunes of the Roman Church in England came with the celebrated synod at Whitby in 664. The debate focused on the celebration of Easter, itself an arid controversy, but underpinning this was a more fundamental question of the relationship between the Celtic and Roman churches and the matter of supremacy, which in turn determined usage, practices and organisation. The Roman Church carried the debate and in doing so the foundations were laid for the subsequent unification of the English Church while not excluding the continued Northumbrian contribution. The authority of the archbishop of Canterbury was now accepted in Northumbria.

Northumbrian decisions had consequences for Mercia; when Northumbrian kings dominated in Mercia they were influential in promoting Christianity there and until the Synod of Whitby they had naturally looked to churchmen trained in the Celtic tradition, and particularly to the Northumbrian monastery of Lindisfarne, to lay the foundations of the early church in Mercia.

Evangelising Mercia

Notwithstanding the presence of Christianity among the British population and the role that they most probably played in embedding Christianity through assimilation, missionaries were dispatched into the region from elsewhere, notably Northumbria, particularly under King Oswiu who insisted that Peada become Christian when he married his daughter, Alchfled. Such marriage arrangements were generally a precursor to the dispatch of missionaries, and so it was here.

Bede relates that in 653 Peada, king of the Middle Angles, was baptised, 'together with his companions and thegns and all their servants', by Finan, bishop of Lindisfarne. With his father Penda's agreement, Peada brought back to his kingdom four priests, among them Diuma, 'chosen for their learning and holy life, to instruct and baptise his people'. Bede subsequently observed that a consequence of Penda's defeat in 655 was that Oswiu 'converted the Mercians and their neighbours to the Christian Faith', overlooking of course the important Christian element already present in the Anglo-British population. Oswiu's dominance of Mercia enabled him to appoint Diuma as the first bishop of Mercia with a see that ran across Mercia, Middle Anglia and into Lindsey, looking more to Lindisfarne than to Canterbury.

Notwithstanding the arrangements already in place to support the British Christian communities of the region, the emerging Roman Church in Mercia needed to establish a diocesan structure, but there was fraught debate on what this should be. The massive dioceses that had taken shape in England were far from those that Pope Gregory had envisaged, detracting from the humility and spiritual obligations expected of bishops.

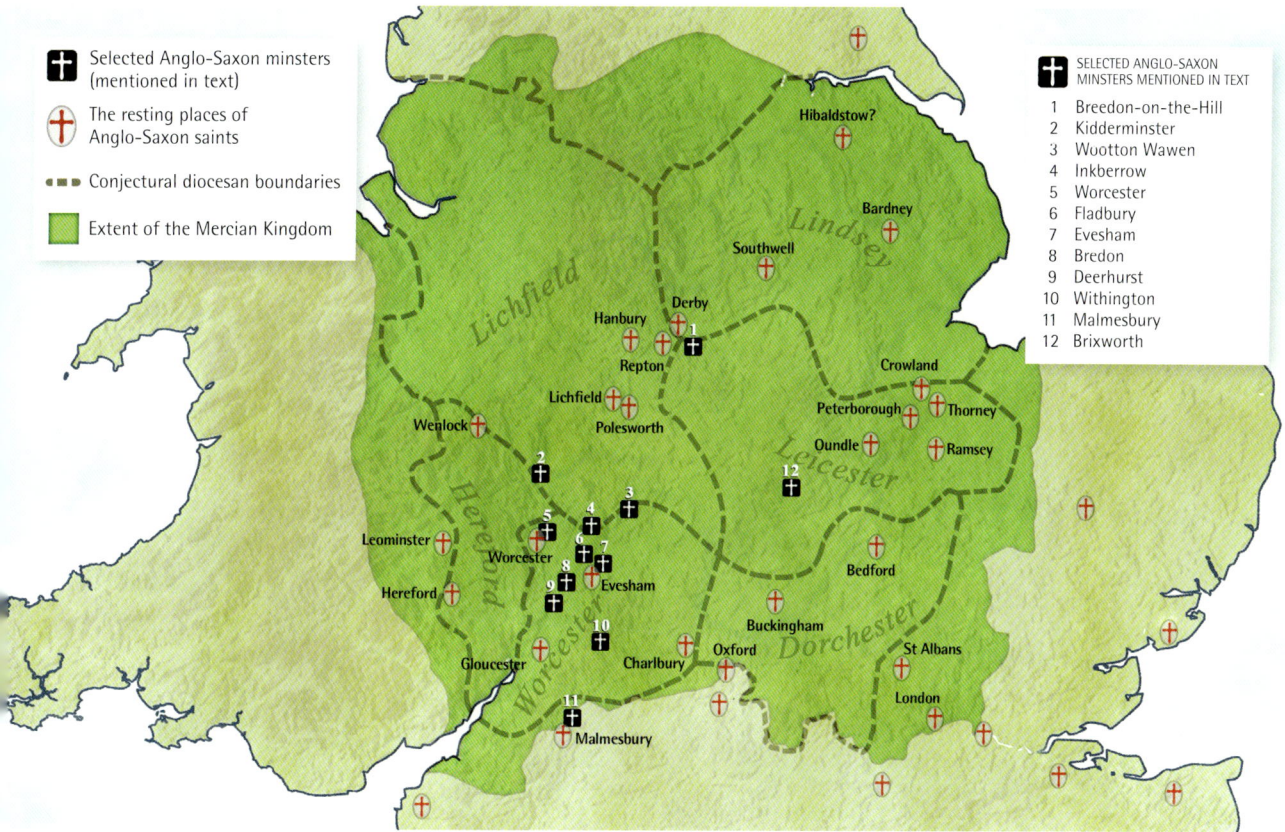

Christian Mercia: the 'resting places' of the saints in Mercia and selected minsters. The dioceses reflect the restructure initiated by Theodore of Tarsus.

The Mercian Dioceses

The arrival in England in 669 of Theodore of Tarsus, Pope Vitalian's appointment as archbishop of Canterbury, was crucial. Informed on papal expectations and aware of the norms within the Roman Church, and undoubtedly aided by an increased stabilisation in political power and kingdom building in England, he immediately started to build a regular diocesan episcopate and embed Roman authority, which had implications for the arrangements in Mercia.

On his arrival he resolved a dispute regarding the bishopric of the Northumbrians, a consequence of which was to bring Chad to Lichfield where in 669, on land given to him by Wilfrid (EN 4), the see

was established at the heart of the Mercian kingdom and close to important royal sites; but the diocese remained massive and in need of restructuring.

Theodore's opportunity came soon after the 672 Council of Hertford when, 'displeased at some disobedience on the part of Bishop Wynfrid of the Mercians' (Bede), he removed him from the bishopric. The subdivision of the see followed, informed not only by the needs of the Church, but also with regard to the political affinities and boundaries of the day. In addition to the see of Lichfield, new bishoprics were created c.680 for the Hwicce focused on Worcester, and for the Magonsæte at Hereford. There was a diocese for Lindsey by 678, but that for the Middle Angles,

Pharaoh ordering an execution, from the Book of Genesis in an Old English Hexateuch (the first six books of the Old Testament), emphasises the role of kings as judges (c.1025-1050).

"From the outset the conversion of the English and the future of an English Church were dependent upon the attitude of kings and of elite society, requiring at best their support, and at worst, their ambivalence."

Minster churches, like Brixworth in Northamptonshire, provided the bedrock for local devotion by the late eighth century.

based on Leicester, was not finally established until 737. Such a restructure could not have been achieved without the support of the Mercian kings for whom these creations were closely associated with the promotion and stability of royal power and collective identity through the royal kin.

Kings and Missionaries

From the outset the conversion of the English and the future of an English church were dependent upon the attitude of kings and of elite society, requiring at best their support, and at worst, their ambivalence. The missionaries did not come empty-handed. Pope Gregory presented Æthelberht of Kent with the idea that by becoming Christian he

joined a prestigious community of Christian kings, at the head of which was the Emperor of Byzantium. Christian kingship brought the 'good gifts' of stability, good fortune and prosperity, while God would 'make your name glorious to posterity'. Gregory hinted that Æthelberht would be England's Constantine, and of course, the Church brought the Anglo-Saxon kings directly into contact with the world of Roman civilisation, of which they stood in awe.

Not only did the Church provide models of kingship, but it also introduced the tradition of written law and with it the book, the cultural impacts of which were immense. The commitment of law to vellum underscored the role of kings as judges and lawgivers; while the book brought literacy and a new vehicle for artistic expression. Christian culture would effectively define the artistic activity and output of much of Anglo-Saxon England in ways not found in the pagan kingdoms.

Despite its frequent turbulence, the relationship between church and royal kin was symbiotic. The church needed protection and patronage, kings providing lands and wealth, rights and opportunity, and protections that came to be enshrined in royal law codes. For their part, through the church, kings enhanced and embedded their authority and reputation, and the fame of their kin, while nurturing their personal spiritual welfare and standing. Furthermore, the skills that were found among churchmen built the capacity of kings to better govern and administer their kingdoms.

The part played by kings, their kin and aristocratic society in establishing the church in Mercia may be eloquently illustrated through two of the most fundamental features in Anglo-Saxon Christianity – monasteries, and the cult of saints.

Monasteries

The 'power-house' of the early English Church, in religious, political and cultural terms, was Anglo-Saxon monasticism whose houses, also known as minsters, were bastions of the faith and focal points for patronage. In the mid-seventh century there were very few such foundations but their number increased considerably from the late seventh and eighth centuries and by the mid-ninth century there were, for instance, at least thirty within the diocese of Worcester alone.

Late seventh-century Mercian charters show Æthelred endowing houses such as Malmesbury and Worcester, sometimes in association with Oshere, under-king of the Hwicce, including a grant to the

bishop of Worcester of land at Fladbury (Worcestershire) so that monastic life might be re-established there. The pace and volume of such benefactions increased massively during the eighth century, among these Æthelbald's grant of land to Æthelric, under-king of the Hwicce, for a monastery at Wootton Wawen (Warwickshire), a church that has been the subject of archaeological investigation.

Minsters varied greatly in size, form and significance, lacking the uniformity associated with later medieval monasticism; they did not have standard layouts and while the 'Rule of St Benedict' had many adherents, it was far from established as the norm, many abbots utilising their own 'Rule'. In its origins monasticism was preoccupied with the personal salvation of the individual monk, but Pope Gregory encouraged less withdrawn models, mixing monks and priests.

Typically, later minsters maintained communities of priests who looked to the spiritual needs of their neighbourhoods or 'parochiae' but in the late seventh and eighth centuries this wider ministry, while not improbable, is difficult to detect. It has been suggested that minsters founded by bishops were most probably established with such pastoral intentions in mind and it seems likely that by the late eighth century minsters provided the bedrock for local devotion, among them Breedon-on-the-Hill (Leicestershire), Brixworth (Northamptonshire), Evesham (Worcestershire) and Deerhurst (Gloucestershire).

Family Churches

Distinctive in Anglo-Saxon monasticism were the numerous houses founded as *Eigenkirchen* or private 'family churches'. These were places specifically associated with the founder and their kin, often their mausolea, offering spiritual and temporal benefits, effectively an investment in the profile and power of the kin. The family generally retained an interest in the affairs and estates of the house, and frequently the head of the community was drawn from the founder's kin. It was not unusual for such foundations to be regarded as part of the family estate, to be utilised as required, an attitude that had resonance into the eleventh century; they could readily become matters of dispute between rival members of a kin.

The mentalité underlying such foundations is revealed in the case of Stour in Ismere when in 736 King Æthelbald gave ten hides of land in Worcestershire for the construction of a monastery, possibly Kidderminster, to his companion, Ealdorman Cyneberht (EN 5). By 757 Cyneberht occurs witnessing charters as an abbot. His son, Abbot Ceolfrith, subsequently gave the estate to Worcester and the bishopric, but in 781 it was among the estates that King Offa complained that Worcester was 'wrongly holding in its power' as it was 'the inheritance of his kinsman, King Æthelbald'.

A 'family monastery' had been established, the founder and his son successively heading it as abbot. Ceolfrith's grant to Worcester was part of a wider pattern where a number of such family foundations were absorbed, among them Inkberrow in

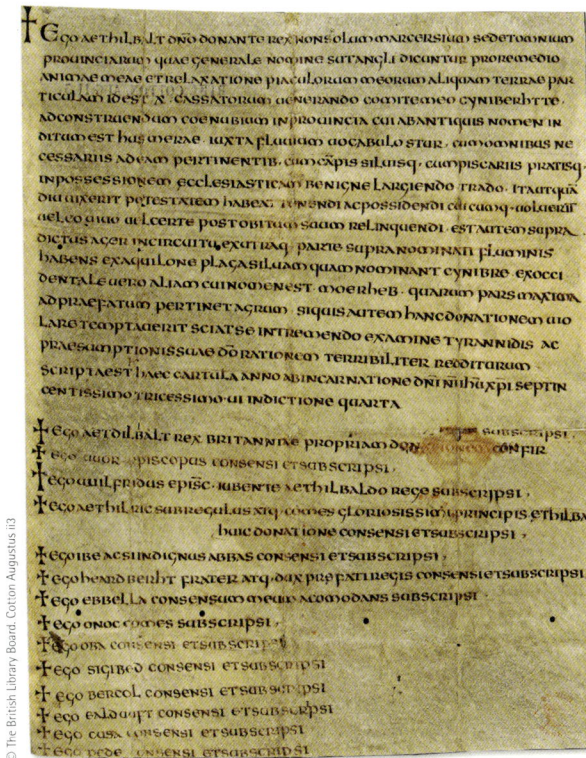

An Anglo-Saxon charter of 736 by which King Æthelbald conveyed ten hides of land for the construction of a monastery at Ismere.

Worcestershire; perhaps concerned that his kin might disapprove, Ceolfrith obtained the consent and licence of King Offa. Thus, Offa's subsequent complaint seems contrived and unjustified but it clearly demonstrates the perspective that land granted to a religious foundation remained with the kin, in this case, his kin.

Similarly, a charter of 780 revealed that St Peter's minster at Bredon in Worcestershire was a church built by Offa's grandfather, Eanulf, on land originally granted by King Æthelbald to his 'companion and kinsman'; land that was required to remain always in the hands of Offa's kin.

At Withington in Gloucestershire, the capacity for such foundations to split a kin is laid bare. Land was granted here by Æthelred and Oshere to two nuns, Dunne and her daughter Bucge, for the foundation of a minster. When approaching death, Dunne transferred the monastery to her young grand-daughter, Hrothwaru, but allowed Bucge, who was then 'a married woman', control until her daughter came of age. When in due course this time arrived, Bucge refused to relinquish the minster until Abbess Hrothwaru's rights were upheld in Holy Synod.

The growth of the Church was closely related to two phenomena – the endowments of secular power,

> *"Saints and relics were a very real force in the Anglo-Saxon world, reflecting the standing and prestige not only of a particular church, but also of a region, and of a kingdom."*

and the reputations of those whose careers and spirituality encouraged such donations. Such men and women were brought into the company of the saints, many of the minsters that buttressed Christian society being the resting places of saints and focal points for their cults.

Mercia and the Cult of Saints

Saints and relics were a very real force in the Anglo-Saxon world, reflecting the standing and prestige not only of a particular church, but also of a region, and of a kingdom. The saints played the role of invisible protectors, of intercessors between Heaven and Earth, and therefore a real equation between saints' cults and the prosperity of a people was perceived. Consequently, places associated with the saints and their relics became centres of pilgrimage.

Notable in Mercia, as elsewhere, was the large number of saints drawn from royal and high aristocratic kin. Generally royal and dynastic, these cults were the creation of a social and political elite rather than the product of popular devotion, although clearly both the people and the church were willing to accept and venerate them. The attractions of such cults are well illustrated by the story of Guthlac (674-714), a saint closely associated with Repton and Crowland, spanning Mercia and East Anglia, and a kinsman of King Æthelbald who had great affection for him and would build 'wonderful structures and ornamentations . . . in honour of the divine power' (Felix). As a young and distinguished warrior, Guthlac led a Mercian warband fighting on the borders of Wales, but one night he resolved to turn his back on that life and devote himself to the service of Christ. He entered the monastery at Repton and

This manuscript illumination of c.1175-1225 shows Guthlac tormented by demons, recalling Near Eastern accounts of the Desert Fathers.

© The British Library Board. Harley Roll Y 6, roundel 7

took the tonsure, where he proved 'the sincerity of his life and the modesty and serenity of his mind'. Around 700 his asceticism led him to leave Repton for the solitary life that he had discovered when studying the 'desert fathers', but in his case departing to the foggy marshes, bogs and black waters of the fens, where he lived on Crowland and did spiritual battle with demons. Revealed here is the vigour of a new culture taking shape as it combined the traditional values of heroic saga with the 'thought-world' of the Desert Fathers, like Saint Anthony, wrestling with devils. This was a world that touched Anglo-Saxon aristocratic mentalité at several levels and it is hardly surprising that Æthelbald could both identify with such a man and derive benefit to the reputation of his kin from it.

Most members of the Mercian royal kin who achieved sainthood in the seventh and eighth centuries did so in obscure and localised circumstances, where promoting the standing of family and kin was an integral motivation. Among the better-known cults was Saint Werburg, a daughter of King Wulfhere, remembered as an abbess of Mercian houses founded by her uncle, King Æthelred, and associated post-mortem with Hanbury (Staffordshire) and Chester; while at Much Wenlock (Shropshire) reposed Saint Mildburg, a daughter of King Merewalh whose cult established a dynastic monastery and devotion that might be identified with the province of the Magonsaete.

By the late eighth and ninth centuries Mercian cults included those of murdered royal kin, such as the youthful princes Kenelm and Wigstan whose murders and subsequent cults reflect dynastic politics, a consequence of the fact that by the ninth century the links with Penda's line, and the legitimacy invested in it, were becoming increasingly tenuous. Competing lineages sought to enhance their standing, like their predecessors, through the promotion of dynastic cults, generally based on family foundations. Kenelm, for instance, was associated with Winchcombe (now Gloucestershire) while Wigstan was buried at Repton (Derbyshire) in the mausoleum of his grandfather, Wiglaf.

Between the seventh and tenth centuries at least thirty saints' cults may be associated specifically with Mercia, as distinct from 'universal' devotions. Some undoubtedly contributed to a sense of Mercian identity that spanned centuries, but many were swept away in the wake of the Vikings and the reforms of the Anglo-Norman Church following the Norman Conquest.

A Transformation

The milieu of Anglo-Saxon Roman Christianity was aristocratic – patrons, bishops and saints being drawn mostly from such echelons. The nature and speed of transformation in Mercia appear remarkable. From Penda's personal rejection of Christianity in the first half of the seventh century, there followed by the end of it two of his sons, Wulfhere and Æthelred, who were every inch Christian kings. They encouraged in Mercia an effective diocesan structure and a network of minsters, and fostered the kingdom's 'spiritual treasury' through the promotion of saints' cults. In 664 the major church synod of the time was held at Whitby in Northumbria; by 672, the next major synod was convened at Hertford, in territory under Mercian authority. By c.731, of the twelve bishoprics south of the Humber, four were essentially Mercian and a further two or three were sometimes under Mercian influence, although one of these, Canterbury, would continue to represent a major challenge for Mercian interests. ✠

Mercia and the Saints: Presenting Relics

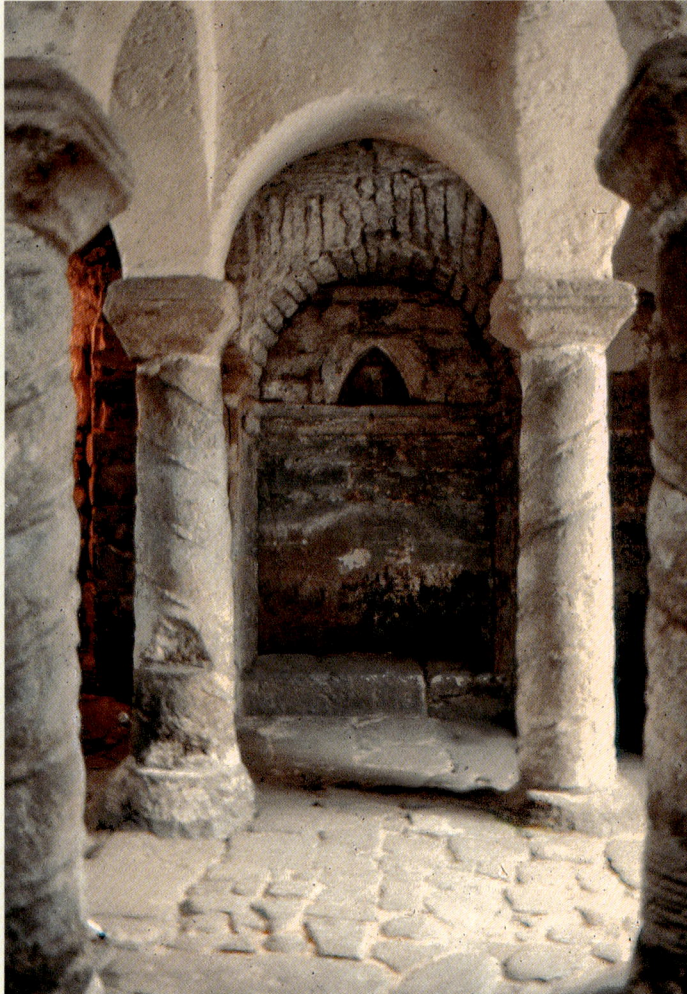

Courtesy John Hunt

The vaulted reliquary-crypt at Repton, a minster closely linked with the Mercian royal house where the cult of a royal saint was promoted.

Saints' relics, objects of veneration since at least the second century, became particularly popular from the fourth century. Sainthood, relics and miracles joined together Heaven and Earth. The saints were protectors and intercessors, close to God because of their holiness but also accessible to humans, whose nature they shared. By the end of the sixth century, in Europe and around the Mediterranean, graves of the saints had become centres of ecclesiastical life in their region.

The cult of Saint Chad, who died in March 672, reflects this phenomenon. The emergence of his cult in the late seventh century may be associated with the purposeful promotion of both his see and Mercia's Christian kings. Bede writes that miracles of healing at Chad's burial place 'attested to his virtues' and when the church of

St Peter was built at Lichfield, his burial was translated to it. Chad's wooden tomb was described as a 'little house' with an aperture in the wall so that the faithful might 'insert their hand and take out some of the dust', reflecting the notion that, in Finucane's words, relics emitted a kind of 'holy radioactivity' pervading all that came into contact, including 'contact relics' like the dust that gathered. This dust was mixed with water to relieve sick men and beasts of their ailments.

Access to relics was vital and demanded careful presentation to the faithful, whose visits and offerings added to the prestige and the wealth of the shrine concerned. These cults were carefully cultivated and managed, not least by mechanisms such as the translation of relics. Recent excavations at Lichfield appear to have revealed such enhancements with the discovery of an accomplished limestone polychrome sculpture of an angel. Representing the Archangel Gabriel, in a sumptuous Byzantine-influenced style of late eighth century date, it is thought to be a panel from Chad's shrine which, it has been suggested, was embellished and promoted when Lichfield was raised to the status of an archbishopric in 787.

The presentation of relics also influenced the arrangements at Repton, a minster closely linked with the Mercian royal house, some of whose members were buried here, and where the cult of a royal saint was promoted. Excavations have revealed a fine free-standing stone mausoleum to the north of the church that preceded developments to the east of the church.

After Æthelbald was murdered at Seckington in 757, he was brought to Repton for burial and a free-standing mausoleum with massive megalithic ashlar walls, perhaps originating as a baptistery east of the church, received his body. Subsequently the mausoleum was joined to the church and remodelled. The addition of a wooden floor enabled a chancel above the crypt, and openings were cut through the plinths of the mausoleum to create barrel-vaulted windows; and pillars, with encircling fillet, and pilaster columns were added, supporting a stone vault. In the mid-ninth century, perhaps following the burials of Wiglaf and the royal saint Wigstan, two access stairways were cut from the west.

The crypt and chancel were now integral to the cruciform church and although the layout to the west is unknown, features in the surviving fabric suggest a gallery level, perhaps to display relics during the year. The transition at Repton from mausoleum-crypt into a reliquary-crypt demonstrates the management and promotion of a royal saint's resting place and his cult. Three 'levels' of engagement between pilgrim and saint were facilitated: veneration at the window of the mortuary chamber; from within the church at a window in the chancel opening onto the chamber; and, most intimate of all, entrance into the crypt itself to approach the shrine. ✠

"Chad's wooden tomb was described as a 'little house' with an aperture in the wall so that the faithful might 'insert their hand and take out some of the dust', reflecting the notion that, in Finucane's words, relics emitted a kind of 'holy radioactivity' pervading all that came into contact, including 'contact relics' like the dust that gathered."

5

The Age
of Æthelbald
and Offa

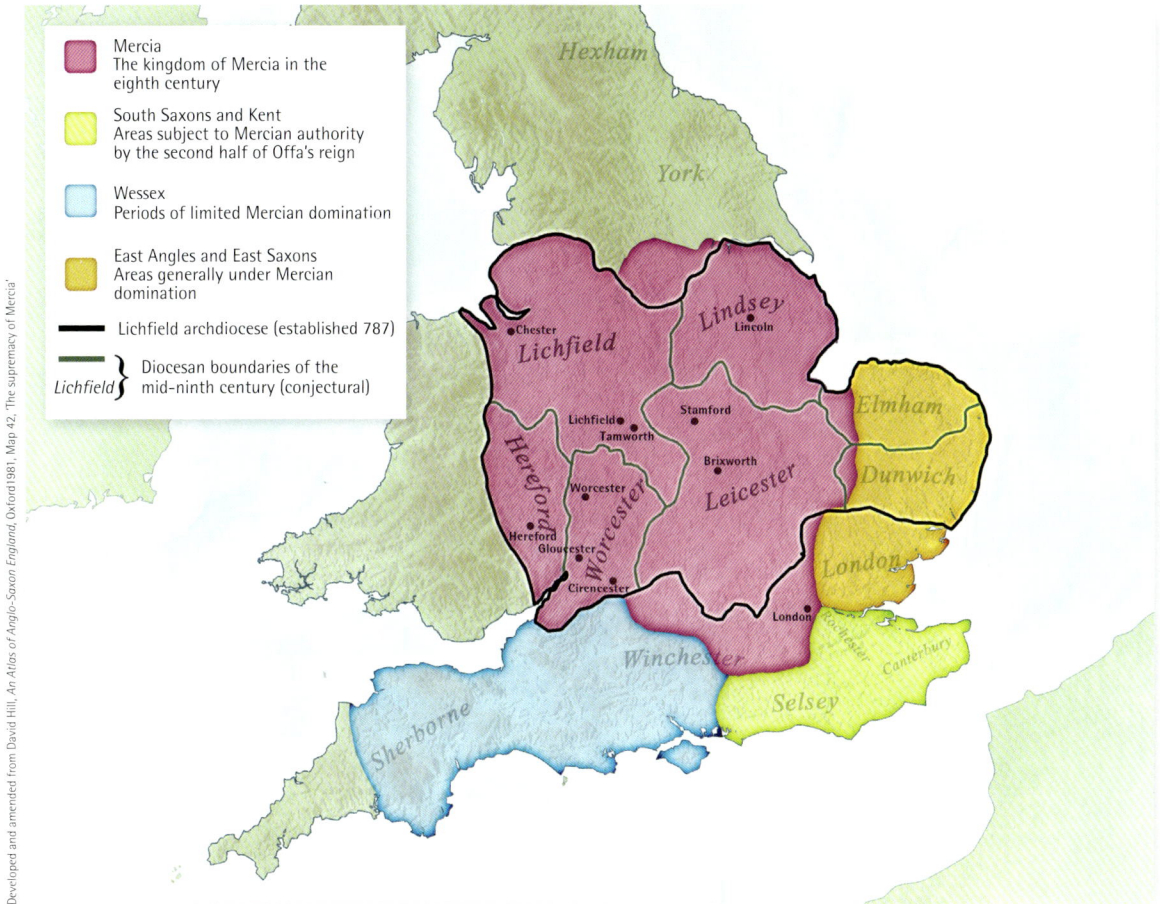

Mercia
The kingdom of Mercia in the eighth century

South Saxons and Kent
Areas subject to Mercian authority by the second half of Offa's reign

Wessex
Periods of limited Mercian domination

East Angles and East Saxons
Areas generally under Mercian domination

Lichfield archdiocese (established 787)

Lichfield } Diocesan boundaries of the mid-ninth century (conjectural)

'Mercian Supremacy' in the eighth century: neither absolute nor of uniform intensity, the creation of the Mercian archdiocese added another dimension focused on the Anglian peoples under Mercian domination.

Since Bede observed in about 731 that the provinces of England's bishops 'south of the river Humber and their kings, are subject to Æthelbald, king of the Mercians', historians have generally looked upon the eighth century as the great period of Mercian domination in Anglo-Saxon England, at least south of the Humber. That Æthelbald was duly followed by the greatest of the Mercian kings, Offa, and that between them their reigns spanned eighty years of the century, merely reaffirms the point.

Over the course of the century the confederation of peoples that Penda and his heirs had forged under their overlordship was to be converted into an enlarged and consolidated kingdom with a strong and increasingly centralised kingship. But how was this achieved, against a backdrop of emerging dynastic rivalries and the scrutiny of churchmen, and what did Mercian supremacy look like?

Previous page: An image of royal power and kin under divine protection, this eighth century figure from Repton may represent King Æthelbald, or his favoured saint, Guthlac.

Mercian Exiles

When Æthelred abdicated his throne in 704 he appointed his nephew Coenred in his place. His reign was short but well-regarded. Mercian authority was maintained in the satellite provinces, Coenred confirming or making grants of land in Middlesex, Worcestershire, Warwickshire and Herefordshire, and contending with attacks by the Welsh; even the demons that Saint Guthlac confronted in the Fens were British-speaking. Coenred's reputation for piety and 'ruling nobly' would seem to be consistent with his decision after five years to abdicate, and with Offa of the East Saxons, to depart for Rome where he took the tonsure and died not long afterwards. No fewer than six Anglo-Saxon kings, two of them Mercian, decided to abdicate their thrones for the religious life between 685 and 710.

Coenred's abdication brought his cousin, Ceolred, to the throne, remembered rather less favourably by posterity. His authority and lordship seem to have echoed that of his predecessor although he also campaigned into Wessex in 716, fighting in Wiltshire. However, his reign marked two developments that pointed to the future. Firstly, as the direct line of Penda weakened and became more 'distant' there are indications of growing discontent among other branches of the royal kin, with their own claims on power and subsequent dynastic rivalries. One of these rivals was Æthelbald, forced into exile and 'driven hither and thither by King Ceolred and tossed about among divers peoples' (Felix). He went into the Fens and sought out the 'holy man Guthlac' from whom he took comfort and the prophecy that with God's help, he would overcome his enemies and gain the Mercian throne. Guthlac had himself been an exile during the reign of Ceolred's father and may have had little love for Penda's descendants.

The second pointer to the future is revealed in Ceolred's reputation. Although not universally adopted, there was a tradition that regarded him as profligate, a visionary at Much Wenlock during the king's lifetime proclaiming that the angels surrounding him had removed their protective shield and abandoned him to demons because of the many crimes that he had committed; the story prompts a suspicion of dynastic interests at play.

At the heart of this uncomplimentary tradition lay the testimony of Saint Boniface, set out thirty years after Ceolred's death in a letter to King Æthelbald. The theme of the letter was a call for reform, in the course of which the example was raised of Ceolred, who, prompted by the devil, set a

In this manuscript of c.1175–1225, Guthlac appears before Æthelbald in a vision; gratitude for the saint's support encouraged the king to promote his cult.

"Fundamental was the absorption of Mercia's former satellite provinces into an enlarged and integrated kingdom, a phenomenon of Æthelbald's reign that was continued under Offa, in both cases reflected by the way in which previously independent rulers became increasingly subordinated in their status."

wicked example with 'an open display of [the] two greatest sins in the provinces of the English'. These sins were described as 'debauchery and adultery with nuns and violation of monasteries'. Personal immorality aside, Boniface was concerned with what he saw as the violation of church privileges, and although there is no further explanation as to what these violations were, it seems probable that the secular 'abuse' of minsters and their lands was among these, a recurrent theme later in the eighth century. As a consequence of his sins, while feasting in splendour with his companions, Ceolred was seized by madness and without repentance or confession he died 'conversing with devils and cursing the priests of God', to be buried, according to William of Malmesbury, at Lichfield.

The last of Penda's direct descendants passed with Ceolred's death in 716. The suggestion in a Worcester regnal list that he was succeeded by a man named Ceolwald cannot be otherwise verified, and if it was the case it can have been only fleetingly as in 716 Saint Guthlac's prophecy, given to Æthelbald while in exile, was fulfilled.

A New Dynasty

Æthelbald's accession marked the triumph of the Mercian royal lineage that traced itself back to Eowa, a brother of Penda, as did his successor, Offa. The two kings were first cousins, twice removed, and so the eighth century saw the replacement of one lineage with another. Barbara Yorke has

suggested that there may have been mutual co-operation between these two branches of the family, and certainly signs of rivalry are lacking. Æthelbald, for instance, made a grant to Offa's grandfather, Eanulf, whom he described as his kinsman and companion.

Æthelbald secured his position by favouring and promoting his kinsmen and friends to positions of power and influence in his service. A '*gesith*' or retainer of Æthelbald during his years of exile was a man named Oba (Ofa) who at one point was healed by the touch of the sheepskin rug in which Saint Guthlac was accustomed to pray. Ofa regularly appeared as a witness to Æthelbald's charters, on one occasion in 742 being described as 'Ofa, *patricius*', a title of distinction that probably signified his charge of the royal household. Another regular witness was the king's brother, Heardberht, often described as '*dux*' but more prestigiously in 749 as '*primatum*', of pre-eminent rank.

In the early years of his reign it is probable that Æthelbald could do little more than ensure his position within Mercia until wider opportunities presented themselves with the death of Wihtred of Kent in 725 and the subsequent partition of his kingdom between three sons; and the abdication of King Ine of Wessex, whose probable ambitions on London and Essex were dissipated by a disputed succession. Even so, historians have recently urged a more considered and 'defined' view of Æthelbald's overlordship around 731.

Securing the Mercian Heartland

Fundamental was the absorption of Mercia's former satellite provinces into an enlarged and integrated kingdom, a phenomenon of Æthelbald's reign that was continued under Offa, in both cases reflected by the way in which previously independent rulers became increasingly subordinated in their status, and their titles, descending from 'king', to 'under-king' and then 'ealdorman'. This latter vernacular title was used of royal kin, formerly autonomous rulers, and distinguished nobles to denote the king's most important and prestigious officers. They had delegated powers of governance, military command and administration in the Mercian provinces, the precursors of the later shires.

The last independent ruler of the Magonsæte was a son of Merewalh, Mildfrith, *regulus* (sub-king) but after about 740 this former province was integrated into the Mercian kingdom under a subordinate ruler, by Offa's time, an ealdorman. Similarly, the Hwiccian royal family was gradually subordinated and their province integrated, reflected by Æthelbald and Offa regularly granting land within their province; indeed one of the earliest of the charters to survive from Æthelbald's reign concerned an exchange of salthouses and furnaces near Droitwich with the church of Worcester. Among the witnesses when Æthelbald granted land at Stour in Ismere to his companion Cyneberht in 736 was Æthelric, 'sub-king and companion of the most glorious prince Æthelbald'.

By Offa's time there was a further but significant shift in how the Hwiccian rulers were described. For instance, there were several charters where Ealdred (fl. 757-790) was described as an under-king of the Hwicce, but in 778, in a charter of Offa granting land in Sedgeberrow (Worcestershire), he was described more precisely as '*subregulus*' and '*dux*' of

the Hwicce, that is, under-king and ealdorman. The transformation of this province into a Mercian *scir* or shire was effectively marked by the synod of Brentford in 781 settling a dispute between Offa and the church of Worcester, but after which there were no further Hwiccian charters. The Mercian kings first made the authority of Hwiccian rulers dependent upon their support and confirmation, which Æthelbald and more particularly Offa took further by completely transforming the basis of their subordinate authority, now entirely derived from the Mercian king until they effectively became his officers. Something similar is thought to have occurred among the Middle Angles and in Lindsey.

Mercia's Neighbours

As in the seventh century Mercian interests were greatly affected by relations with their neighbours, among them the East Anglian and East Saxon kingdoms where international trading networks were focused on the major *entrepôts* of Ipswich and London. Similarly important was the kingdom of Kent, with links to Francia and the seat of the southern archdiocese at Canterbury.

The fact that Saint Guthlac's *Vita* was dedicated to King Ælfwald of the East Angles, and the popularity of his cult in East Anglia, suggests crucially important cordial relations between the East Angles and the Mercians. Beyond the supposed implications of Bede's statement, there is little to suggest direct East Anglian subordination to Æthelbald, other than perhaps his seniority within the community of kings. We might here envisage influence rather than direct control and it was Æthelbald's good fortune that Ælfwald did not die until 749, after a reign of thirty-six years.

Among the East Saxons Æthelbald's authority was more tangible. Mercian control of London was reasserted and Middlesex was effectively annexed into the Mercian kingdom, all at the expense of the East Saxon kings. Æthelbald may be found remitting tolls at London for the benefit of the churches of Rochester and Minster-in-Thanet (Kent) without any need to associate an East Saxon king, at least not in the surviving versions of the grant, although a clause admonishing any future attempts by kings or their deputies to invalidate the gift might prompt speculation. Of course, with London came the

Saint Boniface was critical of Æthelbald's kingship, particularly his dealings with the Church. His martyrdom in Germany in 754 is depicted in the Sacramentary of Fulda, c.1001.

© Staatsbibliothek Bamberg

Kentish kings were subordinate. Mercian influence, however, might be reasonably supposed, as when in 731 the priest Tatwine, from the monastery of Breedon-on-the-Hill (Leicestershire), was elected archbishop of Canterbury. This was not an isolated instance; in 734-5 Nothelm, a priest of London, and again in 740, Cuthbert, a probable former bishop of Hereford, were elected to Canterbury.

Relations with Wessex seem to have been largely framed by border disputes in which Æthelbald was successful in gaining

particular demands of a major trading centre, among these the need for large quantities of coin. From as early as around 720 Æthelbald was striking a silver Mercian coinage with his most important mint in London, but there is nothing to suggest that he sought to enforce or control the minting of coin by other kings.

Mercian control of London and interest in cross-Channel trade must have affected the kingdom of Kent and influenced relations, but the evidence is equivocal and it is difficult to demonstrate that the

territory, perhaps previously contested land. He appears disposing of lands in West Saxon areas and this, alongside the fact that Æthelbald and the West Saxon king Cuthred fought together in 743 against the Britons, leads some to suggest a Mercian overlordship of Wessex at this point; but that need not be so, and in any case, by 752, Cuthred put the Mercians to flight at *Beorhford*. However, Æthelbald still appears witnessing land granted in Wiltshire as 'king not only of the Mercians but also of the surrounding peoples'.

Perceptions of Æthelbald's Kingship

There can be no doubt that royal authority in Mercia itself was strengthened and the kingdom enlarged as former satellite provinces were incorporated with the Mercian heartlands, but what of the rest of southern England?

It has recently been suggested that Æthelbald's ambitions were relatively limited, represented essentially by a 'corridor' of territory that ran south-eastwards along the line of Watling Street towards London. Beyond this, there is little to suggest direct control in Kent, among the South and East Saxons, or in the East Anglian kingdom. Still more limited were Mercian ambitions north of the Humber, with only two raids into Northumbria, in 737 and 740; nor is there much evidence regarding Wales, although the border areas had become more volatile by the early eighth century.

Can we reconcile this more circumspect evaluation with the testimony of Bede, as a direct and well-connected witness, well able to appreciate the contemporary scene; and one subsequently borne out by such as Æthelbald's confirmation of privileges to the churches of Kent in 742, the kind of act that we might associate with a king thought to wield real authority? Direct authority over the lands between the Mercian heartlands and London was essential, but elsewhere negotiation and fluctuation were possible based on influence, friendship and strength. Æthelbald pursued kingdom building in central England and secured its frontiers while elsewhere, to borrow a nineteenth-century phrase, he maintained 'spheres of interest'.

Æthelbald's aspirations and 'profile' may, to some extent, be reflected in the titles that he adopted, but such material must be treated with caution. The practices of individual *scriptoria*, particularly Worcester, played a part here and the styles they used need not have always represented the reality.

The title of '*rex Britanniae*', king of Britain, used in 736 is hardly credible, whereas in the text of the charter is found, 'king not only of the Mercians but also of all the provinces which are called by the general name south English', a description that comes closer to what Bede described a few years earlier. More commonly, as for Offa later, he was styled '*rex Merciorum*', 'king of the Mercians', a more accurate reflection of Æthelbald's authority, status and ambition.

Æthelbald and the Church

The reigns of both Æthelbald and Offa coincided with a period of renaissance in the Frankish Church which impacted on the dealings of the Mercian kings with the Church in England. Central to the tensions of Æthelbald's reign were the concerns laid out in the letter to the king of 746-7 from Boniface and seven other missionary bishops.

Initially it was complimentary in tone, speaking of Æthelbald's imperial rule over the English, his prosperity and faith in God, his giving of alms, maintenance of peace and justice, and his defence of widows and the poor, but thereafter the bishops turned at length to their main concerns. Firstly, Æthelbald was rebuked for the immorality of his personal life. Not only had he failed to take a lawful wife, but he was said to have violated 'holy nuns and virgins consecrated to God', imperilling not only his own soul, but also those of his subjects who might be encouraged to follow his example, giving rise to a degenerate people, 'neither . . strong in secular warfare nor stable in faith'.

Boniface and his colleagues were responding to reports that had been made to them, raising suspicion that there was growing unease over Æthelbald's life and governance, certainly among churchmen. It has been suggested that the king's failure to marry may have been a response to the

Offa's Dyke, an iconic earthwork monument to Mercian kingship.

complexities of Mercian court politics, but this is highly speculative and not very convincing.

The second strand in the bishops' letter was concerned with his violation of the privileges of churches and monasteries, stealing from them 'certain revenues', and complaining that his ealdormen and companions treated monks and priests with 'violence and oppression', and were thus destined for perdition. Not only did Boniface look back to a time when he believed that 'the privileges of the churches in the kingdom of the English remained untouched and unviolated', he was also well aware of the reforming initiatives within the Frankish Church, heightening his worries in England about such things as the behaviour of bishops, secular control of monasteries, and forced labour from monastic estates on royal buildings.

Complaints about secular interests in monasteries gained added force in Mercia from the time of Æthelbald. The traditional practice of granting land to minsters exempted from any future obligations to the kingdom was progressively undermining the resources upon which Anglo-Saxon kings could call. In Mercia, Æthelbald tackled the problem by requiring that certain universal obligations be laid on all lands, particularly the provision of labour; this undoubtedly sharpened Boniface's criticisms although it is doubtful that such demands would have seemed unreasonable to the Frankish kings.

Æthelbald eventually granted privileges to the churches in Mercia that gave them immunity from having to render food-rents and other works and burdens, but critically, he retained the right to demand services for building bridges and defences. Offa would subsequently add military or '*fyrd*-duty' to these 'common burdens'. The military capacity of the Mercian kingdom had been protected!

Coup d'état?

Æthelbald's long reign was clearly one that came to be marked by serious tensions. There may have been concern regarding his personal life and he seems to have been no less inclined than any other Anglo-Saxon ruler to resolve challenges through murder and violence, perhaps all the more so in an environment of competing dynastic ambitions. An atmosphere of division and resentment, and opportunistic ambition, seem likely precursors to his murder at Seckington, near Tamworth in 757, by members of his own household.

Suspicions of an intended '*coup d'état*' are strengthened by the succession to the throne of Beornred, probably to be associated with a rival dynasty that was to have more success in the following century. He lacked broad support, the *Peterborough Chronicle* noting that he 'ruled a short time and unhappily'. Within a year, Offa, representing a more successful rival kin that could associate itself with the successes of Æthelbald, had ousted Beornred from the throne and put him to flight, a second '*coup*' within twelve months.

Making Offa's Kingdom

When Offa took the throne it was again necessary to rebuild Mercian authority. The West Saxons were reversing their earlier losses along the Thames, and East Anglia seems to have drifted away from Mercian influence. In doing so, however, Offa went further than his predecessor in asserting direct Mercian power and influence over its neighbours, particularly in south-east England.

It has been suggested that in the first half of his reign Offa may have been preoccupied with a hostile Welsh border, given that Welsh chronicles record a battle at Hereford in 760 and Mercian campaigns into Wales in the late 770s and early 780s. Of course, historians' perceptions of the threat posed by the Welsh kingdoms have been heavily influenced by their interpretation of the remarkable earthworks known as Offa's Dyke, particularly if seen as a response to unwanted incursions from the west - an interpretation that is now difficult to sustain. Whatever his problems were to the west, Offa could hardly have disregarded a progressive undermining of Mercian interests in the south-east of England, particularly after the death of Æthelberht of Kent in 762.

In Kent Offa displaced the native dynasty. At first he intervened and supported Heahberht's claims on the throne, joining with him in confirming a grant of land at Rochester. How long-lasting or effective Offa's involvement was in Kent at this point is unclear, and while military success bolstered his short-term position there in the mid-770s, the crucial point came in 784-5 when, apparently after the death of King Ecgberht II of Kent, Offa effected a decisive intervention that swept away his Kentish rival, King Ealhmund. For the rest of his reign, with an ealdorman, Offa exercised direct control over Kentish affairs, this representing not the act of an overlord, but of a rival

"*The geography of Offa's power was similar to that of Æthelbald but its intensity was greater. Mercian authority ran from the Humber to the Thames, and extended into the south-east of England.*"

Early thirteenth-century manuscript, 'The Life of Saint Alban', showing the victorious King Offa with his warriors, trampling under their horses' hoofs the decapitated head of Æthelberht of East Anglia.

"In many ways the new archdiocese gave expression to two centuries of Mercian ambition and kingdom building."

for the throne. In 792 he was confirming immunity from secular obligations to Kent's churches, while he also revoked a grant made by King Ecgberht on the grounds that it was not right for his 'minister', or thegn, to make such gifts without his approval and confirmation.

Among the South Saxons however, Offa's authority was enhanced, as it had been among the Hwicce, by reducing the status of their native kings, preceded by military campaigns in 770 and 771. Thus, Osmund who in 770 and earlier had granted land as king of the South Saxons, by 772 was 'dux' or ealdorman of his people, and in the 780s Offa occurs retrospectively confirming the grants of his South Saxon 'duces'.

By differing mechanisms Sussex, and with more difficulty Kent, had been brought under direct Mercian authority by the second half of Offa's reign, but we know rather less about the East Saxons. Although the East Saxon kingdom remained independent, there was no diminution of Mercian control in and around London and Chelsea was a favoured royal residence. Mercian relations with the East Anglian kingdom are also unclear. They seem to have been stable, and sufficiently so for Offa's new archdiocese at Lichfield to embrace the two East Anglian bishoprics, but towards the end of his reign, in 794, Offa is alleged to have had Æthelberht of East Anglia beheaded.

Like his predecessor Offa had little influence north of the Humber although he married his daughter to King Æthelred of Northumbria, and similarly his authority in the south, in Wessex, should not be overstated. Relations between Mercia and Wessex were probably strained, particularly

while Cynewulf was king, and it was not until 779 that Offa was able to defeat the West Saxon king in battle, as a result of which disputed lands between the kingdoms again switched hands, like the Berkshire minster of Cookham first seized by Æthelbald, recovered by Cynewulf and now retaken by Offa. The geography of Offa's power was similar to that of Æthelbald but its intensity was greater. Mercian authority ran from the Humber to the Thames, and extended into the south-east of England. By the 780s Offa's power was at its height, and it was at this point that he sought to redraw the map of ecclesiastical authority in England.

Archdiocese and Kingdom

In 786 England was visited by a papal legation during which Offa pressed his proposals for the creation of a third, Mercian, archdiocese with its seat at Lichfield. The suggestion may have seemed reasonable and desirable among church reformers, concerned about the effectiveness of metropolitan authority in an archdiocese as large as Canterbury. Undoubtedly for Offa, an archbishopric at the heart of his kingdom associated with the cult of Saint Chad, a 'building block' of the Mercian kingdom itself, could only enhance his authority and perceptions of his Christian kingship. Furthermore, in the world of *realpolitik*, such an arrangement would mitigate the debilitating disputes that arose with Archbishop Jaenberht of Canterbury. In 787 the archdiocese of Lichfield was established under Archbishop Hygebald, embracing suffragans at Worcester, Hereford and Leicester, and Lindsey, Dommoc (probably Suffolk) and Elmham (Norfolk).

In many ways the new archdiocese gave expression to two centuries of Mercian ambition and kingdom building. Around the seat of Saint Chad were now gathered, fully and formally integrated in both ecclesiastical and political terms, the former satellite provinces of the Magonsæte, Hwicce and Middle Angles; the province of Lindsey; and now, the two East Anglian dioceses as well. The coherence of what had taken shape suggests that to see this episode simply as a response to difficult relations with Canterbury and the need to ensure that Offa's son, Ecgfrith, would receive his anointing, is to underestimate Offa's statecraft.

The history of the Anglo-Saxon kingdoms has often been perceived by generations of historians as if they were on a journey travelling towards an ultimate goal of unification. Unsurprisingly, Offa's Mercia has been seen as a beacon on this journey, assuming Mercian authority across England, south of the Humber; but in reality this authority was variegated in nature. Still more misleading is the implicit assumption that Offa shared the agenda posited by modern historians. Offa was preoccupied with building a stable and secure Mercia, not with unifying England.

Offa established a coherent and centralised kingship running between the Humber and the Thames, of which London was an integral part, with a natural extension into Kent and its sphere of influence. The engagement of the East Anglian kingdom was crucial to any such ambition, not only to ensure the integrity and security of the Mercian kingdom, but also for the wealth and opportunity generated through commerce focused on the emporia of Ipswich and London. Such associations were further strengthened by the overlay of a shared ecclesiastical jurisdiction. Such transformations of Mercia might be seen as making way for a new

Anglian political community south of the Humber, of the kind that might offer some justification for Offa's occasional use of the style 'rex Anglorum' (EN 6).

If such was the intention, it was short-lived if not still-born. In the nature of the age, much depended upon individuals and their force of personality; personal creations, as such schemes generally were, were prone to crumble when circumstances changed. In 794 the apparently peaceful accord with the East Anglian kingdom came to an end when Offa had Æthelberht of East Anglia killed, an act which post-Conquest historians associated with a plan to take direct control of his kingdom. Then in 796 Offa himself died.

Offa's Legacy

Offa had made preparations for his succession. In 787 his son, Ecgfrith, was anointed 'rex Merciorum', the first Anglo-Saxon to receive this distinction while his father lived, and for which both Insular and Carolingian inspiration has been claimed. Such preparations would have been unwelcome for some at court, as it sought to exclude rival kin from contention, which Offa further ensured by purging potential rivals, occasioning Alcuin's comment on the sins of the father, and the 'blood his (Ecgfrith's) father shed to secure the kingdom on his son'.

In the event, Ecgfrith was to follow his father's death in July 796 with his own in December. While Mercian authority in Kent and East Anglia collapsed, there was a breakdown in relations between Mercia and Wessex, and in Mercia itself the claims of rival kin added to the turmoil. It would be left to Coenwulf to rescue Offa's legacy and to redefine his 'vision'. ✠

Coins, Kings and Trade

A silver penny of Offa: the curled hair may be a deliberate allusion to King David, the Old Testament model for good Christian kings.

The earliest coinage in Anglo-Saxon England, gold and imported, was essentially used as prestige objects or bullion rather than for general commerce. However, coinage emerged from trading bullion, particularly for long-distance trade, and by the mid-seventh century it was being adopted in parts of England.

Although of limited utility in trade because of its high value, the late seventh-century switch from gold to a silver coinage, heralded in Merovingian Francia from the 680s, was prompted primarily by the difficulty of obtaining gold. The gradual debasement of this currency led to its replacement with a lower-valued silver coinage.

The incentive was the growing importance of trade and as trade grew, and with it wealth, kings took increasing interest. The close relationship between the monetary histories of Anglo-Saxon England and Francia reflects not only the significance of their commercial contacts, but also the economic context that necessitated currency reforms.

This early silver coinage, rarely inscribed and known as 'sceattas', also became progressively debased. Æthelbald of Mercia was striking coin by *c*.720, possibly stimulated by the importance of Mercian wool in international trade, and in the 730s and 740s his charters reveal the profits of trade collected through tolls at markets, as at London, described by Bede as an 'emporium of many peoples coming by land and sea.'

Debasement by the mid-eighth century prompted another new coinage, with higher precious metal content and a more uniform weight, now generally carrying the name of the king on whose behalf it was struck. Northumbria led the way in the 740s, followed by East Anglia when Beonna became king in *c*.758.

This reformed currency of silver pennies had room for a legend and design on both sides of the coin, generally with the king's name on the obverse and his moneyer's on the reverse. The new style of coinage came to be closely associated with Offa in the 760s and 770s although he was largely adopting coinage that the Canterbury and East Anglian mints had introduced following Frankish initiatives of 755. Offa again reformed the currency from the early 790s with larger, heavier pennies, in response to similar reforms by Charlemagne.

Offa's coinage is striking for its high standards, artistically and technically. His was the first named Mercian coinage, carrying his name and portrait, although the latter was discarded in his later currency reforms. He also considered a gold coinage, although few examples have survived. One of these imitates a 774 dinar of Caliph Al Mansur, copied around 790 by a moneyer who clearly knew no Arabic. Inscribed 'OFFA REX', it suggests that there was sufficient contact with Arab traders to warrant such a coinage. The gold penny probably represented a '*mancus*' or thirty silver pennies.

Consistent with Offa's style of kingship, he took a close interest in the coinage produced under his authority, moving towards the concept of a royally-controlled and guaranteed coinage, extending further protection to the commercial activity that was so important to the kingdom and to royal coffers. When Archbishop Jaenberht was permitted to mint his own coin around 791, it was still required to carry Offa's name.

Offa's interest was not only economic. The immense numbers of coin produced and in circulation, as the life-blood of commerce, also afforded Offa the opportunity to aggressively promote and enhance his authority and kin. When Offa's portrait utilised curled hair, it was perhaps in imitation of representations of King David, the Old Testament model for good Christian kings; the message was a powerful one for those who could read the imagery.

By the 790s Offa's grasp of the importance of currency was impressive. Canterbury was his most important and productive mint, with others at Rochester and London; and in *c*.795, East Anglian coinage was being struck for Offa, reinforcing the impression that he was now taking direct control of that kingdom following his execution of its king. ✠

"*Offa's coinage is striking for its high standards, artistically and technically. His was the first named Mercian coinage, carrying his name and portrait, although the latter was discarded in his later currency reforms.*"

6

Court, Church and Country

MERCIAN KINGSHIP AT WORK

When Boniface and his fellow bishops wrote to Æthelbald, they were clear on what they both expected, and did not expect, of their kings. His prohibition of theft and iniquities, perjury and rapine, his generous alms-giving and his defence of widows and the poor all earned their approval, whereas his personal life and treatment of the church did not.

There were similar expectations of Offa, as of any Christian king. In a letter of 797 to a Mercian ealdorman, Alcuin, a Northumbrian teacher and scholar, reflected on the kingship of Offa and the needs of the Mercian people. Brorda was told that he should advise the 'whole Mercian people to maintain good, temperate and pure conduct, as Offa of blessed memory laid down for them', so that they might have a stable kingdom and strength against their enemies. While bishops and the servants of God were to serve Christ in 'honesty and self-control', secular powers were to make 'just judgments and pure marriages among the people' and be loyal to their lord, warning that the Northumbrian kingdom was almost destroyed by internal quarrels and false oaths, a point of added poignancy in times of dynastic rivalry.

Alcuin had previously described Offa as the glory of Britain, 'our sword and shield against the enemy', presumably spiritual and temporal, and urged him to act justly and with mercy. For Asser, writing in the late ninth century, Offa had been a 'vigorous king' who 'terrified all the neighbouring kings and provinces around him', while the twelfth-century account of William of Malmesbury noted the king's mixture of vices and virtues, such that he

was not sure whether to 'commend or censure' him; in this he was following Alcuin, who advised Offa's successor, Coenwulf, that he should imitate his predecessor in his modest way of life and concern for reforming the life of a Christian people, but not in his greed or cruelty.

These comments speak particularly to the concerns of churchmen, but they also reach further, revealing the fusion of the traditional expectations of Germanic kingship with those of Christian kingship. Kings were expected to maintain good order and provide justice and protection for their people, while, as Christian kings, in Alcuin's words to Coenwulf, rulers should realise that they are 'a shepherd and steward', expected to promote the faith, protect and honour the Church, and lead by example in their personal lives. There was a long tradition of kings embodying the 'luck' and prosperity of their people, reiterated when Coenwulf was told that the English people were 'worn out' and needed to be restored through the goodness of their kings, the preaching of their priests and the faith of the people.

Shepherd and Steward: Christian Kings

When Alcuin thought about the nature of Christian kingship, there can be little doubt that he turned his mind to his Frankish patron, Charles the Great, also known as Charlemagne (*c.*742-814); or that his Mercian contemporary, Offa, was well aware of the responsibilities that lay on kings. For Alcuin, Charlemagne was '*doctor*' and '*dux*', teacher as well as leader; and his authority was that of a '*ministerium*', a God-given office with the responsibilities of guidance, correction and protection. No less was

Previous page: Alcuin, Northumbrian teacher, scholar and counsellor of kings, depicted in a medallion from the ninth century Bamberg Bible.

Offa was a devoted patron of the cult of Saint Alban, having the saint's body placed in a magnificent shrine and founding the monastery of St Albans.

expected of any Christian king, who themselves had the guidance of their bishops and the models of kingship presented in the Bible.

By the late eighth century this sophisticated model of kingship was firmly established at the Mercian court, reinforced through contacts with the Frankish church and kingdom. The anointing in 787 by Offa of his son Ecgfrith, investing in his successor sacerdotal acknowledgement, is one illustration of how this Mercian king saw the nature of royal authority, but not the only one.

Although disputes arose, kings were not hostile to clerical expectations as they strengthened and legitimised them and gave them a voice in the affairs of the church. Accusations of personal immorality were certainly avoided by Offa who promoted his marriage to Cynethryth; the queen regularly attested his charters and, without parallel elsewhere in Europe, minted coin with the legend

'regina Merciorum'. Churchmen at least expected kings to lead by example; in the words of Alcuin, 'a king who is above others in rank should be above them in moral perfection, justice and goodness', in their daily lives, honouring the saints and supporting the church.

Æthelbald, for instance, was generous in almsgiving and honoured Saint Guthlac by building a shrine of 'wonderful structures and ornamentations', and was credited by the twelfth century with the foundation of Crowland Abbey. Offa likewise gave land for the foundation or endowment of minsters, several established by him, and many dedicated to Saint Peter, for whom he seems to have held a particular affection. His correspondence with Charlemagne regarding measured black stones may reflect an interest in the patronage of buildings, while his gift of a great Bible and two gold bracelets to Worcester demonstrates another aspect of his patronage. Offa also gained a special association with the cult of Saint Alban, Britain's first Christian martyr and the only martyr of the early church to be generally recognised on the Continent; such associations were, of course, prestigious for Offa. Twelfth-century writers record that Offa reputedly had the body of Alban exhumed and placed in a magnificent shrine, decorated with gold and jewels, and around the small church on the site was founded the monastery of St Albans, building there a 'church of most beautiful workmanship'.

Despite these associations, both Æthelbald and Offa were regarded as rapacious 'despoilers' of the church, breaching the very privileges that kings were expected to protect. In fact, patronage and despoliation were two sides of the same coin, arising from the prevailing custom for family monasteries and the view that no land was alienated from the kin granting it. Of course, Æthelbald and Offa sharpened criticism further by their reservation of certain key obligations from lands held by the church, but as the basis of sustainable power now lay with obligations vested in the land, the Mercian kings were left with few alternatives.

While Offa could argue that the rights he asserted were those rightly enjoyed by all patrons, he nonetheless strengthened his claims by obtaining from the papacy, in perpetuity, for himself, his wife and his offspring, a privilege permitting the possession of monasteries and monastic properties. That Offa also surrendered some minsters when the bishop of Worcester objected to religious communities under lay control may hint at some personal ambiguity or unease attuned with the concerns of the church.

The integration of church and kingdom made inevitable the engagement of kings in church affairs, nowhere more so than in the church councils of the second half of the eighth century. In 747 Æthelbald attended a synod at unlocated *Clofesho* and heard discussion on the dress, immorality and drunkenness of the clergy, and the thorny issue of lay interests in monasteries. Two years later he was at the synod of Gumley, defending his impositions but agreeing a compromise on the question of church immunities, so he was not entirely out of step with the concerns

An early medieval court where the enthroned Frankish king, Charles the Bald, is surrounded by his courtiers and counsellors (mid-ninth-century Carolingian Bible).

that Saint Boniface had raised; and from 781 there were regular meetings between the archbishop and bishops of the southern ecclesiastical province and the Mercian king and court, continuing into the ninth century.

Particularly momentous for Mercia was the legatine commission of 786 which met initially under the presidency of Offa and Cynewulf of Wessex. Not long before, Pope Hadrian had been alarmed at rumours that Offa was urging his deposition, but the primary purpose of the mission was to investigate the condition of the church in England. Their enquiries returned twenty canons on matters for correction, ten dealing with questions of faith and ecclesiastical order, and ten directed towards the laity, including prohibitions on the killing of kings as the Lord's anointed; all were appropriate to royal oversight. However, Offa also took the opportunity of this mission to promote his proposals for an archdiocese at Lichfield, plans which were at least partly motivated by the difficulties he faced in dealings with Archbishop Jaenberht of Canterbury regarding Mercian control of Kent, a timely reminder of the ever-present 'political' undertones in royal dealings with the Church.

The Court and the King's Men

The earliest English court for which we have significant information is that of Alfred of Wessex in the second half of the ninth century, with several texts that offer insights into it and into the king's thinking. Among these Alfred used his translation and additions to Boethius' 'Consolation of Philosophy' (*De Consolatione Philosophiae*) to make the point that he 'desired tools and materials' to undertake the work that he was charged to perform. In what appears to be the earliest statement of the 'three orders' familiar from medieval society, Alfred noted the need for priests, soldiers and labourers, as 'without these tools no king can reveal his power'. These orders must be sustained, through land, gifts, weapons, food, ale and clothes, as 'without those things he cannot hold those tools, nor without these tools do any of the things that he is charged to do'.

While details of the court might differ, the needs of the Mercian kings were little different. Indeed, in 797, Alcuin advised Coenwulf to have 'wise counsellors who fear God, love justice, desire peace with friends, and show faith and goodness in a devout way of life'. While kingship was an intensely personal affair, it could not function effectively without the support and advice of trusted men, in the court and in the country. A fine visual image of this reality may be found in a mid-ninth century Carolingian Bible, the *First Bible of Charles the Bald*, where Charles II is depicted enthroned, surrounded by his counsellors, receiving the presentation of a bible created in the *scriptorium* of the abbey of St Martin at Tours.

So important were these roles that kings looked to family, friends and kin to fill many of them. The court brought together men of various talents and standing from the household and beyond, from both the laity and the church. Some impression of these assemblies may be glimpsed in the witness lists to charters, while, albeit at a later date, we can detect from royal wills specific roles in the royal

"While kingship was an intensely personal affair, it could not function effectively without the support and advice of trusted men, in the court and in the country."

Courtesy MOLA (Museum of London Archaeology) Northampton

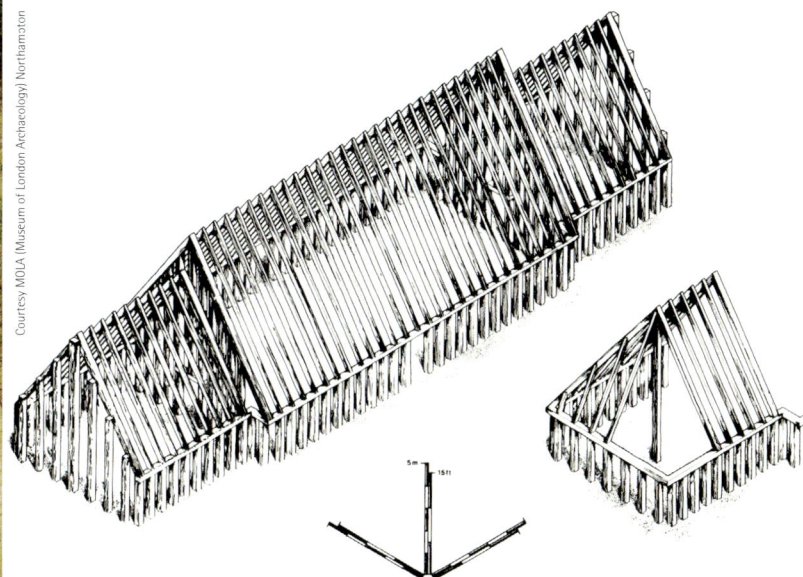

A probable timber royal hall excavated in Northampton, dated before c.820.

household; men such as ealdormen, reeves, stewards and seneschals, keepers of the wardrobe and butlers, mass-priests, sword polishers and stag-huntsmen. Bishops, abbots and priests brought considerable skills to the practice of government, not least in the needs of diplomacy, although some could find their position difficult. In the early eighth century the bishop of London complained that through involvement in government, churchmen had become divided by a dispute between the West Saxon and Mercian kings, while later in the century the tensions between the Mercian king and the archbishop of Canterbury must have been uncomfortable for some.

The royal household comprised 'tried men' and young men, and for the latter in particular the Mercian court must have seemed a place of splendour and opportunity with ceremonial and display, given what we know about the Northumbrian court, and Mercian familiarity with Carolingian and perhaps Byzantine practice. The court was a busy and sophisticated place, dealing with diplomacy and intrigue, administration and justice, hospitality and advancement. Gifts were exchanged and relationships built; such was the gift to Offa of a Hunnish sword from the Avar treasure taken in 795, one of Charlemagne's gifts. The court of a powerful king was expected to dazzle and impress, not only in the authority it reflected, but also as a place where a rich material culture was evident; in fine clothes, gold embroideries, wall hangings in silk and other textiles; stuccoed and

© Cambridge University Collection of Aerial Photography

Aerial photograph of a hall site at Atcham in Shropshire.

painted walls, rich personal adornments and possessions, such as swords, belt fittings, rings and brooches, and fine metalwork.

The court was a place of learning. We may suppose a library in the Mercian court, and perhaps, by the time of Offa, a court school. Alcuin congratulated Offa in the late 780s on his eagerness to promote learning and reading in his kingdom, and he sent him his pupil, requesting that he be given pupils to teach. In the Mercian court were muniments, an interest in written genealogies and books, among them a manuscript copy of Bede's *Ecclesiastical History*, and

"The court of a powerful king was expected to dazzle and impress, not only in the authority it reflected, but also as a place where a rich material culture was evident."

although the date and provenance remain a matter for debate, the final stages in the composition of *Beowulf* may have been undertaken here, where an appropriate audience would certainly have been found. Nonetheless, literacy at court, in the technical sense of being conversant with Latin, was restricted. Documents addressed to Æthelbald and to Offa's court, were explained or also read in the vernacular to ensure that all understood. Of course, some of those unable to read Latin may well have been able to read the vernacular.

Fundamental to king and court were the making of law and the provision of justice, which under the influence of the Church gave rise to written law codes. Clearly Mercia had laws, but no texts have survived. In his own laws King Alfred noted that he had been informed by those of his forebears, including Offa, although it has been suggested that this may refer to the legatine decrees of 786, issued in Mercia under Offa's name.

Mercian royal households included servants at all levels, from messengers, ushers and scribes to great men who advised, commanded and dealt justice. The title of '*patricius*' in some charters may refer to the head of the king's household, while in the early ninth century the titles of '*pedes sessor*' or '*pedisecus*' occur, meaning 'one who sits at the feet'. The titles of '*praefectus*' or '*gerefa*' were used to describe some royal officers, such as the '*wicgerefa*' or 'town-reeve' of London mentioned in Kentish laws. Reeves, who could be wealthy and powerful individuals, often had charge of royal halls and estates, Saint Boniface complaining to Æthelbald about the conduct of his 'reeves and *gesiths*' (warrior companions or retainers). Some '*praefecti*' had wider, regional responsibilities, as ealdormen. The detail is unclear before the tenth century, but there were at least eight ealdormen in the late eighth century, and twelve in the early ninth century,

several of whom were probably associated with provinces also defined by the dioceses that served them.

Sword and Shield

Early medieval kings were constantly on the move. Even with the support of trusted officers, the personal nature of kingship meant that kings were well-advised to be seen around their realm. Generally, royal itineraries were related to royal estates and other principal places, sometimes favouring certain residences. Offa and Coenwulf, for instance, were often at Chelsea or Tamworth, although the latter was a particular favourite between 781 and 857, numerous charters being issued or ratified there. Described in some as '*in sede regalis*', 'at the royal seat', or as the 'royal palace', the king and court regularly spent Christmas and Easter here, reflecting both favour and tradition. The great festivals were favourite times for summoning councils, and to do so in the traditional heartland of the Mercian kingdom, at the chief place of the Tomsæte, perhaps had symbolic significance. However, Tamworth was not a 'capital' in the modern sense of the word, but was rather one of many royal estates.

These estates were the personal possessions of the king rather than attached to his 'office', King Alfred naming sixty such places in his will. These royal vills, often known as *tūnas* (plural of *tūn*), were estate centres with other lesser places dependent upon them, and from these networks were drawn the food and services needed to support the king. He did not necessarily progress between these vills in turn, but their resources could be summoned to where the king was. Similarly, through the obligation of '*feorm*', the king could make demands on the estates of others for provisions, including hospitality for his officers, servants and messengers, although these obligations

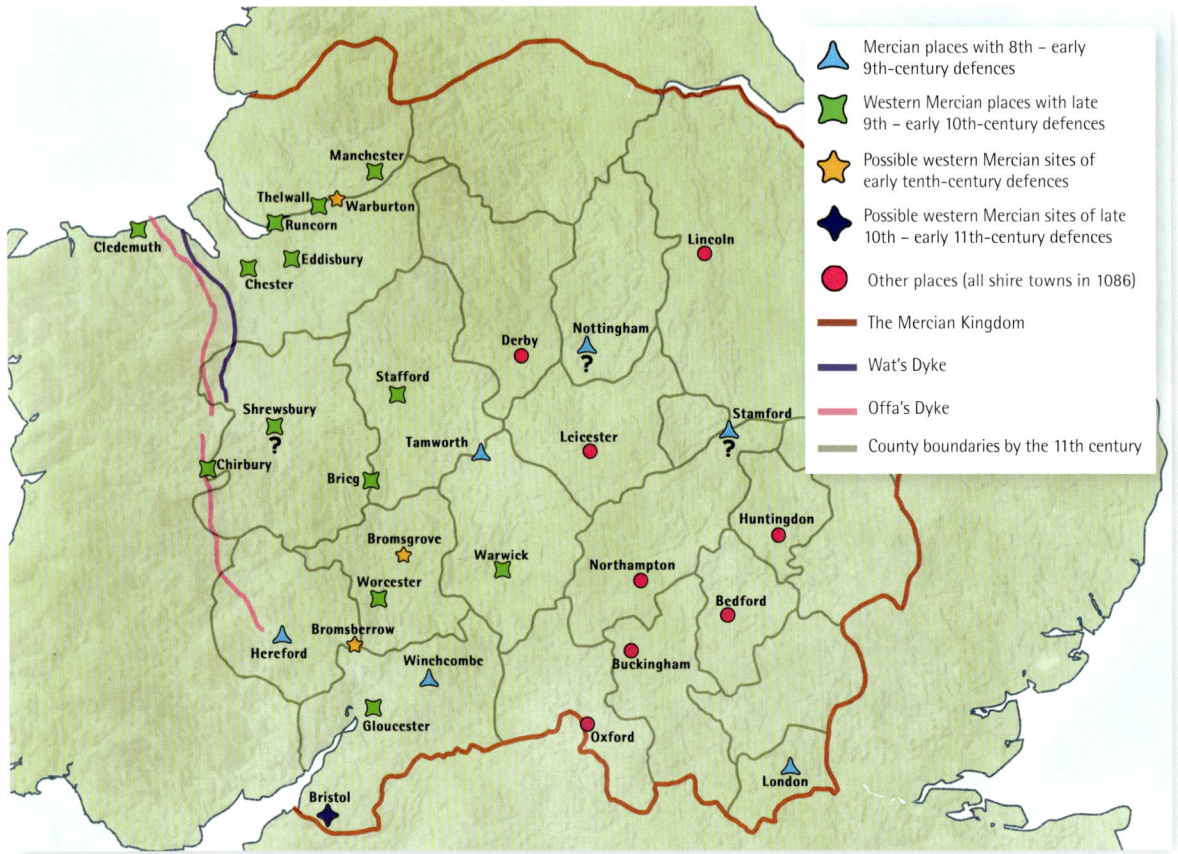

After S Bassett, with additions, 'Anglo-Saxon Fortifications in Western Mercia', Midland History, 36, No 1, 2011, Figure 1

Legend:

- ▲ Mercian places with 8th – early 9th-century defences
- ▣ Western Mercian places with late 9th – early 10th-century defences
- ★ Possible western Mercian sites of early tenth-century defences
- ◆ Possible western Mercian sites of late 10th – early 11th-century defences
- ● Other places (all shire towns in 1086)
- ▬ The Mercian Kingdom
- ▬ Wat's Dyke
- ▬ Offa's Dyke
- ▬ County boundaries by the 11th century

Fortifications in Mercia

were increasingly the subject of exemptions, particularly on church estates.

Royal residences were scattered across the Mercian kingdom; some, like Tamworth and London, are known from documents while others are suggested by events such as councils, as at Wellesbourne in Warwickshire. The best known archaeological sites are Yeavering in Northumberland and Cheddar in Somerset, but in Mercia a probable royal hall was excavated in the early 1980s at *Hamtun*, or Northampton. The earliest building, dated to before c.820, was a timber-built rectangular hall of robust construction, with annexes at each end. This building was succeeded in the ninth century by a large and distinctive stone hall, part of a site that included a minster church. Recent investigations at Drayton in Oxfordshire have added what may be another timber palace site, while aerial photographs have revealed high-status, but not necessarily royal sites, at Atcham (Shropshire), Long Itchington and Hatton Rock (both in Warwickshire), although

"Mercian success was reliant upon military power and Æthelbald and Offa were the first Anglo-Saxon kings to seek to 'codify' this capacity and move it away from dependency upon the person of the king."

"Mercian kingship was sophisticated, innovative and powerful. Embracing the opportunities afforded by Christian models, and well aware of Frankish and Byzantine practice, it was built upon the standing and reputation of the kin, the mutual support of king and church, and a more integrated kingdom with effective governance and strong military power."

royal and episcopal halls differed little. These halls were generally part of a complex of buildings, grouped in ranges and often within enclosures, in some cases better described as defences, as at Tamworth, which by 781 was known as *Tamworthy*, denoting an important, fortified settlement. This highlights a crucial factor in the success of Anglo-Saxon Mercia.

Alongside giving justice, ensuring defence and protection were the bedrock upon which early medieval kingship was built. Mercian success was reliant upon military power and Æthelbald and Offa were the first Anglo-Saxon kings to seek to 'codify' this capacity and move it away from dependency upon the person of the king. Central to this was the reservation of the 'threefold obligations' on all estates, begun with Æthelbald's demands for the building and repair of defences and bridges that prompted complaint in the 740s. The Mercian system developed incrementally as Offa later added a third demand, for '*fyrd*' or military service.

These developments were integral to the Mercian military system. Border disputes and displays of power aside, Mercian military actions in the eighth century were not expansive campaigns of conquest but rather were intended to achieve well-defined and specific objectives. Mercian territory was secured by establishing a number of substantially fortified settlements, supported by their hinterlands, which the 'obligations' ensured

could be built, maintained and manned, with armies moved rapidly around the kingdom.

Steven Bassett in particular has explored the importance and role of early Mercian fortifications and demonstrated that at Hereford, Winchcombe and Tamworth there were substantial defences built in the eighth or very early ninth century. It is improbable that these were the only ones; an extensive network of fortifications, generally based on existing settlements and royal residences, seems probable. These may only be discovered through excavation, but seem likely to include places such as Leicester, Lincoln, Chester, Gloucester, and certainly London, with reutilised Roman walls; and later towns like Nottingham, Northampton, Bedford and Huntingdon (EN 7). Offa's Dyke has also been traditionally seen as a part of Mercia's military defences but there are now strong reasons to doubt this.

Power, Kin and Prosperity

Mercian kingship was sophisticated, innovative and powerful. Embracing the opportunities afforded by Christian models, and well aware of Frankish and Byzantine practice, it was built upon the standing and reputation of the kin, the mutual support of king and church, and a more integrated kingdom with effective governance and strong military power. Mercia prospered, but much still depended upon the person and personality of the king himself. ✠

Offa's Dyke

Offa's Dyke is best understood as an ambitious and symbolic statement of King Offa's power and imperial pretensions.

The massive earthwork that Welsh sources referred to as *Clawdd Offa*, or Offa's Dyke, is the largest archaeological monument in Britain, marking a frontier of some 150 miles, with about eighty miles of surviving earthworks. This remarkable monument was of sufficient note for Asser to record in the late ninth century that Offa 'had a great dyke built between Wales and Mercia from sea to sea'. The rampart was in places up to twenty-five feet high, topped with a timber palisade or stone wall, and fronted to the west by a ditch about six feet deep. Notwithstanding its prominence and celebrity, it remains enigmatic. Despite the massive organisational feat that it represented, no contemporary accounts or administrative records have survived to inform on its construction, context or purpose. Nor has the work of archaeologists yet provided a definitive interpretation.

In the mid-twentieth century (EN 8a) it was argued that this was a negotiated frontier running from the Severn estuary to Prestatyn on the north Wales coast, seen as a progression from earlier smaller earthworks that had attempted a localised settling of boundaries. The many gaps in the line were associated with forest, rivers, ravines or unfinished work (EN 8b). Implicit in this interpretation of the Dyke as an agreed frontier was the assumption that it was forged out of peaceful diplomacy.

However, more recent research challenged these views (EN 8c) and has even 'shortened' the dyke, refuting Asser's description. The only section that may be safely associated with Offa runs for sixty-four miles from Rushock Hill in Herefordshire to Treuddyn near Mold; it has been argued that Wat's Dyke was used to the north, an earthwork traditionally associated with Æthelbald, but excavations in 2006 of a length of Wat's Dyke have proposed a later date, in the 820s, when Offa's successor, Coenwulf, and after him Ceolwulf, were campaigning against the Welsh. The idea of 'gaps' integral to the original construction has also been rejected, traces of the western ditch having been detected in places. These discoveries have encouraged some (EN 8d) to see the Dyke not as an outcome of peaceful negotiation, but as a response to war, with suggestions also that there was a series of Mercian forts along the line of the Dyke by the early ninth century, if not earlier.

Thus it has been proposed that the Dyke was not so much an attempt to define the Mercian border in general, but rather a short-term response to an aggressive and expansive kingdom of Powys under King Eliseg. However (EN 8e), the argument has not proven persuasive. The reality of this threat may be questioned and in any case such earthworks were not the customary Anglo-Saxon response to external threat. Nor can we certainly demonstrate that it was manned or part of an integrated system of frontier defence in the way that Hadrian's Wall had been, or indeed that it was maintained beyond initial construction.

What is undeniable is the powerful symbolism of this earthwork, fulfilling in the Mercian landscape a function akin to monumental architecture. It encapsulated and projected Offa's lineage and his ambition. A passage in the poem *Widsith* attributes a dyke along the Eider to Offa's Continental ancestor, Offa of Angeln, while in Britain the imperial associations of such linear frontiers were obvious. The Dyke may be seen primarily as a statement of Offa's power and imperial pretensions, consistent with other expressions of how he saw his kingship. The message inherent in the Dyke was probably intended more for Offa's Mercian subjects than for the Welsh to the west. ✠

7

Merchants,
Markets and the
Carolingians

On Christmas Day in the year AD 800 there occurred in Rome one of the 'milestone' events in the history of early medieval Europe, the imperial coronation of Charlemagne by Pope Leo III, reviving the title of 'Emperor' in Western Europe. This marked the mastery of Europe that the Frankish king had achieved, driven by his sense of Christian kingship, sustained by the intimate relationship between the Church and the Carolingian state, and his determination to fashion a domination that politically and culturally reawakened the image of Rome, but now Christian and recast through Frankish eyes.

These were events of consequence for Anglo-Saxon England as well. Mercia, a dominant power in England, was also actively part of an international community brought together by the Roman Church and its culture, by shared perceptions of Christian kingship, and through trade. Anglo-Saxon kingdoms did not exist in isolation from the Continent, nor were they able to stand aloof of its influence; indeed, they generally embraced it. It seems probable that Offa looked upon his contemporary, Charlemagne, with guarded admiration and certainly the Mercian kings could never afford to disregard such powerful and influential near-neighbours.

A fine ninth-century sculpture of Charlemagne in the monastery church of Saint John in Müstair, Switzerland.

© Wladyslaw Sojka at the German Language Wikipedia, CC BY-SA 3.0

Charlemagne, the Frankish Empire and Mercia

In a reign of over forty-five years, Charlemagne organised around sixty military campaigns that extended his authority into Saxony, annexed Bavaria and the Lombard kingdom in northern Italy, cast his influence across most of the Italian peninsula, and dominated the 'marcher' areas that bordered his empire, reaching into the Balkans, Bohemia and northern Spain. Beyond these frontiers lay the Emirate of Cordova, dominating the Iberian Peninsula save for the Christian princes of Galicia who with Navarre and the Spanish March looked northwards to Francia. In the eastern Mediterranean, the Eastern Roman Empire, with outliers in southern Italy, Sicily and Sardinia, was ruled by an emperor who was heir to, and the model for, Roman imperial heritage; while north Africa and the Near East were dominated by the Abbasid Caliphate. Charlemagne's diplomatic links and 'allies' embraced all of these neighbours, and extended westwards as far as the 'kings of the Irish', bonds of friendship that Einhard, Charlemagne's 'biographer', thought 'augmented the glory of his realm'.

Previous page: The importance of international trade is reflected by the depiction of a Frankish merchant ship on a silver denier of 814–840, minted at Quentovic.

© Genevra Kornbluth

Mercia and the Frankish Empire: Mercian trading links with north-western Europe, which in turn connected with wider networks.

It is against this background that Charlemagne's links with England, and more specifically with Mercia, must be seen. Contact between Anglo-Saxon England and the Continent reached back to the early days of the Conversion and English missionaries, like Wilfrid, Willibrord and Boniface, proselytised the Faith among the Frisians, Franks and Germans during the late seventh and early eighth centuries. Moreover, the career of Alcuin illustrates the attractions of the Frankish court to English churchmen and scholars. The primacy of Rome drew the English and Frankish Churches together, and Charlemagne corresponded with English kings and bishops, dispatching

> *"Mercia, a dominant power in England, was also actively part of an international community brought together by the Roman Church and its culture, by shared perceptions of Christian kingship, and through trade."*

representatives as required. Indeed, Abbot Gervold of Saint-Wandrille (France), a friend of Offa, was sent by Charlemagne on many occasions as his ambassador to the Mercian king. Thus through embassies and correspondence, including the letters of those in the 'court circle' like Alcuin, the Frankish court maintained considerable contact with Mercia and her neighbours.

Carolingian Influence in Mercia

Contact between the Mercians and the Carolingians, and the prevailing trends among 'state-builders', were sufficient to encourage shared perspectives and inspiration but not necessarily direct indebtedness. Frankish and Mercian elites shared very similar outlooks on the world and their place within it, familiar with rank and status, the dynamic of lord and man, and the rights and expectations that came with that; the nature of wealth and the basis of power; the exercise of authority within the context of an ordained Christian order and society; the symbolic power of reference to a Roman imperial past, and an appreciation of a rich and vibrant artistic and intellectual culture receptive of new influences, particularly prestigious ones. Frankish and Mediterranean influences were not hard to find in Mercian culture, as sculpture in the church of Breedon-on-the-Hill illustrates.

The Franks and the Mercians saw the necessity of rooting obligations such as military service in the land and applying it universally, and of embracing the church as integral to the fabric of the state. However, the fact that Offa and Charlemagne both revalued their coinages within a year of each other was not so much a matter of imitation as responsiveness, both protecting royal revenues by ensuring that foreign coin would need to be exchanged for commerce. If 'Offa's laws' were actually the decrees of the Legatine Mission in 786, then Carolingian influence must be accepted here as the men behind them had close Frankish associations, among them Alcuin. More certainly suggestive of Carolingian influence was the use of the Roman Church to assert legitimacy and possession of royal power through anointment, as Offa sought to establish the

© National Maritime Museum, Greenwich, London

The late ninth-century Graveney boat carried goods such as hops and quernstones from the Rhine Valley.

Courtesy CBA /Robert Meeson

Tamworth's horizontal watermill of at least the mid-ninth century, and possibly earlier, used millstones of imported Rhineland lava.

succession of his son by direct descent, a new departure for Mercia. Charlemagne's own sons had been consecrated by the Pope some six years earlier.

Charlemagne and Offa: the Nature of their Relationship

The Carolingians clearly had the power to impress, but while the scarcity of reference might not do justice to the levels of contact between the two royal courts, the suggestion of some historians that Offa was regarded as Charlemagne's equal is improbable and unsustainable. Charlemagne's hegemony encompassed some 1,200,000 square kilometres with an intensively governed and bureaucratic state at the heart of it. Offa's hegemony ran to around 100,000 square kilometres which, lacking the advantageous inheritance of functioning Roman imperial institutions, was developing its identity as a state. Based fundamentally upon two letters speaking of 'brother' and 'friend', the idea confuses the language of diplomacy with that of equality.

However, there are some indications as to the nature of their relationship. Charlemagne took under his protection a number of exiles from Offa's Mercia, like those returned to their land following the death of their lord, Hringstan. The Carolingian court sheltered Ecgberht, rival of Offa's protégé Beorhtric of Wessex, and the Kentish claimant, Eadberht Praen. The exiled Northumbrian King Eardwulf looked to Charlemagne for help and both he and Ecgberht may have received direct and material assistance. Charlemagne, and his heir, evidently had the capacity to interfere and pose a threat to Mercian kings. In 821 Coenwulf declared that he would not stand for the interference of either Pope or Emperor in his dispute with Archbishop

Wulfred. The threat, however, was not reciprocal; Mercia was hardly in a position to challenge Carolingian interests.

Such a perspective explains the diplomatic indignation that followed Charlemagne's proposal in 790 that Offa's daughter might marry his son, Charles. Royal marriages were diplomatic tools, claims on influence and expressions of alliance or authority, where the husband's affiliations were recognised as dominant. Offa responded by stating that he would not agree unless Charlemagne's daughter married his own son Ecgfrith, implying a parity that was in reality illusory, and for Charlemagne, insulting. The Franks broke off their dealings with Mercia and closed their ports and trading places to the Angles, causing disruption that Alcuin noted in his letters, sailings forbidden to traders on both sides.

Trade with the Franks

Charlemagne's emissary in these marriage negotiations was Abbot Gervold, who for many years had served as superintendent of the Frankish kingdom's trade, collecting taxes and tolls from various ports and cities, particularly from the important port of Quentovic (near Étaples in France). The taking of taxes and tolls from trade was no less important to the Mercian kings, served by their great emporium at London, so the imposition of a trade embargo underscored the importance attached to commercial links.

It is not clear how long the embargo lasted but a letter of 796 from Charlemagne to Offa reveals that trade had by then been restored. The letter is couched in the diplomatic language of Christian kings and its central concern is with the exile Eadberht whom Charlemagne had sent to Rome under his protection to be examined by the Pope. The letter closed with reference to Charlemagne's gifts to the bishops of Offa's kingdom and a request that prayers of intercession be offered for the soul of the late Pope.

However, there is also much about trade and some have looked upon it as virtually a 'commercial treaty'. Charlemagne sought to ensure that the tolls due were paid by Mercian traders coming into his kingdom, as some had been posing as pilgrims in order to secure concessions and avoid payment. It was also agreed, by the 'ancient custom of trading', that merchants would enjoy royal protection; such customs were well-established in Anglo-Saxon England, including protection on the king's highways; trade was sufficiently important to warrant royal oversight and regulation.

There was also comment on the items traded. The Mercians were importing 'black stones', the length of which was being specified. These were most probably for building purposes rather than the imported millstones frequently assumed in discussions of the horizontal watermill excavated at Tamworth, dating from at least the mid-ninth century, possibly earlier, and which utilised millstones of imported Rhineland lava. For their part, the Franks were importing textiles, an important Anglo-Saxon export, and particularly cloaks which it would seem were now being skimped upon. They were no longer as long or as warm as they had been previously, yet one suspects that the price of them had not been reduced accordingly; Charlemagne complained elsewhere,

"London, a major international market, was at the heart of Mercia's economic growth and the quickening of commercial pace in the late seventh and eighth centuries."

London was a major focus for international trade with a densely occupied commercial centre, laid out with houses and workshops along streets (Royal Opera House site of c.730-770).

'What's the use of these little bits of cloth?' They did not cover him in bed, or protect him from the wind and rain when riding, or from the cold when answering a call of nature!

Emporia and Long-distance Trade

Archaeology confirms that there was a busy and profitable trading network moving luxury goods and valuable raw materials across Europe and beyond, reaching into Scandinavia, into Slav lands and the Eastern Roman Empire, and into the Mediterranean and the Abbasid caliphate. In Europe this commerce was focused around several key sites, many of which included the place-name element 'wic', denoting a trading settlement or harbour, typically undefended, situated on navigable rivers.

Possibly developing from seasonal beach markets, by the late seventh century these emporia were sustained by permanent trading activity, attracting in turn a range of specialist crafts and industries that added to their mercantile capacity. Anglo-Saxon 'wics', like those at Ipswich, York and Southampton, linked into the Frankish trade networks through the great trading settlements at Quentovic and Dorestadt (near Utrecht, Netherlands), respectively about two and three days sailing time from the Mercian trading port at *Lundenwic* (London).

London, a major international market, was at the heart of Mercia's economic growth and the quickening of commercial pace in the late seventh and eighth centuries. A growing settlement with waterside embankments, roads and close-packed buildings, it had links to Normandy, the valleys of the Seine and the Meuse, and the Rhineland. By the mid-eighth century textile production, present from the outset, had developed into a major activity, and was joined by new industries such as tanning, together with artisanal workshops associated with jewellery-making and bone and antler working. London was an active slave market trading with the Frisians and it seems probable that salt exports were important to the activity of London and the economy of Mercia (EN 9).

Matching this archaeological picture of a vigorous and prosperous trading community was the widespread growth in the use of silver coinage and charter evidence for the collection and remission of tolls. Furthermore, between 672 and 674 King Wulfhere confirmed a charter conveying lands to the monastery of Chertsey, among them ten hides on the Thames 'by the port of London, where ships come to land, on the same river on the southern side by the public way'. Apart from illustrating the role of kings and monasteries in the growth of trading places, this grant also reflects their prosperity, as ten hides in this case suggests a relatively small area with a high value. It might be compared with King Burghred's charter of 857 granting to the bishop of Worcester, a 'profitable little estate in the town of London', and with it the liberty 'to use freely the scale and weights and measures as is customary in the port', at a place called *Ceolmundinghaga*; a '*haga*' was an enclosed residence or compound. The two grants suggest that the abbot and the bishop were actively engaged in trade, holding parcels of land that were reckoned to be profitable, and taking back to the seventh century an arrangement widely found in *Domesday Book*, namely that estates might have urban residences attached to them, acquired for the commercial access that they afforded.

The Mercian Hinterland

As with later medieval towns, emporia were sustained commercially by the consumers and suppliers of their hinterlands, where they interlinked with a hierarchy of smaller places engaged in trade and production. Although the River Trent may have been part of the network serving northern Mercia from the east coast, it was London that engaged with most of Mercia, which provided the port with a very large commercial hinterland reaching into the west

midlands, the Thames serving Mercia as a major artery. The rural estates of Mercia supplied the raw materials that London manufacturers, such as tanners and bone-workers, required, while the burgeoning textile trade could look to the sheep flocks of the Chilterns and the Cotswolds.

The ability of the Mercian kings to harness the commercial activity of their kingdom and its wealth through taxes and tolls was one of the foundations upon which Mercian supremacy was built, so it is unsurprising that their interest seems far from passive. It was managed, as the important salt works at Droitwich in Worcestershire illustrates. Salt was a vital commodity for food production and the purity of the Droitwich product, which allowed prolonged periods of storage, together with the extensive complex of productive brine pits, beckoned the Mercian kings to take direct control of it. The excavation of ten stone-built boiling hearths, with wattle screens, demonstrates Mercian salt extraction by the late sixth or early seventh centuries, which continued throughout the Anglo-Saxon period. Mercian charters, particularly of King Æthelbald, suggest careful management of the complex, granting salt rights to encourage increased production and developing royal salt works.

The value of this production was exemplified in the 890s when gifts made to the religious community at Worcester explicitly excluded the 'wagon-shilling and the load-penny', that is the payments made on every cart-load or pack-load of salt, which went to the king 'as they had always done at Droitwich'. While there were many Mercian consumers, among them royal estates and monastic communities, ensuring demand across the region, it is probable that much found its way via the salt ways and the River Thames into London for domestic use and export, and that consequently Mercia dominated the salt trade in southern England.

"The ability of the Mercian kings to harness the commercial activity of their kingdom and its wealth through taxes and tolls was one of the foundations upon which Mercian supremacy was built."

'Productive' Sites

As the element '*wic*' suggests, Droitwich was itself a trading place, reflecting a sometimes elusive inland trading network. The surge in metal-detector finds may have helped identify some sites, known as 'productive' sites because of the concentrations found there of coins and non-ferrous metalwork, such as pins, strap-ends and hooked tags. These are generally situated inland on important routes, and may also have ferrous metalwork and industrial activity; localised trade in commodities and foodstuffs was probably an important ingredient for many of these places, given their strong links into the local economy.

Such a site has been found at Bidford-on-Avon in Warwickshire, possibly linked with marketing Droitwich salt. By 2010 the parish had yielded sixty-one objects comprising silver coins and copper-alloy items, seventy-seven per cent of which were found on the site itself; the site was in use from the late seventh to the late ninth century, and in the early eighth century may have been attracting foreign traders, given the finds of Continental coinage. Such sites may have served as resting-places on internal trade routes, route centres and places of internal regulation by royal officers. Although not currently well represented in Mercia, Bidford-on-Avon will not have been alone.

A combination of factors stimulated the expansion of commercial activity. The unprecedented growth in religious communities, alongside royal and aristocratic estate centres, created consumer demand and the capacity for active participation in estate development and wealth generation, particularly through the production of surpluses for the market. Trading centres and networks developed and stabilised as these factors gained pace, presumably fostered by the elite, although Bidford has betrayed no evidence of a high-status presence; emporia, rural hinterlands and distributive networks came together for trade and supply. The Mercian kings may have had the particular good fortune not only to recognise such potential from an early date, but also to have had monastic establishments, and the '*wics*' of Droitwich and London around which to promote it, and profit by it.

Decline and Change

London was in decline by the late eighth century, symptomatic of a wider economic malaise that saw European emporia in decline by the ninth century, the 'ripple effect' impacting upon smaller centres of local exchange and production across the commercial network of Anglo-Saxon England. The reasons for this, at least in part, may be related to increasing fragmentation and regionalism in the Carolingian economy, exacerbated by declining supplies of Arabic silver and the impact of Viking raiders who were offsetting their own difficulties by attacking emporia already in decline. Mercian kings sought to manage and regulate their economy but English long-distance trade was part of an international network and vulnerable to disruption and its changing circumstances. By the second quarter of the ninth century the volume of coinage in circulation south of the Humber was in decline, although this did not make southern England a 'poorer' region than it had been previously, as the mid-century attentions of the Vikings amply illustrate.

The Mercian kings, with much to lose, attempted to revive commercial activity, at least in London, with grants of exemption from toll, trading opportunities, and a rejuvenation of the Mercian mint in London and an increase in Mercian moneyers, but there was progressive debasement of both Mercian and West Saxon coins. London's commercial activity survived on a new site, and the town was 'restored' by King Alfred in the late ninth century, but this was in the context of a new political order and a changing commercial network that was more closely associated with a series of fortified centres, or burhs.

Burhs and Towns in Mercia

By the ninth century English affairs were dominated by the Viking onslaught, whose early raiding had turned into sustained campaigns of conquest. Integral to countering the military threat posed by the Vikings was the building of fortified centres around Mercia and the West Saxon kingdom, thirty-three of which were recorded in a document known as the *Burghal Hidage* together with the hides, or taxes, assigned to their maintenance and binding them into their localities. Generally dated between 911 and 914, it records a system put in place in the late ninth century, although arguments have been advanced dating the document, and some burhs, earlier than is usually suggested.

Burh sites tend to exhibit high levels of internal planning and deliberate layout and as most of these places subsequently developed as towns it has been argued that they were inherently intended and planned to stimulate urban activity and attract specialist manufacturers and merchants. This has recently been claimed for London, dating Alfred's

burh here to late 879 or early 880 (earlier than most would allow), arguing that it was intended to accommodate the nucleus of a garrison and nascent trading community.

That so many burhs emerged by the eleventh century as urban places with diverse commercial economies suggests that the promotion of trading networks through them proved successful, but it also 'blurs' the process of urban growth. In Mercia, it was not the fortified site *per se* that stimulated towns and trade.

The burhs established or refortified in late ninth- and tenth-century Mercia were generally focused on places that were already of significance, as the sites of royal estates, minsters, or existing market and production centres. Pre-burh combinations of such roles can be claimed for Worcester, Hereford, Shrewsbury, Gloucester, Warwick, Tamworth and now Stafford, where recent excavations have shown it to be developing by the late eighth or early ninth century and home to a sophisticated pottery industry by the mid-ninth century. Was Stafford associated with efforts by the Mercian kings at commercial revival?

These became places for urban growth not because they were fortified but because they were focal points intimately associated with the regions that looked to them, and had been so for a long time. However, provision for defence intensified and perhaps broadened these associations. Although the middle-Saxon evidence of occupation and trading is more elusive than on some east midlands sites like Northampton, Bedford and Nottingham, it seems probable that most were also centres for local trade and production. As these functions strengthened, they become more visible to archaeology from the later tenth and eleventh centuries, and by 1086 these sites emerge as the towns opening the folios of their shires in the *Domesday Book*. ✠

Lundenwic: the Mercian *entrepôt*

After 'The Site of 7th century Saxon London', Museum of London Blog, and Julian Ayre and Robin Wroe-Brown, 'The Post-Roman Foreshore and the Origins of the Late Anglo-Saxon Waterfront and Dock of Æthelred's Hithe: Excavations at Bull Wharf, City of London', Archaeological Journal 172, 1, 2015, illustration 3

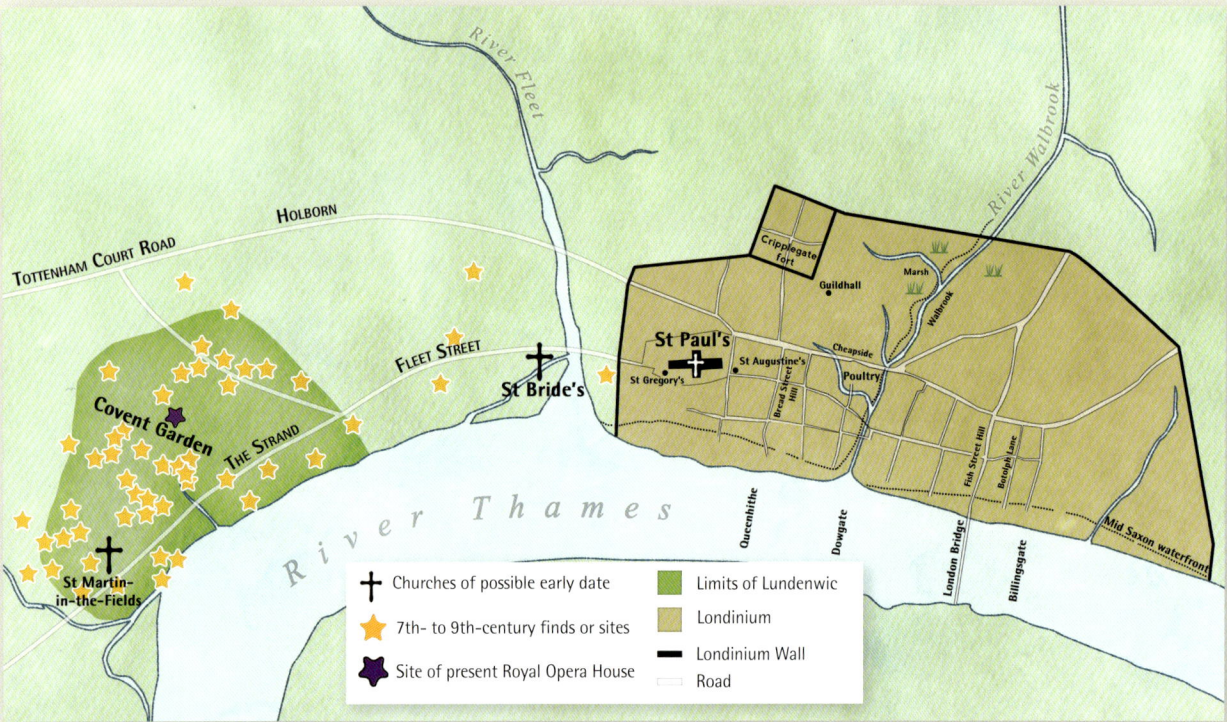

Mercian London: the commercial focus shifted westwards from Roman Londinium to Lundenwic, and subsequently back to the walled city and the establishment there of a burh, Lundenburh.

Our understanding of Anglo-Saxon London was transformed in the mid-1980s when it was realised that there were two 'Londons'. The Roman walled city, *Londinium*, largely abandoned in the early fifth century but reused by the early seventh, was of immense symbolic importance for its Roman and imperial associations. Within the intramural area was St Paul's cathedral, founded by Mellitus in 604 on or near the site of Wren's cathedral; later burials and possible evidence for a monastic enclosure have been excavated here.

The two churches of St Augustine and St Gregory may also have earlier precursors, but no evidence has yet been found for middle-Saxon period buildings in the intramural area, restricted perhaps to an ecclesiastical establishment and a royal hall. *Londinium* therefore cannot be the vibrant and teeming place that Bede described.

However, about 800 metres upstream, in the area of the Strand and Covent Garden, an extramural trading settlement,

Lundenwic, was established. It may have begun in the late sixth or early seventh century as a seasonal beach trading site, but by about the time of King Wulfhere, the settlement was growing with an expanding riverside embankment. Densely occupied into the eighth century, space became increasingly restricted and property boundaries more clearly and permanently defined. The settlement comprised a network of narrow gravel streets, about three metres wide and flanked by narrow drains, which were well-maintained, with some being resurfaced at least ten times.

Aligned on the streets or around yards were rectangular timber buildings, about 12 x 5.5 metres, built using posts set into the ground or sill beams, with wattle walls plastered with daub, and some lime-washed. Used as habitations and as workshops by bone, antler and metal workers, they had hearths made from reused Roman brick and tile and generally had external doors in their long walls. Extensive contact with Scandinavia and Continental Europe, and with local and regional trade, is evident. Wheat and barley were acquired partly processed, and fruit was consumed, probably wild; animal bones indicate the importance of cattle bred for beef.

However, by the last quarter of the eighth century the emporium was in decline and was transformed into a scatter of smaller settlements along the river bank. Excavations on the site of the Royal Opera House showed a general decline with only three new buildings constructed after about 770, the roads falling out of use or into disrepair. While manufacturing and industrial activity continued, it was much reduced on its eighth-century levels, although sword-hilt fittings suggest the manufacture of high-status items in one building. Textile manufacture too was declining and tanning pits at the northern edge of the site had fallen out of use by the ninth century and the area given over to dumping. Pottery suggested an intensification of links with the Rhineland but reduced contact with regions further south.

In the early ninth century a large defensive ditch was dug on the northern edge of the site, passing through earlier abandoned buildings, apparently part of a wider scheme, as traces of similar ditches have been found elsewhere in London. This may partially explain why the focus of activity now shifted back to the walled area and by the mid-ninth century *Lundenwic* was effectively abandoned.

In the burh of London which followed, *Lundenburh*, a beach market traded in the vicinity of Æthelred's hithe' with settlement concentrated in the area behind the waterfront, but this did not expand northwards until the late tenth century. Although excavations at Bull Wharf point to Rhineland contacts *c.*900, the wider picture suggests little maritime trade taking place before *c.*970. ✠

"Densely occupied into the eighth century, space became increasingly restricted and property boundaries more clearly and permanently defined. The settlement comprised a network of narrow gravel streets, about three metres wide and flanked by narrow drains…"

8

Art and Society in Anglo-Saxon Mercia

Since early prehistory, mankind has expressed itself through art, providing revealing insights and marked by a sense of the 'power' with which it was imbued. Alongside pleasure in its aesthetic qualities, the ability of art to convey complex ideas and to build a bridge between a seen and an unseen world has always been an inherent dimension. Art holds a mirror to the society that produced it, reflecting its interests, beliefs, values and aspirations, which in turn reveal the relationship between art and society. What was the nature of this relationship in Mercian society?

Art and Society in Mercia

The relationship was a complex one, rich in ideas. Art and architecture eloquently expressed power, authority and status, and, of course, wealth. In early medieval societies, such symbolism and display was important; it confirmed, enhanced and projected the status of individuals and institutions, and the relationship between them, directly and through prestigious associations. Imagery that resonated with imperial authority or with Carolingian Europe was particularly important.

From the late seventh century our knowledge and appreciation of Mercian art is derived primarily from religious contexts, such as churches, funerary and commemorative monuments, and illuminated manuscripts. Through such works patrons expressed their piety and standing in this world and hoped for the salvation of their souls in the next. Mercia's Christian art also revealed something of this world to come, inspiring devotion among the faithful; it was used to make 'sacred spaces' and to mediate access to them, helping the worshipper to enter and to witness the 'divine landscape'.

However, Mercia's exuberant artistic production was not restricted to the church alone. The sophisticated tastes of Mercia's rich and powerful elite are well illustrated by the elaborate silver-gilt dress-pin set found in the River Witham (Lincolnshire), a complete set reflecting a fondness for showy dress-pins. Decorated with distinctive crisp interlace, sprightly beasts and paired creatures with pricked ears and pointed wings, they may be linked with several major works of the second half of the eighth century that fuse the Anglo-Saxon tradition of zoomorphic decoration with Eastern influences. Such rich, exquisite and fashionable items, together with the large numbers of strap-ends, rings, pins and brooches that metal detectorists have revealed over the last thirty years or so, demonstrate the importance of this secular market for Mercian metalworkers.

Similarly illustrative, fine timber halls and prestigious palaces, like the ninth-century stone hall at Northampton, with their rich furnishings, textiles and hangings, examples of which survive, reveals that from buildings to belt buckles, art and the display associated with it was integral to Mercian secular life.

What follows introduces the main classes of Mercian art, considering its place in Mercian society through the themes of power, display and piety. Furthermore, whether 'religious' or 'secular', art had the capacity to promote a sense of 'belonging' and shared identity; the possibility of a Mercian art style by the eighth and early ninth centuries will also be examined.

Previous page: A gold plaque probably part of a book cover, with the eagle-headed image of Saint John the Evangelist (early ninth-century, Brandon, Suffolk).

The Witham Pins, a set of intricately decorated silver-gilt dress-pins of the second half of the eighth century (Lincolnshire).

Patronage, Art and the Mercian Church

Mercian kings, and those around them, were familiar with the wider influences of north-west European society and culture, promoting an ambitious and accomplished cultural environment whose legacy survived the kingdom itself. Even allowing for the artistic virtuosity of the seventh century Staffordshire Hoard, the eighth and early ninth centuries have good reason to be regarded as a 'golden age' for Mercian art and architecture, as a period of experimentation and receptiveness, absorbing influences from the Mediterranean and Eastern Christian decorative art. Mercia's political dominance, the variety of contacts and networks that supported it, together with the aspirations of her secular and ecclesiastical elite, brought opportunity for cultural exchange and influence.

At the heart of this creativity was the art of the Mercian Church. Most Anglo-Saxon monasteries received gifts from lay benefactors, often objects of gold and silver rather than manuscripts, wood and stone, although Offa is believed to have given to Worcester a great Bible, possibly one of the great Ceolfrith Bibles produced at Wearmouth/Jarrow (Tyne and Wear) before the abbot departed for Rome in 716. Monastic communities included artists and craftsmen among their number, and not only scribes and illuminators. Mannig, the abbot of Evesham who died early in 1066, was noted as a master craftsman, a goldsmith who produced numerous works of art, often working with a layman named Godric who later became a monk at Evesham. The artistic riches of a church may be sensed in the monk Hemming's description of the

"…the eighth and early ninth centuries have good reason to be regarded as a 'golden age' for Mercian art and architecture, as a period of experimentation and receptiveness, absorbing influences from the Mediterranean and Eastern Christian decorative art."

94

From *The Anglo-Saxon Church of All Saints, Brixworth, Northamptonshire*, David Parsons and D. S. Sutherland, Oxbow Books 2013, Fig 11.3, drawings Maggie Kneen

Alternative reconstructions of the church at Brixworth as it might have appeared late in the reign of King Offa.

gold and silver altar-frontals, chalices, crucifixes and precious bindings at Worcester, broken up in order to meet payments of the Danegeld.

Mercian Churches: a 'Golden Age'

Relatively little is known about the earliest church buildings and monastic layouts in Mercia. It is probable that many were located on the sites of Roman public buildings, as at Leicester and Lincoln, or used former villa sites. A building excavated at Much Wenlock has been variously interpreted as re-used Roman or of the seventh century, while recent excavations in Lichfield revealed a stone structure of fifth- or sixth-century date, across which was constructed a sunken-featured building in the seventh to eighth centuries. The stone structure, comprising two roughly square chambers, is currently unique in Britain. Its purpose is uncertain, and there are problems with reconstructions of it as a church, mausoleum or habitation; it may have been used by the Mercian episcopal community for the storage of unprocessed cereal crops, as was its successor.

However, from the mid-eighth century and into the early ninth century, monumental and richly furnished churches became prominent features in

"Brixworth was consciously engaging with a sense of 'romanitas', that is, deliberately associating the church, its patron and the kingdom with the prestige and ambience of the Roman legacy, past and present."

the Mercian landscape. A prevailing environment that combined ambition, piety, inspiration and wealth gave rise to impressive buildings like that at Brixworth in Northamptonshire.

This 'basilican' church comprises two distinct early periods. The main body of the building, consisting of a rectangular nave and square 'central space', flanked by *porticus* entered through arches on rectangular piers, dates to the late eighth century. Before the end of the ninth century the *Westwerk* was remodelled to form a western tower and stair turret, while the apse, with a crypt below, was rebuilt in polygonal form.

© Humphrey Bolton www.geograph.org.uk/photo/653902

The crosses at Sandbach in Cheshire formed an impressive monument in the landscape that projected the power and authority of the Church.

architectural models.

The early church at Brixworth dates to late in the reign of King Offa and was probably established under royal patronage, possibly as a kind of model religious community, consciously engaging with a sense of *'romanitas'*, that is, deliberately associating the church, its patron and the kingdom with the prestige and ambience of the Roman legacy, past and present.

Brixworth was not alone. In Gloucestershire, still more sophisticated was Cirencester, a large church whose western complex and probable

Features such as the western forebuilding indicates the importance of Carolingian influence and it has been suggested that Brixworth reflected trends current in the Carolingian Renaissance on the planning of major monastic churches, epitomised in the plan of St Gallen. Brixworth may be seen in the context of mid-eighth century reform within the Anglo-Saxon Church and the fusion of liturgy with architecture as the adoption of Roman liturgical models was reinforced by the use of Roman ring crypt again point to Continental influences. At Deerhurst, a major rebuilding programme encompassed the polygonal apse, east wall of the nave, east and south walls of the south *porticus* and the western porch up to and including the second-floor chapel; integral to this fabric was sculpture and polychrome decoration, including animal heads and a Virgin panel, dating this phase to the early ninth century. The external walls of the apse carried decorative panelling of pilaster strips rising from a

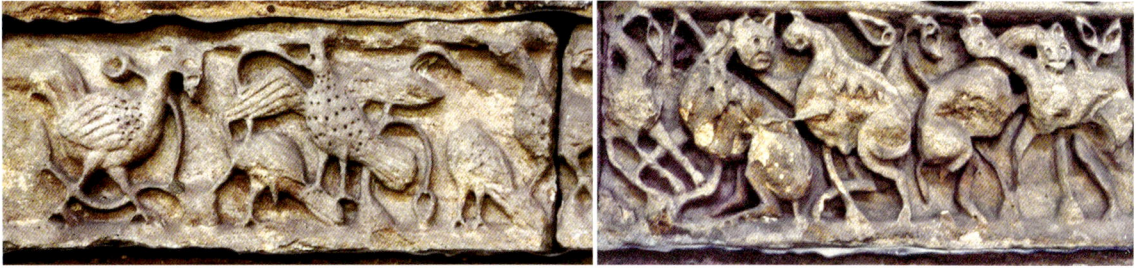

Much of the sculpture at Breedon-on-the-Hill is arranged in long narrow friezes using plant or vine scroll motifs, some inhabited by birds and beasts, dating c.800-810.

double plinth to a string course, above which were gabled areas carrying sculptured panels: winged archangels that once stood guard over the church and its community. The font, with Celtic trumpet spiral bordered with vine scroll of *c.*800, may be one of the earliest made-for-purpose fonts in England.

These and other churches, like Wing (Buckinghamshire), Leicester and Repton, reveal in Mercian architecture of the eighth and early ninth centuries a period of unusually high ambition, paralleled most readily not by English structures, but by those built by Carolingian kings at places like St Denis, Aachen and Paderborn.

Mercian Sculpture

Among the most dynamic and cosmopolitan of artistic output in Mercian art was that of its sculptors, whose work permeated the kingdom. A particularly accomplished group of related figure sculptures occurs at Peterborough, Castor, Fletton and Breedon-on-the-Hill, the latter being the largest corpus of eighth- and early ninth-century sculpture in Mercia and full of innovation. Originating in early Byzantine and Carolingian sources, much of the Breedon sculpture is arranged in long narrow friezes and panels, dated *c.*800-810, in which plant or vine scroll is the dominant motif, some inhabited with birds and beasts, while others have human figures, among them horsemen with spears and a

vineyard scene; depicted here are striding and long-necked birds, quadrupeds and lions, all with characteristic drilled eyes and considerable freedom of movement and expression.

Another innovation are panels depicting human figures in architectural frames, the earliest being the 'apostle panels' of *c.*780-90, interpreted as originally part of a sarcophagus although they may alternatively have been from a baptistery scheme. Dating to the early ninth century, the Breedon sculptors also carved a naturalistic paired figural panel whose long flowing garments articulate their bodies, while a fragment of the Cana miracle, probably based on an ivory carving of mid-eighth century from Syria, Palestine or Egypt, is a relatively rare example of biblical narrative sculpture from Mercia. There are also panels of early ninth-century date depicting the Angel Gabriel and, slightly later, the Virgin Mary.

This whole group of sandstone carvings, with influences looking back to late Antiquity, stands apart from other Mercian sculpture of the period, but drawing on the same corpus of influences are the figures at Castor and Fletton. As Richard Jewell (EN 10) observed, 'the delicate blend of tender humanism and exquisite linear design' in the Castor panel makes it a masterpiece of Anglo-Saxon art, a sculptural counterpart to the Evangelists' portraits in the 'Barberini Gospels' (see below).

In western and south-western Mercia, surviving

Portrait of Saint Matthew from the *Book of Cerne*, produced in central or western Mercia (c.820–840).

sculpture is more commonly represented by fragments of cross-shafts and cross-heads, like those from Wroxeter (Shropshire), Acton Beauchamp (Herefordshire) and Cropthorne (Worcestershire), decorated with animals and plant scrolls, here possibly the product of one man. The use of trefoils with oval leaves is one detail that suggests stylistic influences moving westwards from eastern Mercia in the early ninth century.

The delicate and elegant modelling of the Lichfield angel demonstrates the quality and creativity of major west Mercian ecclesiastical centres, with access to Byzantine models, as does the painted sculpture at Deerhurst which includes a depiction of the Virgin and Child that is unique in England and rare in Europe. This full-length depiction of Christ in an oval frame is taken from a Byzantine-inspired model, probably brought back to Gloucestershire by pilgrims to Rome; among them was Æthelric, the patron of Deerhurst, who made a pilgrimage to Rome between 802 and 807 and could have brought back a painted Roman or Byzantine icon of the Virgin for his church.

In northern Mercia too the sophistication of Mercian art is reflected by the Sandbach crosses (Cheshire), which undoubtedly formed an impressive monument in the landscape. Influenced by metalworking techniques, one also carried a metal *appliqué*, recreating in stone a gem-encrusted metal cross, a '*Crux Gemmata*', while laid out in various compartments was an extensive and complex iconography proclaiming the presence of the Church and its sacraments, with themes of revelation, universal adoration and the establishment of the Church on earth. The '*Traditio Legis cum Clavis*' scene is particularly unusual in including Peter and Paul with the keys and the Law, the two apostles responsible for spreading the Gospel and founding the Church; in this the only other site to compare in *c*.800 is Müstair in Switzerland, under the direct patronage of Charlemagne. This remarkable scene in an early ninth-century Anglo-Saxon context represented a direct iconographic reference to the establishment and authority of the earthly Church, while the Transfiguration symbolised confirmation of the Church in Christ. The message of the Sandbach crosses focused on power, authority and the working of the Church and it may be that senior churchmen were invoking and imitating Carolingian images of ecclesiastical authority in support of their new archdiocese.

Piety, Spirituality and Sacred Space

Mercian art in churches created 'sacred space' and built bridges between heaven and earth, and among the most popular of images to mediate access to the sacred and the holy was the angel. Such was probably the intention of the Lichfield angel, dating to the late eighth or early ninth century and displayed on Saint Chad's shrine, although it might alternatively have been situated in the wall of the church. Accomplished in style, richly decorated and most probably part of an Annunciation scene, the angel's colouration was a symbolic reference to the divine. Clothed in bright yellow, modelled with red, with white edging around the borders of the garment, this colouring was suggestive of gold and silver, producing a shimmering effect of red-gold, intensifying the visual experience and what it prompted emotionally and psychologically. This rendered the mediation all the more effective, especially in a figure associated with attendance upon the heavenly throne.

In the visually sophisticated and well-connected culture of Lichfield in the early ninth century, the Annunciation scene recalled the Virgin's purity, humility and obedience, qualities to be admired by the viewer and a focal point for contemplation and meditation.

In a similar way, the wealthy and the privileged with access to a prayer book like the '*Book of Cerne*', with its theme of salvation and the communion of saints, could call upon its imagery to evoke a mystical relationship with the divine. For most, however, it was the painted and sculptured imagery that they found within their churches that conjured the spiritual atmosphere, particularly after a decree of the Synod of Chelsea in 816 required in churches an image of the saint to whom the church was dedicated.

Mercian Books

Although there is a reluctance to attribute manuscripts to specific monastic *scriptoria*, there can be no doubt that Mercia was served by centres that were well-connected and capable of calling upon Byzantine influences and Carolingian models, while also drawing upon Insular traditions to produce books of high quality. It is probable that Worcester was among the major centres of manuscript production in Anglo-Saxon England, and the role of Lichfield may well have been underestimated until relatively recently (EN 11). Attention has been drawn to the 'Tiberius' group of Mercian manuscripts with their distinctive use of animal ornament, such as biting beasts, like those used in metalwork (discussed below), suggesting that a Mercian 'scribal area' might be claimed in areas under Mercian domination, based on the use of stylistic features and script in the eighth and ninth centuries.

The late eighth century 'Codex Bigotianus', a Gospel Book that might be a Worcester product, may represent the earliest occurrence of these Mercian bird and beast motifs, but particularly impressive are the sumptuous 'Barberini Gospels', probably produced at Peterborough. The Barberini Evangelist miniatures call on Byzantine sources in their portrayal of well-modelled bearded figures within stylised spatial settings while Celtic scroll, animal ornament, and interlace perpetuate Insular traditions. Described as a 'de luxe' product that one might expect of Offa's reign, its rich colours imitate those of Italian and Byzantine manuscript painting.

© The Trustees of the British Museum

A silver-gilded and niello inlaid sword hilt (later eighth-century, London).

The 'Tiberius' group includes several prayer books, three of which have female associations and two may have been produced at Worcester. Such books, owned perhaps by Mercian royal or aristocratic women in the early ninth century, mark a milestone in the development of devotional tradition, becoming the principal focus for private and public prayer. The 'Book of Nunnaminster', a meditation on the life of Christ, may have been produced within the diocese of Worcester in the early ninth century, but a manuscript firmly attributed to central or western Mercia, possibly Worcester, is the 'Book of Cerne'.

Dating to c.820-840, the 'Book of Cerne' has a less naturalistic and more linear figural style, but uses elegant arcading. Intercourse between the arts is reflected in the use of distinctive triangular folds of drapery, as in the figure sculpture of the Lechmere Stone and the Breedon panels. Similarly, an exquisite gold plaque found at Brandon in Suffolk displays the same linear style; the eagle-headed image of Saint John the Evangelist that may have been part of a book cover, or from the arms of a cross, also reveals the links between the metalworker and the scriptorium.

Such prayer books seem to herald the arrival of a more intimate level of artistic patronage, while their knowledge of Greek and Hebrew reflects learning and cosmopolitanism; Mercian skills were later called upon to support the Alfredian revival of learning.

"The ability of art and architecture to convey messages of power and authority was well understood by Mercian society, from the display of wealth and status through the possession or gifting of prized items, to more specific and targeted messages within artistic schemes."

Power and Authority

The ability of art and architecture to convey messages of power and authority was well understood by Mercian society, from the display of wealth and status through the possession or gifting of prized items, to more specific and targeted messages within artistic schemes. The Staffordshire Hoard epitomised such display in the mid-seventh century, with its richly decorated fittings from around ninety swords and seaxes, as did the swords of later generations of warriors, like that represented by the silver-gilded and niello inlaid sword-hilt found in Fetter Lane in London, dating to the later eighth century and decorated with tendril pattern, bird heads, a beast and a spiral of four snakes. Although personal dress adornment appears to be largely absent from the material in the hoard, items such as belt-fittings and brooches were also display objects, for both men and women. They are well known from early burial sites, among them two 'Mercian jewels' of mid-seventh century date from a barrow in Derbyshire, one a silver-gilt and garnet round brooch, and the other a filigree decorated pectoral cross. Although neither can claim Mercian origins, the elegant ninth-century Strickland and Fuller silver disc brooches with niello and gold inlay, the former decorated with animal masks and the latter with representations of the Five Senses, together with the late eighth-century silver-gilt dress-pin from Brandon in Suffolk, decorated with confronted birds, or the exquisite eighth- / early ninth-century silver-gilt finger-ring decorated with

an animal and interlace, found in the River Thames at Chelsea in 1856, all convey a sense of the rich ambience of personal display.

The distinction modern society claims between the 'religious' and the 'secular' is misleading if applied to early medieval societies, where the two were inextricably entwined. Images displayed in religious contexts were frequently intended to have an impact in the secular world, while clearly secular objects might carry religious imagery, as on the Staffordshire Hoard sword pommels, or like the late ninth-century sword from Abingdon (Berkshire) inlaid with silver and niello and evangelist symbols. Here we see art invoking divine power and protection. This was not unique to Christianity, as the symbolism of the Mercian Benty Grange helmet called upon both the boar and a Latin cross, and the image of the boar was much used at Sutton Hoo and in the hoard; similarly, the Coppergate helmet from York, dating *c*.750-775, carried a prayer for the protection of its owner. Such concerns may in part explain the presence of some Christian objects in the hoard, particularly the folded cross set with garnets which may have served as a processional cross, leading warriors into battle as readily as a liturgical procession.

Dating perhaps a century later, the Repton Stone illustrates a more specific example of art in a religious context with secular impact. This powerful image of an equestrian figure has generally been interpreted as a warrior king, presumably Æthelbald, drawing on Roman imperial imagery

"Prominent in the style was the use of animal heads as features in their own right, occurring frequently, for instance, on silver-gilt fittings as three-dimensional heads, with ribbed muzzles and gaping jaws…"

and gravestones. However, the depiction of a warrior saint has also been credibly argued, such as Wigstan or Guthlac. The latter seems particularly appropriate to Æthelbald's burial, given their close association and the role that Guthlac reputedly played in aiding and protecting both the king and his dynasty. This was the imagery of royal power under divine protection.

Identity

Can we think in terms of a Mercian style? Probably so, based on the distinctive animal art found in Mercian manuscripts, sculpture and metalwork, with characteristically quirky and playful animals adopting a range of stances and attitudes. The tradition of Anglo-Saxon zoomorphic decoration was influenced by Eastern models through textiles and ivories, and the two fused to produce the style. Not only do these animated creatures occur in religious contexts, they also appear in secular metalwork such as strap-ends, rings, pins and brooches. The style combines in a fairly consistent way a range of animal, plant and abstract motifs; frequently paired, these animals, some 'high-stepping' and others 'lizard-like', appear in interlace, or among the stems and berry bunches of vine scroll and other plants. The middle disc of the Witham Pins, for instance, has panels filled with winged animals, both confronted and back-to-back pairs, and a single beast, all with lightly incised collars and set within crisp interlace, with punching on their bodies. It has been described as a refined, lively and teasing style even when applied to less

accomplished pieces such as an early ninth-century incised disc brooch from Leicester. A particularly accomplished example of the style is the whalebone chrismatory known as the 'Gandersheim Casket', probably made at Peterborough in the late eighth century (EN 12).

Prominent in the style was the use of animal heads as features in their own right, occurring frequently, for instance, on silver-gilt fittings as three-dimensional heads, with ribbed muzzles and gaping jaws, as on strap fittings or the gold ring found at Berkeley Castle, or stone-carved versions like those at Deerhurst. The marked coincidence between the occurrence of this refined and lively style and the extent of Mercian power raises the possibility that this might be regarded as a 'Mercian style'.

Aftermath: A Legacy

The end of the Mercian Supremacy certainly did not mean the end of artistic achievement in Mercia. Described as an 'unparalleled' monument (EN 13), the Wolverhampton round shaft of late ninth- or tenth-century date brought together the acanthus leaf ornament of the Carolingians with the Mercian repertoire of the previous century, with lozenge-shaped panels occupied by 'Mercian beasts', above them foliage, bird and beast carvings. The similarity in the motifs used on the Wolverhampton shaft with ninth-century metalwork suggests inspiration may have come from such a source, perhaps some kind of processional cross with applied metalwork plaques. ✠

The Lichfield Gospels (Gospels of Saint Chad)

Commonly associated with Mercia are the '*Gospels of Saint Chad*', dated *c*.725-50, whose patronage and place of production are not certainly known; Northumbria, Iona and Wales have all been suggested but a Lichfield origin is entirely possible. However, the name 'Lichfield Gospels' derives from their known associations since the tenth century.

Although parts of the Gospels have been lost, it is clear that they were conceived with an ambitious and rich decorative scheme matched by the accomplishment and quality of their production. The colours of the illuminations are particularly striking, using purple and mauve, with some application of blue, yellow, orange and brown. The Gospel of Saint John has been lost, as has most of the text from Saint Luke; the Gospels of Saints Matthew and

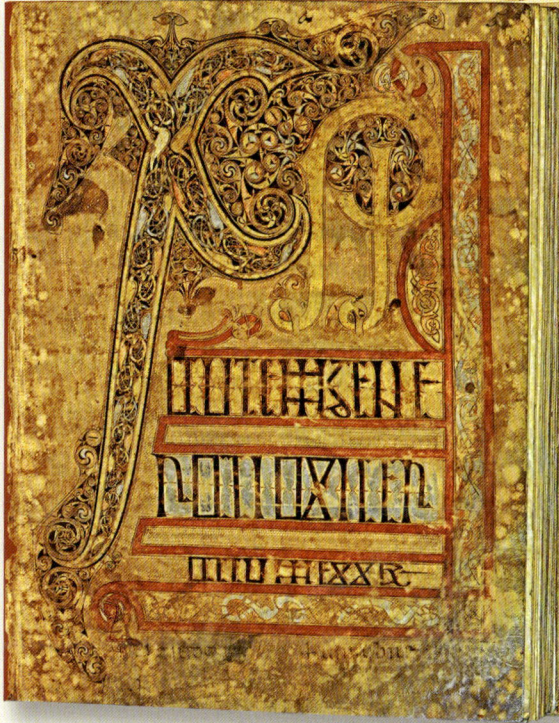

Used by permission of the Chapter of Lichfield Cathedral

The vibrant incarnation initial (the first two letters of the word Christ in Greek) dated to c.725-750, opening Saint Matthew's Gospel, is marked by intricate and inventive use of zoomorphic interlace and scroll work.

Mark preserve their initial pages and a portrait of the latter.

Only Saint Luke's Gospel still retains the complete original decorative sequence, comprising an evangelist portrait with his symbol, opposite a page of all four symbols, followed by a 'carpet page' and a decorated page opening the Gospel with a large and elaborate initial. The other Gospels no doubt shared the same arrangement.

The Chad incarnation initial opening the Gospel according to Saint Matthew is indebted to the Lindisfarne Gospels, as is perhaps the only surviving 'carpet page' with its dense and tightly-packed animal interlace, reflecting the longstanding Anglo-Saxon fondness for zoomorphic design. This page writhes with activity, filled with birds characterised by entwined necks and tails, and richly coloured in purple-mauve with a large cross almost subsumed into the scene but setting the frame for it.

The evangelist figures, Luke and Mark, were probably derived from late Antique models. The Lion symbol of Saint Mark recalls the '*Imago Leonis*' in the late seventh-century '*Gospels of Saint Willibrord*' (Echternach Gospels), probably produced in the Northumbrian abbey of Lindisfarne. ✠

9

The Vineyard of the Lord Devoured by Foxes

A CHANGING WORLD

The ninth century was a period of dramatic, and traumatic, change for Anglo-Saxon England, effectively sweeping away the 'old order', familiar for some two centuries. It was dominated, particularly from mid-century, by the arrival of the Vikings and the consequences of this for the political geography of the Anglo-Saxon kingdoms. Not long before his death Offa was strengthening his defences against Viking attacks and Kentish charters as early as 811 were making specific reference to military service against the pagans, and in 822 to the destruction of their fortresses. Across the Channel the Frankish rulers too were looking to their defences.

The 'fury of the Northmen' was challenge enough for any European kingdom, but for the Mercians it was part of complex adjustment and repositioning as their own 'world' changed. The eighth century brought Mercia problems both familiar and new in maintaining the kingdom's prominence, not least major shifts in the military and political balance between the kingdoms south of the Humber. However, these 'external' threats were compounded by a serious vulnerability that arose from dynastic instability of a kind not previously so prominent in Mercia.

Dynastic Rivals

In 796 Offa's son Ecgfrith was succeeded to the Mercian throne by a distant cousin, Coenwulf, who reigned until 821. Perhaps the son of Cuthbert, one of Offa's ealdormen, Coenwulf claimed descent from a brother of Penda named Coenwealh, not known beyond the Mercian genealogy. Descent from Penda and his brothers remained a measure of legitimacy for Mercian kings, but the links were becoming ever more tenuous and Alcuin, who clearly had reservations about Coenwulf, observed that 'scarcely anyone is found now of the old stock of kings'. It is not improbable that, as the member of a very powerful kin, Coenwulf effectively seized the throne and consolidated his hold through the appointment of relatives to key positions. His kin were represented among Mercian ealdormen and in the upper echelons of the church; one kinsman was the abbot of St Augustine's, Canterbury, while his daughter Cwenthryth was abbess of Minster-in-Thanet, one of the richest of the Kentish royal nunneries. He assigned another wealthy foundation, at Glastonbury, to his son Cynehelm, and established a major proprietary monastery at Winchcombe, this 'shire' becoming a major focus of family interests and resources; indeed, the kin might have been of Hwiccian descent.

Since at least the closing stages of Offa's reign, Mercian dynastic rivalry and uncertainty were rife and in the ninth century it worsened. Coenwulf's own son fell victim to this instability around 811, as one of the murdered royal princes of the ninth century who gave rise to a saint's cult. With its main centre at Winchcombe, the kin took full advantage of the cult to enhance the prestige of their house. Coenwulf was succeeded by his brother Ceolwulf, but the hard-won stability that he had inherited quickly evaporated. His short reign seems to have been generally one of dissension, a document of 825 noting that after the death of Coenwulf 'much discord and innumerable disagreements arose between various kings, nobles, bishops and ministers of the church of God on very many matters of secular business' and Ceolwulf's own

Previous page: The martyrdom of King Edmund at the hands of the Danes in 869 or 870, from the 'Life, Passion and Miracles of St Edmund, King and Martyr', c.1130.

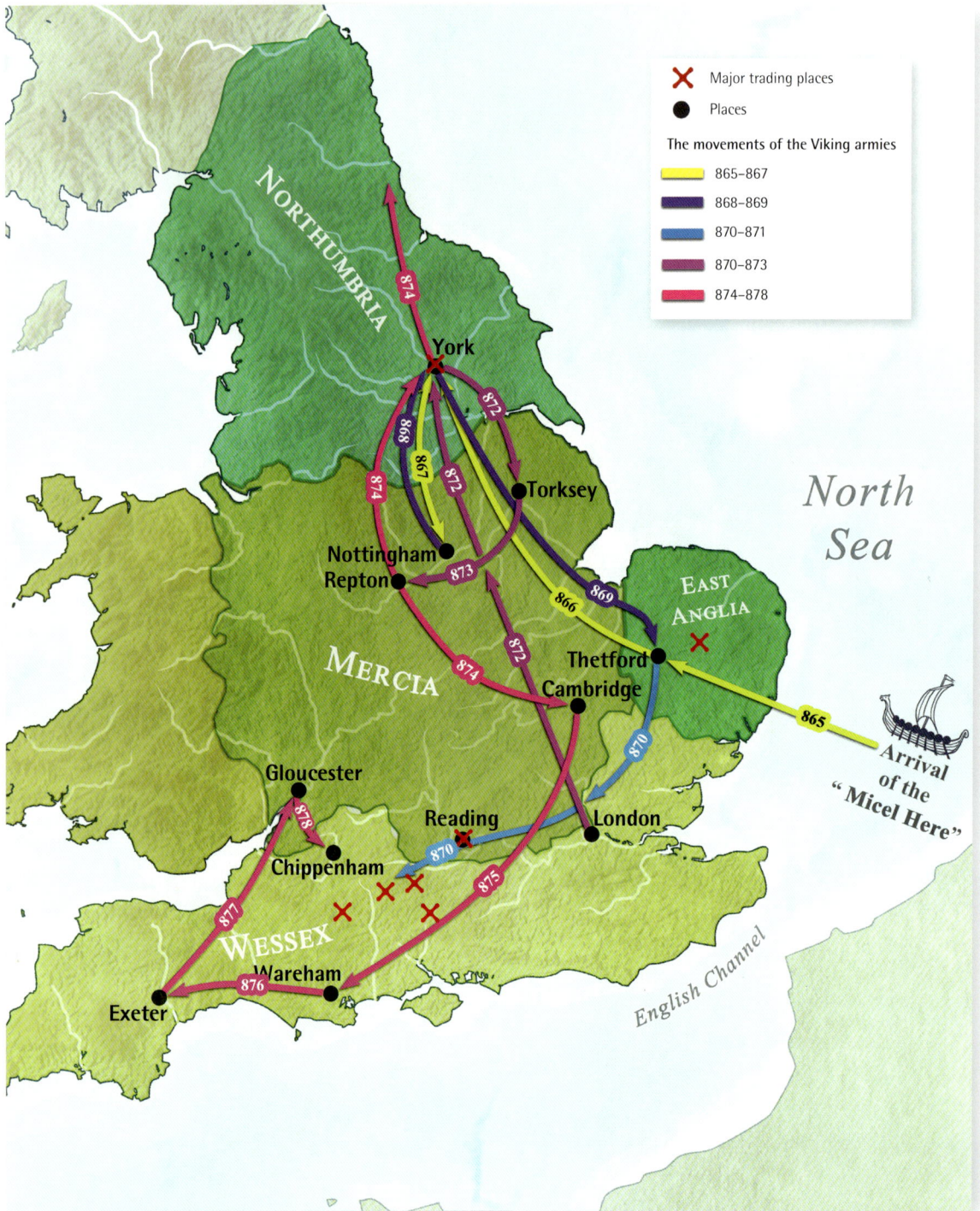

The movement of Viking armies between 865 and 878, in the wake of which Mercia was partitioned.

consecration was delayed until September 822. It may be that this discord owed much to the legacy of Coenwulf, and there clearly were those who exploited it as in 823 Ceolwulf was deposed and in the following year two ealdormen were murdered, one of whom at least had been a leading member of Ceolwulf's court. The kingdom passed to Beornwulf and not until the very 'last act' of Mercian kingship in the 870s did Coenwulf's dynasty reappear, in the person of Ceolwulf II.

The identification of vying Mercian families is largely based upon their usage of alliterative personal names, families which Barbara Yorke has traced back to representatives in the late seventh century. While the house of Coenwulf might be referred to as the 'C dynasty', based on the distinctive first elements of their names, there was another house that may be described as the 'B dynasty', perhaps represented at an early stage by Berhtwald, a nephew of King Æthelred, and in the early ninth century by a relatively undistinguished ealdorman. Mercian military strength remained impressive and Beornwulf used it, but his reign, from 823 to 826, also marked a watershed in Mercian fortunes, following defeat by the West Saxons.

Beornwulf died in 826 while campaigning against the East Angles, as perhaps did his successor Ludeca in 827. Ludeca witnessed charters in 824 as an ealdorman of Beornwulf's court, but the supposition that he was a kinsman of the deceased king is speculative. After Beornwulf's death in 826 his dynasty fell silent until it reappeared with King Beorhtwulf in 840, to be followed by Burghred in 852.

Between 827 and 840 a third ambitious kindred took power in Mercia with the reign of Wiglaf; the origins of his family are uncertain although Yorke has associated the line with a *subregulus* named Wigheard. This was another Mercian royal line to promote itself through the establishment of a saint's cult, that of Wigstan, son of Wigmund, another murdered prince and victim of dynastic strife.

Presumably mindful that his lineage did not demonstrate links to the house of Penda, Wiglaf married his son, Wigmund, to Ælfflaed, the daughter of King Ceolwulf, whose dynastic credentials and family wealth must have seemed attractive. The succession of Beorhtwulf in 840 suggests that Wigmund had either died or been passed over. No doubt aware of the benefits that had attracted Wiglaf, Beorhtwulf's son, Beorhtfrith, sought marriage to Wigmund's widow, a match that Wigstan opposed on the grounds that Beorhtfrith was his father's kinsman and his own godfather. Clearly there were some links of kindred between the 'B' and the 'W' families, which, as Yorke observed, might have its origins in Penda's practice of placing sons over satellite and conquered provinces. Beorhtfrith responded by inviting Wigstan to a council where he killed him.

"*The Anglo-Saxon Chronicle ... was created by the West Saxons to serve their own interests, primarily to promote the achievements of Alfred and his family and to underpin West Saxon aspirations to supremacy south of the Humber. The presentation of Mercia as a failing kingdom and a 'spent force' played very much to this agenda, undermining our impressions of ninth-century Mercia.*"

Significantly, Wigstan was taken *c*.849 to Repton for burial, where the cult subsequently developed, promoting the family in the same way as that of Cynehelm at Winchcombe. Cnut later had Wigstan's relics translated to his reformed monastery at Evesham, but the parish church remains dedicated to the saint. That Wigstan was buried in such a special place for the Mercian royal kin, as had been his grandfather Wiglaf before him, suggests that he was acknowledged as a member of it, and despite the fact that he died at the hands of Beorhtfrith, the 'B' family perhaps felt sufficient kinship to not feel threatened; indeed, perhaps quite the contrary. Still more speculatively, the burials of Wiglaf and his grandson at Repton suggest that they claimed, or sought to infer, links with the early Mercian kings. At Evesham Wigstan was remembered as a descendant of Coenred, grandson of Penda, a link that may have been transmitted through his mother's line.

The arrival of the Vikings as shown in the 'Life, Passion and Miracles of Saint Edmund, King and Martyr', c.1130.

Coenwulf successfully countered these challenges, such that his kingship might be favourably compared with that of Offa. In a charter of 798 to his *dux* and *minister* Oswulf regarding land in Kent, Coenwulf was described as, by the grace of God, '*rector et imperator Merciorum regni*', the first official use of the term 'emperor' in Britain since the Roman Empire. Caution is called for, but as Eric John speculated, like later medieval kings, Coenwulf perhaps claimed imperial power *within* Mercia.

However, his successes delayed rather than averted the gathering storm, in which the resurgence of West Saxon fortunes, with the return to Wessex in 802 of the exile Ecgberht, was critical. King Ecgberht's defeat of Beornwulf in 825 at the battle of *Ellendun* in Wiltshire has been described as 'one of the most decisive battles in Anglo-Saxon history', marking the end of the ascendancy of the Mercian kings (EN 14), but this perspective with its inference of Mercia's terminal decline from this point onwards is one that is based on an uncritical acceptance of the narrative in the *Anglo-Saxon Chronicle*. Although a crucial source, it is one that was created by the West Saxons to serve their own interests, primarily to promote the

The Mercian Hegemony: Offa's Inheritance

When Offa died Mercian kingship, and the Mercian kingdom, had never been stronger, but already this position was under threat with the kingdoms of Kent and the East Angles reasserting their independence.

achievements of Alfred and his family and to underpin West Saxon aspirations to supremacy south of the Humber. The presentation of Mercia as a failing kingdom and a 'spent force' played very much to this agenda, undermining our impressions of ninth-century Mercia.

Ecgberht immediately seized the opportunity to challenge and supplant Mercian authority in the south-east of England, and then, in 829, he invaded Mercia itself, expelling King Wiglaf and taking the kingdom and the title of '*Rex Merciorum*'. Wiglaf had come to the throne in 827 in the wake, and accompanying psychological impact, of several military defeats and the loss of two Mercian kings in battle that no doubt had undermined Mercian resilience and morale. However, despite the fact that the West Saxons may have advanced as far as the Mercian border with Northumbria, Ecgberht's domination cannot have been secure as in 830 Wiglaf 'obtained the Mercian kingdom again'.

Although more circumscribed, Mercian authority and prestige was still considerable. In 836 Wiglaf presided over an assembly of 'my bishops, *duces* and magistrates' at Croft in Leicestershire, attended by the archbishop of Canterbury and eleven bishops of the southern province. Wiglaf's authority embraced London, Middlesex and possibly Essex, and the Mercians still held disputed land along the middle Thames. The transfer of these Berkshire lands into Wessex was eventually agreed by Wiglaf's successor, Beorhtwulf, who fostered a *rapprochement* if not an alliance between the two kingdoms.

Defending Mercian 'Supremacy'

The continued vibrancy of the Mercian kingdom in the ninth century was attested by the vigour with which the Mercian supremacy was defended in both England and Wales. Although *Ellendun* was clearly a setback in Mercian fortunes, when viewed against a wider canvas there was no reason to suppose either the demise of the kingdom or West Saxon ascendancy.

Upon his succession in 796 Coenwulf had turned immediately to the situation in the south-east of England where in Kent Eadberht Praen had returned from exile and established himself as king, forcing Mercia's ally, Archbishop Æthelheard, to flee. As Eadberht was a priest, Coenwulf delayed until the papal position was clear, but once the papacy had denounced him he retook Kent in 798. Eadberht, his eyes put out and hands cut off, was taken in chains into Mercia and imprisoned at Winchcombe. Possibly as an act of reconciliation, Coenwulf restored some lands to Canterbury and entrusted Kent to a king, albeit his own brother, Cuthred, who reigned until his death in 807 whereupon the Mercian king took direct control.

Coenwulf's tight grip on the south-east survived him, lasting until 825 when the West Saxon king Ecgberht sent a large army into Kent, forcing Baldred, the delegated ruler of Kent and probable kinsman of Beornwulf, to flee. By 826 Mercian authority in the south-east of England had been compromised, the men of Kent, Essex, Surrey and Sussex submitting to Ecgberht who claimed, in line with the objectives that informed the *Chronicle*, that he was restoring what had been 'wrongfully forced away from his kinsmen'. West Saxon success was adjusting the political balance.

The East Angles too had reasserted their independence, reflected by coinage minted in the name of King Eadwald, and again cut short by Coenwulf. But in the wake of *Ellendun* the East Angles again rose against Mercia, asking Ecgberht for his protection. King Beornwulf died in 826 campaigning to subdue them; so too did his successor Ludeca, in 827, together with five of his ealdormen, although alternatively an internal dispute in Mercia may have been responsible.

West of Offa's Dyke, Coenwulf invaded Gwynedd in 798, killing its king, Caradog ap Meirion. In 816 the Mercians returned, raiding between Clwyd and the Elwy, reaching into Snowdonia and taking Rhufuniog, while in 818 Dyfed was ravaged. Coenwulf may have been planning a further campaign when he died at Basingwerk in 821, perhaps realised in the later expeditions that destroyed the stronghold of Degannwy at the mouth of the Conway in Gwynedd, and conquered Powys. These latter successes are generally associated with Ceolwulf but given the difficulties of his reign, the uncertainties of dating, and his deposition in 823, David Kirby has suggested a more realistic association with the early months of Beornwulf's reign, launched as a demonstration of Mercian power. These proved to be the last of Mercia's major military achievements.

King, Pope and Archbishop

The uncertainty of Mercia's authority in Kent undoubtedly persuaded Coenwulf to revisit the matter of the Mercian archdiocese. He advised Pope Leo III of the unease that his bishops and counsellors felt regarding the failure to fulfil Saint Gregory's intentions for archdioceses at York and London, no doubt genuinely felt by many. He also added, rather unhelpfully if not entirely incorrectly, that Offa's advocacy of an archdiocese at Lichfield had been driven by a hatred of Archbishop Jaenberht and the men of Kent. Of course, the intention was to persuade the Pope to suppress both Lichfield and Canterbury and establish a new archdiocese on London, a town that was securely Mercian, strengthening Mercian influence over the Church within a structure that could claim legitimacy from Saint Gregory. The papacy delayed but proved unpersuaded and in October 803 Canterbury was restored to its former authority and the archdiocese of Lichfield suppressed; the Mercian recovery in Kent, however, mitigated the impact of the decision.

When Æthelheard was succeeded as archbishop by Wulfred (805-832), Coenwulf's relations with Canterbury deteriorated drastically. Between 805 and 817 Wulfred is found witnessing royal charters but thereafter a major dispute erupted. Its origins are obscure but it is likely that the long-running debate on secular interests and jurisdiction in monasteries lay at the heart of the matter, and there clearly were inherent political overtones. As heir to the Kentish kings, Coenwulf took control of the important monasteries of Reculver and Minster-in-Thanet, wealthy houses which Archbishop Wulfred claimed should be under his jurisdiction.

In 816, at the Council of Chelsea, Coenwulf's right to appoint to vacant nunneries and monasteries was directly challenged, even though he had a papal dispensation to do so. Coenwulf countered this challenge to royal authority by laying before Pope Paschal I serious charges against the archbishop, who was suspended. So divisive was this long-lasting and traumatic dispute that for six years the bishops of the province refused to perform baptisms.

"When Burghred came to the Mercian throne in 852 his world was rather different from that familiar to his predecessors only two generations earlier."

The Vikings overwintered at Repton in 873-4 within a 'D-shaped' earthwork enclosure alongside the River Trent. It is possible that the stone-built church was used as a strongpoint in the defences, while to the west lay the royal Mercian mortuary chapel re-used by the Vikings.

Not until 821 did a solution emerge, in the form of an imposed settlement on Coenwulf's terms. Wulfred was required to surrender an estate of 300 hides and pay a fine of 120 pounds, or forfeit everything and be irrevocably exiled. Wulfred reluctantly agreed and was restored, but the matter rumbled on after Coenwulf's death with both Ceolwulf and Beornwulf reaching agreements and it was not until about 827 that the matter was finally settled.

"The occupation of Repton, a royal estate centre, dynastic mausoleum and cult centre was a well-calculated psychological blow that hit at the credibility and reputation of the Mercian royal dynasty itself."

'Hungry Wolves take big Bites': the Arrival of the Vikings

When Burghred came to the Mercian throne in 852 his world was rather different from that familiar to his predecessors only two generations earlier. Mercia and Wessex had settled into an alliance, issuing compatible coinage, and sealed in 853 by Burghred's marriage to Æthelswith, the daughter of Æthelwulf. This marriage followed a joint expedition into Powys earlier in the year, we are told at Burghred's request, an alliance demonstrating the two kingdoms' shared interests.

Among these, the threat posed by the Vikings to both kingdoms was already very apparent by the 850s. Raids along the English coast in the 840s were followed in 851 by a large fleet sailing into the mouth of the Thames, storming Canterbury and London. Both Mercia and Wessex were shaken by these events, their defensive capabilities questioned, and royal capacity to mint coin affected.

In the 860s the intensity of the threat increased massively, particularly after 865 when the '*micel here*', the 'great army', arrived in East Anglia threatening sustained campaigning and conquest. In 866 the army crossed the Humber into Northumbria and took York, and in 867 moved into Mercia, taking up winter quarters at Nottingham. Although Mercian military strength was far from negligible, Burghred sought the West Saxons' support; they joined him at

Nottingham in 868 and forced the Danes to buy peace and withdraw. In the same year the Mercian-West Saxon alliance was further strengthened by the marriage of Alfred of Wessex, the king's brother, with Ealhswith, the daughter of ealdorman Æthelred Mucil and a descendant of King Coenwulf through her mother.

In 869 the Danes crossed Mercia into East Anglia, killing Edmund, king of the East Angles and in 870 or early 871 went into Wessex where a West Saxon victory at Ashdown (Berkshire) was followed by defeat at Basing (Hampshire). The same year saw the death of Æthelred and the accession of Alfred. Their withdrawal having been purchased, the Danes crossed back into Mercian territory to take up winter quarters at London, where the Mercians also bought peace, suggesting that in 872 the Mercians and West Saxons were unable to assist each other. The demands being made on Mercian resources were considerable and deep-felt, one charter of 872 referring to land at Nuthurst in Warwickshire leased by Bishop Waerferth of Worcester on account of 'the very pressing affliction and immense tribute of the barbarians, in that same year when the pagans stayed in London'. Unlikely to be unique, the impact of these events bit deep into the kingdom. Indeed, the situation had worsened in 871 with the arrival of reinforcements, the 'Great Summer Army', now leaving two Danish armies campaigning across England.

Revolt in Northumbria in 872 drew the Vikings

northwards again, but it was not long before they again ventured across the Humber into Mercia. In 873 the combined Danish armies wintered first at Torksey, near Lincoln, where the Mercians bought peace, and then in 874 they moved further south to Repton in Derbyshire. The occupation of Repton, a royal estate centre, dynastic mausoleum and cult centre was a well-calculated psychological blow that hit at the credibility and reputation of the Mercian royal dynasty itself. Burghred fled Mercia and travelled to Rome where he died in exile. Danish practice in their subjugated territories was to appoint dependent 'caretaker' kings and this they did in Mercia. Ceolwulf II gave hostages and swore an oath that he would serve the Danes and surrender the kingdom to them whenever they might wish.

This came a few years later, in 877. After Repton the Viking armies divided, Halfdan returning to Northumbria with the army that had been campaigning since 865, and where in 876 he 'shared out the lands of Northumbria and they were engaged in ploughing and making a living for themselves'. England south of the Humber was left to the army of Guthrum, part of whose force moved to Cambridge, and then in 875 or 876 into Wessex, returning to Mercia by 877 and wintering in the Gloucester area. Ceolwulf II was now called upon to honour his sworn oaths with arrangements made for the division of Mercia; as the *Anglo-Saxon Chronicle* records, 'some of it they shared out and some they gave to Ceolwulf'. While Guthrum returned to Wessex in 878, part of the army remained behind intent, as in Northumbria, on settling the lands that they had won. The character of the Danish campaigns had changed from plundering to settlement, exemplified when Alfred negotiated a treaty with the Danes, leaving

Guthrum in possession of the East Anglian kingdom and effectively acknowledging the partition of the Mercian kingdom, the Danes holding the eastern provinces of Mercia while western or 'English Mercia' had the old territory of the Hwicce at its core.

The 'Last Act'?

Traumatic as these events were, there is no reason to think that contemporaries saw them as the 'death throes' of the Mercian kingdom, having faced radical readjustments since the mid-830s and successfully found a new equilibrium with their neighbours.

While the West Saxon account inevitably ridiculed Ceolwulf II as a 'foolish king's thegn', his position was far from unique and, as a probable kinsman of Coenwulf and Ceolwulf, he may have seized upon an opportunity to re-establish his kindred on the Mercian throne. Reigning until 879, or perhaps the early 880s, he was described in one of his charters as 'Ceolwulf, by the grant of the gratuitous grace of God, king of the Mercians', and he issued joint coinage with King Alfred. The 2015 discovery of a probable Viking hoard, deposited near Watlington (Oxfordshire) around the end of the 870s, included double-figured coins depicting both Alfred and Ceolwulf, suggestive of an alliance between the two kings. Ceolwulf's reign was clearly recognised as legitimate, supported by the church and served by at least some of Burghred's ealdormen. When in 875 he freed the diocese of Worcester from the service of feeding the king's horses and grooms, in return for spiritual commemoration and the lease of land at Daylesford to himself and his heirs for 'three lives', there was no thought that the Mercian kingdom might not continue. ✠

Repton and the Vikings

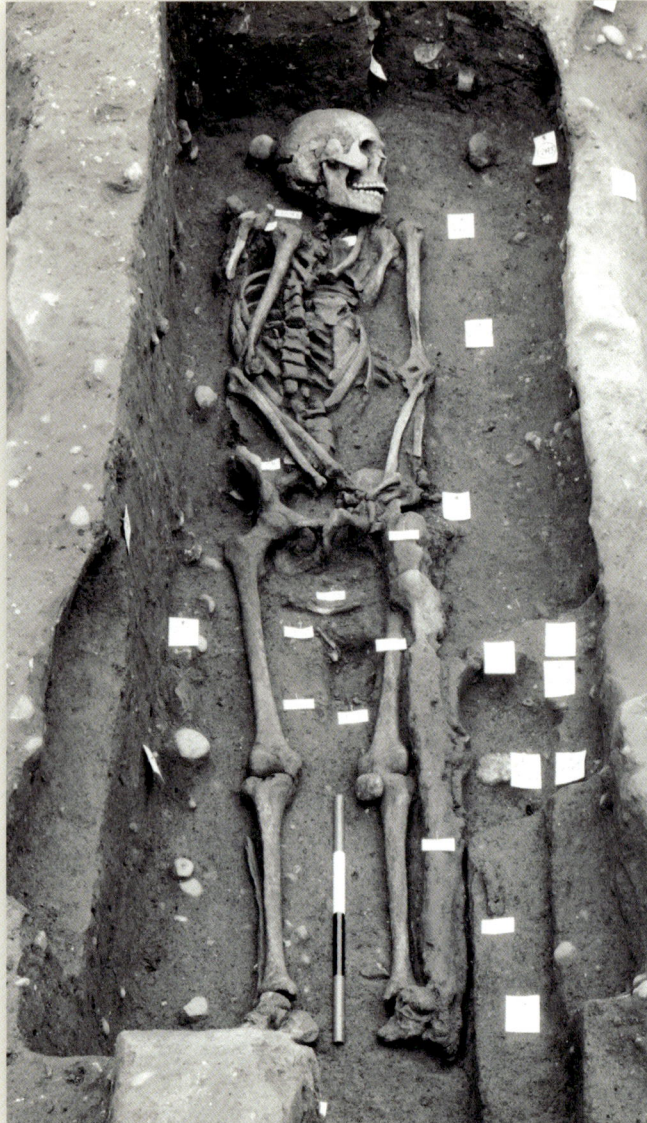

Grave 511 supplied by Derby Museums Trust

Grave 511, a Viking warrior burial excavated at Repton, whose possessions
included a boar's tusk and a silver hammer pendant which suggests that
he was a devotee of the Norse god, Thor.

*"The excavations at Repton provide a dramatic entrée not only into a
critical episode in Mercian history, but also into the mentalité of the age,
conjuring up a place at the heart of Mercian sensibilities."*

114

Repton stands on a prominent bluff of Bunter sandstone and pebble on the south side of the Trent valley which in the early medieval period was navigable. The excavations between 1974 and 1988 (and 1993) are among the most important of the late twentieth century on an Anglo-Saxon site. The central place for the region of the Hreppingas, Repton was the administrative centre of a royal estate and the site of a royal minster established in the seventh century. Its special place at the heart of Mercian kingship and dynastic identity was reflected by its role as a royal mausoleum, possibly since the seventh century and certainly from the eighth, and the emergence in the second-half of the ninth century of a saint's cult rooted in the Mercian royal kin.

The Repton project was initially concerned to investigate the structural history of the Anglo-Saxon church and its crypt, but excavations at the east end of the church discovered a major ditch and rampart. Subsequent seasons revealed details of the Anglo-Saxon monastery and the Viking overwintering of 873-4.

The monastery comprised a number of buildings, some of stone, which the Danes took full advantage of when fortifying their winter encampment. Using the church as a strongpoint and apparently as a hall and gatehouse, they enclosed a 'D-shaped' area of a little under two acres. The line of the ditch, about 30 feet wide and 12-15 feet deep near the church, was traced to the bank of the Old Trent where a 'V-shaped' ditch was excavated.

Excavations around the chancel uncovered a long series of burials, some associated with the Viking overwintering. Grave 511 was the burial of a warrior around 35-40 years of age, apparently killed by massive weapon cuts to his thigh and arm. He was buried with his sword and scabbard, a silver Thor's hammer pendant, boar's tusk and, between his legs, a wooden box containing bird bones. Also in this area on the south side of the chancel was another burial, Grave 529, a male aged 25–35 years, buried with a gold ring and five silver coins dating the burial in the mid-870s.

Equally remarkable were the discoveries made within 'The Vicar's Garden' to the west of the church, beyond the fortified enclosure. Excavation revealed a burial mound, at the heart of which was a rectangular stone building, about 20 feet by 10 feet, aligned east-west. This sunken two-celled structure, dating to the late seventh or eighth century, was a mortuary chapel. This fine building was decorated with white plaster and stucco, probably glazed, and may have served as a royal mausoleum, perhaps accommodating Æthelbald before the new mausoleum was built to the east of the church.

The excavation of this structure produced the disarticulated remains of at least 249 people, about 80% of whom were male, aged 15–45, and robust in character. The building, in decay by the ninth century, was cut down to ground level and used by the Vikings to form a chamber for a high-status burial of c.873/4 within a mound, possibly with sacrificial burials at the corners.

With its important additions to the corpus of Viking burials known from Mercia, and the rare opportunity to examine a well-documented fortified Viking campaign camp and its impact, the excavations at Repton provide a dramatic *entrée* not only into a critical episode in Mercian history, but also into the mentalité of the age, conjuring up a place at the heart of Mercian sensibilities, the attack upon which was calculated psychologically and militarily to debilitate the Mercian kingdom. ✠

10

Mercia, Wessex
and the Vikings

Alfred, and the West Saxon monarchy, emerged from the Viking onslaught of the ninth century with immense prestige, presented in the *Anglo-Saxon Chronicle* as the only kingdom to have successfully withstood the Danes, and as the only English dynasty that had not been supplanted. England was left divided between those areas to the north and east that had succumbed to Danish conquest and settlement, where an Anglo-Danish society emerged, and Anglo-Saxon culture and polity broadly focused on Wessex. Mercia was in the 'frontline' of what followed.

The tenth century witnessed the recovery of Anglo-Saxon society from these tumultuous events and the forging of a single English kingdom, only to again face renewed Danish raids by the end of the century. English history remembers this extension of West Saxon authority across Danish-occupied and settled England as the 'Saxon Re-conquest', as if it was a restoration of the *status quo*; in fact, it was far from this. It was a specifically West Saxon campaign of aggrandisement that left Wessex as the dominant power, with West Saxon kings of England, and the possibility of a resurgent Mercian kingdom quashed for ever.

Mercia Partitioned

The extent of Viking settlement in England is graphically illustrated by the pattern of Scandinavian place-names, which while in need of careful interpretation, reveals Mercia cut in half. There is no record of what the Vikings agreed with Ceolwulf in 877 and therefore historians have often looked to the treaty negotiated between Alfred and Guthrum for guidance. Although undated and debated, it is generally placed between 880 and 890,

traditionally at around 886 following Alfred's 'restoration' of London and the acceptance of his overlordship by the English.

The boundary between Alfred and Guthrum's territories was defined using the rivers Thames and Lea and 'up the Ouse to Watling Street', but applying these boundaries to Mercia is problematic. Some historians have inferred that the boundary ran along the Watling Street as far as Shropshire, while others have rejected this on the basis that the Mercian frontier lay beyond the scope of this treaty. The south-eastern midlands would certainly have been of interest to the Mercians, but extending the agreement into the north-west midlands is more contentious, and it seems probable that rather than follow the Watling Street westwards, the boundary turned northwards from Warwickshire, perhaps following the line that later became the boundary separating Staffordshire, Cheshire and Lancashire from Derbyshire and Yorkshire. Irrespective of its inclusion or otherwise in the treaty of *c*.886, it is probable that a 'de facto' boundary did run along the Watling Street at least as far as Tamworth, which became a 'border town' as a result. The road provided a clear border between the area dominated by the Danish army of Leicester and English Mercia, but near Tamworth the boundary turned north, ensuring that together with Lichfield these two key Mercian places remained within English Mercia, albeit in a vulnerable frontier zone.

Mercia was thus divided; a northern and eastern area under fragmented Danish authority, a part of Danish-settled England or 'Danelaw'; and the south and west under English lordship. By the early tenth century the Danish territory was controlled by armies based on what later became known as the confederacy of the 'Five Boroughs', fortified centres

Previous page: Æthelflæd, the 'Lady of the Mercians', from the Cartulary of Abingdon Abbey, *c*.1220.

at Leicester, Nottingham, Derby, Lincoln and Stamford, with armies also at Bedford, Huntingdon and Northampton. The focus of political authority in English Mercia also shifted, moving to Gloucester and the Severn Valley, but those borders thought convenient in the late ninth century rapidly dissolved in the early tenth with a changing balance of power.

The 'Lord and Lady of the Mercians'

There is much about the period between 877 and 910 that cannot be recovered in detail but this was when Mercia's last king disappeared from history and the lordship of Mercia passed to an ealdorman named Æthelred. His origins are unclear but when in 883 he granted privileges to Berkeley minster, he did so with the consent of the Mercian *witan* and of King Alfred, whom he clearly regarded as his lord and to whom he had apparently sworn an oath of obedience. Alfred may have assumed direct authority over Mercia when Ceolwulf left the scene and therefore played a part in Æthelred's appointment. However the Mercians may have viewed him, he was Alfred's man and was obliged to

accept the status of an ealdorman, but he was singled out from the others by distinguished titles (*patricius; procurator*) and by associating his status with the divine grace and gift of God. Alfred clearly had confidence in him. London was recognised as Mercian and entrusted to the ealdorman's care and not later than 887 Æthelred married Æthelflæd, Alfred's eldest daughter, whom the *Mercian Register* referred to as the 'Lady of the Mercians'.

Æthelred ruled in Mercia with the circumscribed powers of a client king. He sometimes acted independently but mostly it was in association with, or with the permission of, King Alfred, and while he was allowed to issue charters, his remit did not run to the minting of coin. Often in association with his wife, Æthelred, like all Mercian rulers, supported religious communities, as at Berkeley, Worcester and Much Wenlock, actions that did as much to enhance their authority as to satisfy their piety. A charter of 887 transferring estates in Oxfordshire to the see of Worcester states that this was done for the redemption of his soul and for the safety and stability of the kingdom of the

An enthroned King Alfred, who negotiated a treaty with the Danish king Guthrum, from a manuscript of 1321.

© The British Library Board. Cotton Claudius D.ii, f.8

"While Mercia and the Mercians remained an identifiable entity throughout the tenth and eleventh centuries, the vicissitudes of this period did not realistically offer the prospect of a reawakened Mercian kingdom in the way that a resurgent kingdom remained possible north of the Humber."

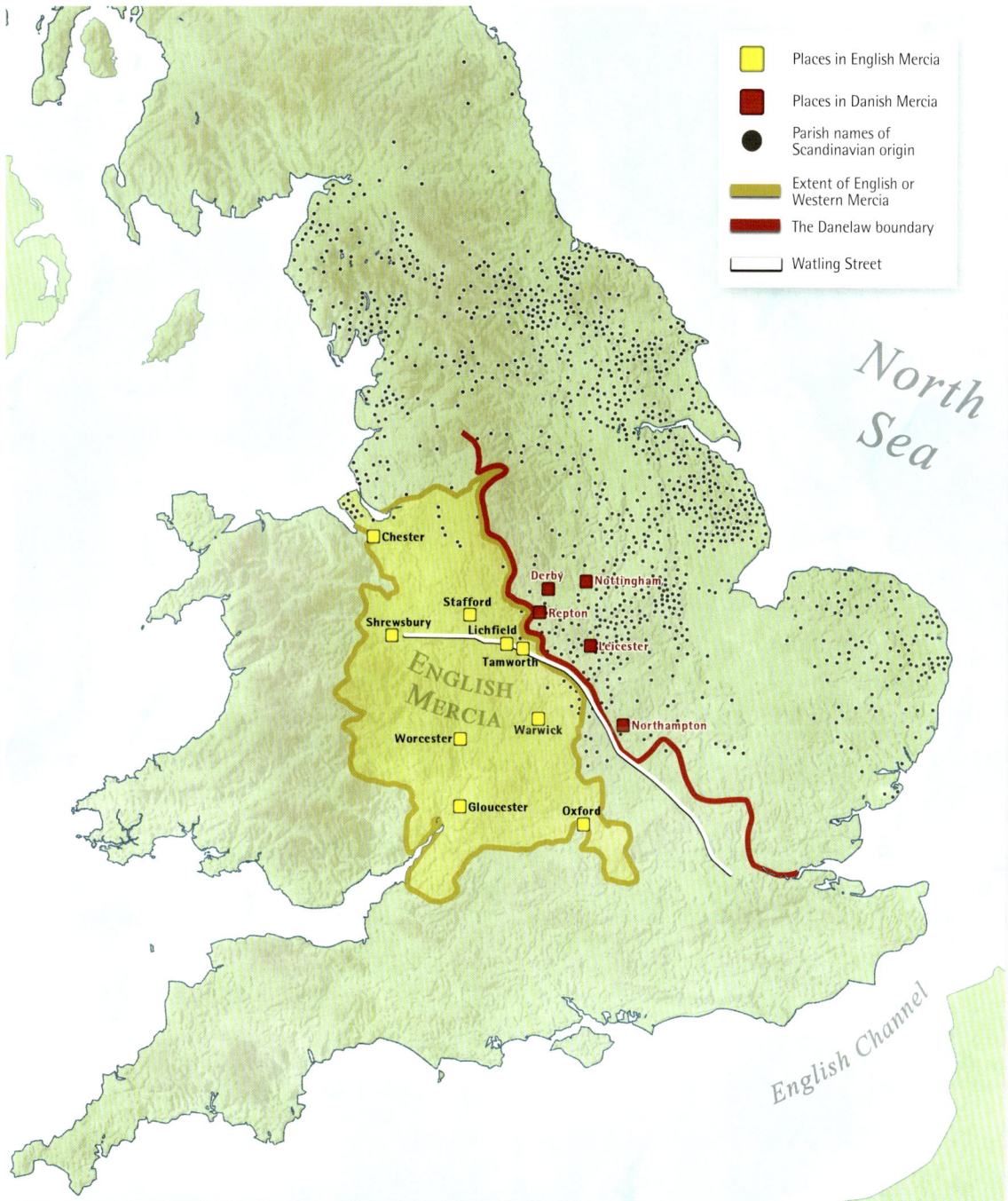

Legend:
- Places in English Mercia
- Places in Danish Mercia
- Parish names of Scandinavian origin
- Extent of English or Western Mercia
- The Danelaw boundary
- Watling Street

North Sea

English Channel

ENGLISH MERCIA

Chester, Stafford, Shrewsbury, Lichfield, Tamworth, Worcester, Warwick, Gloucester, Oxford

Derby, Nottingham, Repton, Leicester, Northampton

English Mercia: Mercia was partitioned with the areas to the east falling under Danish domination. The extent of the Viking settlement is reflected by the distribution of Scandinavian place-names.

"Fundamental to the exercise of royal authority in the locality, shires, originating in Wessex and introduced into Mercia in the early tenth century, suggest the assimilation of territory rather than its domination."

Mercians. Undoubtedly conscious of the prestigious implications and inherent symbolism, near their palace in Gloucester Æthelflæd founded the New Minster of St Oswald, possibly on an existing royal cemetery site, to which in 909 she brought relics of Saint Oswald from Bardney (Lincolnshire), a house closely associated with the Mercian royal kin.

West Saxon concessions to Mercian autonomy suggest an awareness of Mercian sensitivity and identity rooted in its past, pragmatically avoiding distractions that might otherwise undermine efforts to contain and turn the Danish threat. However, it may also have been about Alfred fashioning a new political order, a kingdom of the Anglo-Saxons that brought together the Anglian and Saxon people outside of Danelaw, with common interests, under West Saxon rule. As Simon Keynes has argued, this was not so much the combination of two ancient kingdoms or the domination of one by the other as the creation of something different and new that subsumed both.

Æthelred and his wife, as allies of the West Saxon kings, played a central role in the reassertion of English authority across the midlands. Their strategy mirrored that of Alfred's son and successor, Edward, who most probably orchestrated the military campaigns of the early tenth century against the southern Danelaw. They responded to incursions but otherwise made incremental progress with limited and focused campaigns, co-ordinating their operations and consolidating successes by extending the network of fortified centres or burhs. This latter process is reflected in a

remarkable charter of the 890s, also demonstrating the extension of royal authority. At the request of Bishop Waerferth, Æthelred and Æthelflæd ordered the construction of a burh at Worcester 'for the protection of all the people, and also to exalt the praise of God therein'. The seemingly generous clause granting the bishop a half of all their rights of lordship in the city 'whether in the market or in the street, both within the fortification and outside' disguises the fact that the bishop had effectively surrendered his lordship of the city in the process. These arrangements, including the provision of divine offices on behalf of the 'donors', were witnessed and confirmed by King Alfred and the councillors of the Mercians. In 907 Æthelred also re-established Chester as a burh to counter the threat posed from the Vikings in Ireland.

The Mercians achieved a notable success when in 910 a Viking army from Northumbria raided as far south as the West Country, during which 'the fields of the Mercians were ravaged on all sides ... and deeply, as far as the streams of the Avon'. As they returned northwards they were pursued, caught and defeated by Mercian and West Saxon forces at Tettenhall in Staffordshire, dealing a serious blow that left several Viking leaders dead and undermined Northumbrian support for the southern Danes. Æthelred died in the following year, buried 'in the fortress known as Gloucester', and the lordship of Æthelflæd was acknowledged by the Mercians. This rare commitment to a female ruler suggests confidence in her 'track record' and can as readily be seen as an assertion of Mercian

Courtesy John Hunt

The New Minster of St Oswald's, Gloucester, at the focus of English Mercian political power in the late ninth century. Æthelflæd may have intended that she be buried here but the *Mercian Register* records the eastern chapel of Saint Peter's as her place of burial.

independence as the imposition of a surrogate ruler on behalf of her brother, Edward the Elder.

While Edward campaigned northwards, Æthelflæd moved west. To Mercia's network of fortifications she added burhs at Bridgnorth (912), Stafford (913), Tamworth (913), Warwick (914) and Runcorn (915), often enhancing existing centres. Tamworth was already a defended royal residence; Warwick the location of a probable minster complex, trading settlement and royal residence; and Stafford, a developing production centre since the mid-ninth century.

In 917 she received the submission of the Danes of Derby, followed by the army of Leicester in 918. Her brother meanwhile had secured the south-eastern midlands and much of eastern England, forcing the submission of the armies of Northampton, Huntingdon, Cambridge and East Anglia, so that by 918 lands to the south-east of a line from the Severn estuary to the Wash were controlled by Edward, and those east of the Welsh border, and towards Nottingham and Leicester, by Æthelflæd.

In June 918 Æthelflæd died at Tamworth and was taken to Gloucester for burial in the east chapel of St Peter's Church. In the following year, just before Christmas, King Edward seized her daughter Ælfwynn, depriving her 'of all authority in Mercia' and taking her to Wessex.

Mercia, Annexation and the English Kingdom

Edward had determined upon a different approach from that of his father Alfred, even if still true to his vision. In 912 he had taken possession of the Mercian centres of London and Oxford and their lands and now he secured his position by displacing a potential focus of challenge from within Mercia, assuming direct control. It is a moot point as to whether this might be seen as annexation, or simply

> *"Existing boundaries, political, geographical and tenurial, some of considerable antiquity, influenced the making of shires and preserved memory and identity in the landscape and Mercian tribal names continued to be used in tenth-century charters."*

an inevitable step in a process that had commenced in the late ninth century. Notwithstanding the survival of a sense of Mercian identity, it was a process of 'incorporation' that confirmed one kingdom under the West Saxon dynasty, and a process of imposition rather than response to any form of popular demand.

When he died in July 925 Edward was established as king of England south of the Humber, encompassing both English and Danish territories, and had received the submission of the Northumbrians. These were foundations on which his successors could build, and by Easter 928 his son, Athelstan (925-939), had annexed Northumbria and brought Wales and Cornwall into submission.

But there were also reverses. Between 939 and 941 Olaf Guthfrithsson crossed from Viking Dublin, was accepted as king of York, and extended his bid for power into the east midlands where he found ready support among the Danes. By 941 he had the 'Five Boroughs', his authority in the eastern midlands running as far south as the Watling Street; Leicester became his base while in Derby coins were struck in his name. It was only his death that gave King Edmund (939-946) an opportunity to recover the situation and regain what had been lost.

While Mercia and the Mercians remained an identifiable entity throughout the tenth and eleventh centuries, the vicissitudes of this period did not realistically offer the prospect of a reawakened Mercian kingdom in the way that a resurgent kingdom remained possible north of the Humber. However, these years heralded a developing

characteristic that would become increasingly influential - the cultural and kinship ties that Northumbrian society shared with much of Mercia.

Mercian Shires

The impact of 'incorporation' upon the administrative geography of Mercia eloquently illustrates penetrating change. Notwithstanding the continued influence of earlier boundaries and arrangements, an administrative framework based upon '*regiones*' and '*provinciae*' was eclipsed by one based upon the '*scir*' or shire. Fundamental to the exercise of royal authority in the locality, shires, originating in Wessex and introduced into Mercia in the early tenth century, suggest the assimilation of territory rather than its domination. The shire was a basic area of local jurisdiction overseen by a royal officer, the 'shire reeve' or sheriff, and further subdivided into areas known as hundreds which, based on places of assembly, probably often reflected much older units.

Existing boundaries, political, geographical and tenurial, some of considerable antiquity, influenced the making of shires and preserved memory and identity in the landscape and Mercian tribal names continued to be used in tenth-century charters; the Magonsaete in a charter of 958; the Wreocensaete in a Shropshire grant of 963; and the Pecsaete in another charter of 963, for Ballidon in Derbyshire. Traditional associations were slow to relinquish their hold.

However, the emerging infrastructure was not entirely novel in Mercia. Since the mid-eighth century the Mercian kings had promoted a defensive system with fortified places at its heart. These burhs had hinterlands that supported them, the territories from which public renders and obligations, such as labour and military service, were drawn. Their system may have been more extensive than previously thought, but even so the network was intensified in the early tenth century with the further construction of fortifications or the revitalisation of existing ones.

Across Mercia, including eastern Mercia where fortified boroughs played the same vital role in the military strategy of the Danish armies, these places became the centres of recast local administration, giving their names to the shires. In a relationship that was entirely reciprocal and symbiotic, these were the territories dependent upon the protection of the burh concerned.

Many of the places fortified already had distinction as religious or royal estate centres with territories focused upon them, so the creation of a shire simply added another, perhaps broader layer of responsibility. In western Mercia, Worcester was a longstanding centre of the Hwicce, fortified by the late ninth century if not earlier, with royal and ecclesiastical roles. Warwick too had religious, royal and trading functions before the burh was created, while in Staffordshire, Tamworth's border location led to its decline in favour of Stafford, a place which recent excavations have demonstrated was developing from the late eighth century. Shrewsbury was

probably defended by the late ninth century if not earlier, and the burh at Hereford by the mid-eighth century. The fortified Roman city of Gloucester enjoyed particular importance by the early tenth century as English Mercia's political 'centre' and the residence and burial place of Æthelred and Æthelflæd.

In eastern Mercia, shires formed on boroughs frequently situated at key points on roads and river crossings, and sited, as at Derby, Nottingham, Stamford and Lincoln, in anticipation of an attack from the south.

Dating the origins of shires in the east midlands is particularly difficult, but, as Pauline Stafford has observed, they were not the result of a single administrative decision. She suggests that Northamptonshire, Bedfordshire, and Huntingdonshire were formed in the first half of the tenth century, with Derbyshire, Leicestershire and Nottinghamshire following slightly later. Not all shires succeeded; Winchcombe and Stamford 'failed', the latter being incorporated into Lindsey.

The focus of many shires was therefore largely pre-determined, and as the shire and its court grew in importance during the tenth and eleventh centuries, forming the 'backbone' of royal governance and administration in the provinces, they became inevitable centres of activity and a focus for the local aristocratic community.

Silver coin of Anlaf (Olaf) Guthfrithsson minted at York 939–41 with its distinctive bird of prey, perhaps an eagle or a raven.

From Ealdormen to Earl

From the middle of the tenth century, Mercia was dominated by its magnate families, particularly its ealdormen, later known as earls. While generally active on a wider stage, they were also subsumed into the world of regional politics as it was here, in region and locality, that the basis of their power really lay. These were the men to whom Mercians gave their allegiance, fostered through 'good lordship'.

A mass burial of male skeletons at St John's College Oxford may represent victims of the brutal Saint Brice's Day Massacre.

King Edmund revived the office, most probably to bolster his attempts to contain and reverse the advances of Olaf Guthfrithsson. Ealhhelm was made ealdorman in central Mercia, most probably the old territory of the Hwicce, and in order that he might have the resources to fulfil his duties he was granted the lands of a failing Evesham Abbey, for which he was remembered by monastic chroniclers as a despoiler. He was not alone. Ealdorman Æthelmund held the north-western provinces of Mercia and Æthelstan in the south-east.

A complex web of land tenure, patronage and kinship bound aristocratic society together and focused it on the Mercian magnates, promoting at the same time a continuing sense of Mercian identity. Consequently, given their range of delegated powers, the appointment of ealdormen could be a sensitive business.

English kings, whose itineraries reflected a 'centre of gravity' south of the Thames, fostered loyalty in the regions through patronage and appointments; they made grants to local families and promoted those whom they trusted to hold their allegiance, like Ælfhere of Mercia and Æthelwold of East Anglia, both from West Saxon families. The intensely loyal new monasteries of the tenth century further reinforced their positions regionally.

The appointment of ealdormen in Mercia fell into abeyance after the death of Æthelred but in 940

In 956 Ælfhere, appointed by his kinsman King Eadwig, followed his father as ealdorman and subsequently became ealdorman of western Mercia, stretching from Cheshire to Gloucestershire, with others as his subordinates. Like his father, he too was criticised for his abuse of monastic estates to appropriate 'enormous revenues.'

The ealdormanry of Mercia again fell into abeyance following the death of Ælfhere and the abortive term of his brother-in-law, although ealdormen with more restricted remits, like Leofwine 'of the Mercian provinces', continued. But under pressure from Viking attacks, the Mercian ealdormanry was reinstituted in 1007 and given to a royal favourite, Eadric Streona.

The Vikings Return

From about 980, the reign of Æthelred II, popularly known to English history as 'Æthelred the Unready', saw the return of the Vikings to England. For the most part these new incursions were initiated by the Danish royal kin leading national levies in pursuit of political and economic objectives.

Fearing for his life and his throne, in 1002 Æthelred ordered what became known as the 'Saint Brice's Day Massacre'. A charter of 1004 in favour of the monastery of Saint Frideswide in Oxford looked back on these events, recalling that a decree was sent out 'to the effect that all the Danes who had sprung up in this island, sprouting like cockle amongst the wheat, were to be destroyed by a most just extermination'. In Oxford persecuted Danes sought sanctuary in the church, which the people set alight 'with its ornaments and its books', necessitating the replacement charter.

Who were the victims of this slaughter? They may be represented by the thirty-five skeletons found in Oxford in 2008, all males aged between sixteen and twenty-five years and marked by some charring and weapon-wounds, mostly to the back of the head and interpreted as inflicted while running away. A similar mass grave has been found at Weymouth in Dorset.

Although referred to as a 'massacre' it is probable that the killing was relatively selective and limited to those areas within the king's immediate jurisdiction. Most of those living within the Danelaw, some four generations on from the ninth-century colonisation, had settled into the towns and countryside as artisans and farmers, and it is unlikely that they were directly targeted. However, in a prevailing atmosphere of accusation and distrust, Danish merchants, more recent settlers and some prominent individuals who were suspected of aiding and informing the Viking raids were natural targets, particularly within English communities. Those who died at Oxford were probably traders and perhaps some members of a small Danish community in Oxford attracted by the town's dynamic and varied mercantile activity. The few Scandinavian finds from Oxford, including a postulated furnished equestrian warrior grave, may be associated with the activities of Danish armies and a garrison rather than with a community.

By 1013 the Viking attacks forced Æthelred into temporary exile and the Danish king's authority was consolidated among the Danes of Northumbria, Mercia and East Anglia. The narrative of Mercia's part in these years is overshadowed by the apparent enmity, or at least mistrust, between Eadric Streona and Edmund Ironside, Æthelred's son and the leader of the English military campaign. The *Anglo-Saxon Chronicle* presents the ealdorman as a treacherous and untrustworthy figure who undermined English efforts, first by joining with Cnut in 1015 and then, after re-joining Edmund, by fleeing the battle of Ashingdon (Essex) in 1016 with the men of the Magonsæte, precipitating an English rout, after which he counselled a treaty with Cnut.

The Chronicler's judgments on Eadric were neither neutral nor disinterested, resented for his rapid success as a royal protégé. protégé. However, Eadric's role clearly left its mark, testimony to severe disunity among the English and to a sense of separatism still evident among the Mercians.

The kingdom was partitioned rather than conquered, with Edmund ruling Wessex, but his death in November 1016 left Cnut as king of all England. In 1017 Eadric was confirmed in his possession of Mercia when England was divided into four large earldoms, but this arrangement proved short-lived and Eadric was himself murdered later in the year, guilty or suspected of treason, clearing the way for more reorganisation in Mercia. ✠

The *Anglo-Saxon Chronicle*, Mercian identity, and the *Mercian Register*

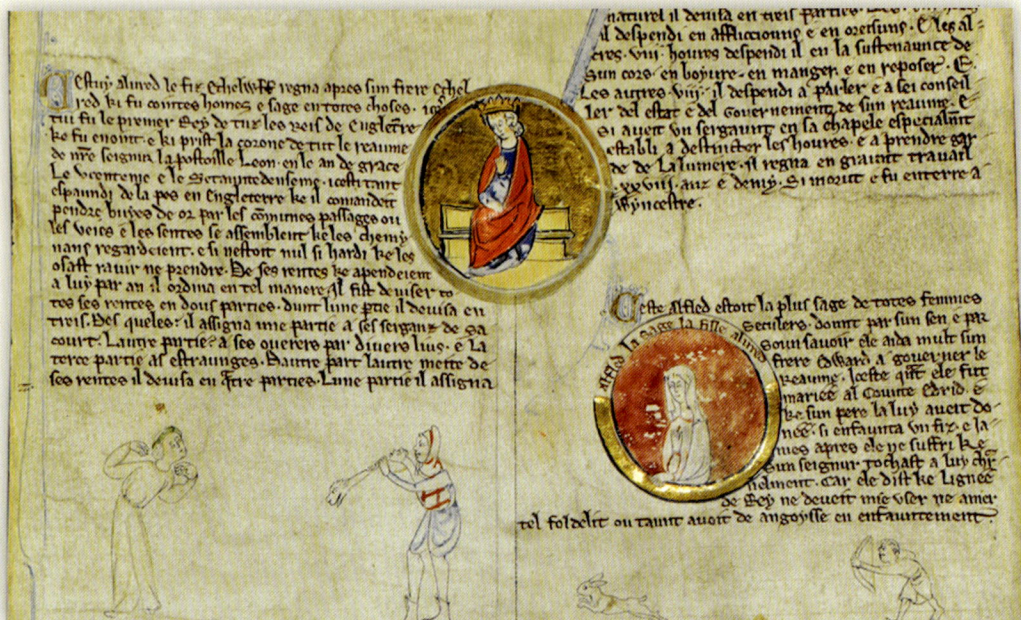

King Alfred and his daughter Æthelflæd, the 'Lady of the Mercians', a detail from a *Genealogical Chronicle of the English Kings* dating to 1275-1300.

Although essentially a West Saxon work, a distinctively Mercian 'voice' may be detected within the *Anglo-Saxon Chronicle*, a vital source offering a narrative framework and chronology for much of the period. It was initially devised under Alfred's patronage as dynastic propaganda, to promote his achievements and the authority of his kin, and to build a sense of unity within and beyond the traditional boundaries of Wessex. With their continuations, the *Chronicle* presents English history from Julius Caesar to Henry II, but it is not a single text. A series of separate but related Old English annals, it survives in seven different manuscripts with fragments of an eighth, produced at various centres around England but originating with the initial 'Alfredian Chronicle' of the 890s. Consequently, there is a strong regional flavour in much material, revealing how the Anglo-Saxons saw themselves and their history.

Of these texts, the 'B' manuscript (together with 'C'), known as the *Mercian Register*, whose Mercian associations are especially evident in the early tenth century, focuses on Æthelflæd from 912–918, justifying their alternative description as *The Annals of Æthelflæd*. Providing a distinctively Mercian perspective, the annals focus on and celebrate Æthelflæd in her role as 'Lady of the Mercians', particularly her military activities, ranging across her burh-building, her campaign against the king of Brycheiniog, the capture of Danish forts and the submission of Danish armies, including pledges made to her by the people of York.

These annals convey an impression of Æthelflæd's independence, with little reference to Edward the Elder, and very different from that found in Manuscript 'A' which sees these years from the perspective of Edward, with sparse reference to Æthelflæd, and then as Edward's sister rather than as ruler of the Mercians. The distinctiveness of this Mercian account is underscored by the fact that women feature rarely in such vernacular chronicles; this is the longest sustained treatment of a woman anywhere in the *Anglo-Saxon Chronicle*.

With God's support and without reference to Wessex, Æthelflæd's activities as ruler of Mercia, her effectiveness and legitimacy, emphasised qualities generally associated with masculine rule, but more importantly, demonstrated that Æthelflæd delivered what the Mercians expected of effective lordship.

The Anglo-Saxons were very conscious of what we might now

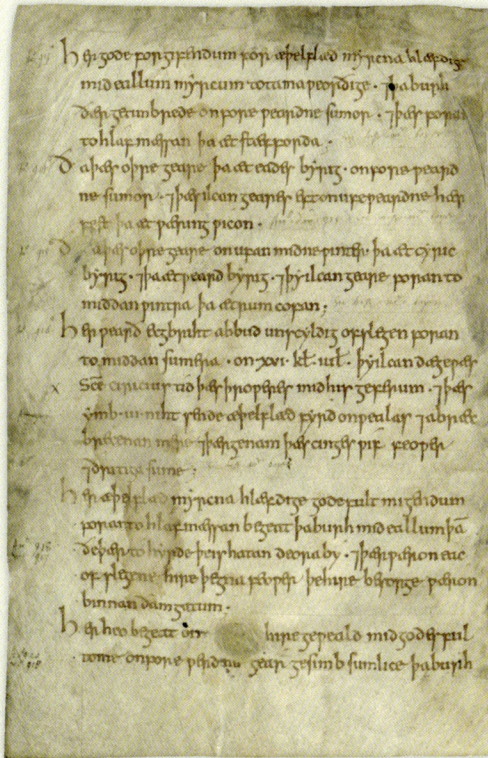

A page from the *Mercian Register* recounting events between 913 and 918.

think of as the 'flexibility' of history and the significance attached to how the past was presented. Like the annals of Edward's activities in the 'A' manuscript, *The Annals of Æthelflæd* were a response to the key political questions of the day, namely Alfred's inheritance and the question of the succession to both the individual and combined kingdoms of Wessex and Mercia. England was still perceived as a collection of kingdoms, each with their own identity, rather than a single unified

kingdom. It was not impossible that Alfred's vision, if such it was, and Edward the Elder's progress could still unravel.

However, nor were the Mercians necessarily separatist; they had co-operated in West Saxon rule and the reality was that for all of Æthelflæd's considerable achievements, the powers of Mercian rulers in the early tenth century were more limited than those of their royal predecessors. But, the West Saxons needed to make their rule in Mercia acceptable to the Mercians, and that is what these annals did, finely balancing Æthelflæd's West Saxon dynastic links with her Mercian heritage through her mother, and her success as a Mercian ruler.

In the event, these preparations were not really tested. When Edward the Elder died, Athelstan was accepted as king by the Mercians, but the potential implications were averted when Edward's son Ælfweard died at Oxford within days of his father, leaving Athelstan unchallenged and potential divisions avoided. ✠

"Providing a distinctively Mercian perspective, the annals focus on and celebrate Æthelflæd in her role as 'Lady of the Mercians'."

11

People and Settlement in Anglo-Saxon Mercia

Running broadly from the Humber to the Thames and from the Welsh borders to the Fens, the Mercian kingdom embraced many different landscape types and economic regimes, ranging from lightly settled areas of upland or woodland where pastoral farming dominated, to more intensively occupied and farmed lowland areas where mixed farming regimes became increasingly arable in their emphasis. Sheep flocks were particularly important, given the significance of textiles and wool exports for Anglo-Saxon wealth, possibly as early as the eighth century, while many woodland areas accommodated elite interests in hunting. There were large areas characterised by open woodland which accommodated a scattered population and flexible economy, such as that which perhaps ran from the Humber estuary down to Gloucestershire; but some regions, particularly those where clearance for arable use could be traced back into the Romano-British period, supported denser populations with an increasingly specialised arable economy.

Across this landscape was laid a pattern of early territories and great estates, largely focused on minsters and royal vills, each embracing a range of landscapes and resources; some of these places might be geographically distant from their estate centres, recalling patterns of transhumance or seasonal activity. Gradually, from the eighth century, these large, or 'multiple' estates, fragmented to form the smaller estates and manors that characterised the countryside by the tenth and eleventh centuries. The kingdom was served by a network of roads and rivers, with some places, like the major salt-producing centre of Droitwich,

served by multiple routes. Also settled into this landscape alongside minsters and royal vills were artisanal production centres, royal fortifications and growing towns. How did Mercian society settle and live in this landscape?

Early Anglo-Saxon Society

The archaeology of early Anglo-Saxon inhumation burials suggests a society familiar with hierarchy and a sense of 'one's place' within the community. The arrangement of cemeteries points to the influence of ethnicity, kindred and status as well as of religious practice, while the deposition of grave goods reveals a population marked by considerable variance in status and wealth, both as individuals and as whole communities. Early Anglo-Saxon communities in Mercia included well-equipped warrior burials suggestive of a male elite and richly furnished female burials reflecting the apparent prominence of powerful women, but there were many cemeteries characterised by relatively poor grave goods and low-status populations.

The complexity of early English society that is suggested by the archaeology is further revealed in the corpus of surviving Anglo-Saxon law codes which also take us beyond the kings and noblemen familiar from other documents. These law codes date from the seventh century and later, the earliest from Kent, and although none survive from Mercia there is sufficient commonality to gain some impression of early Mercian society.

Characteristic of these laws was the concept of 'wergeld' or 'blood-price', inherent in a system of keeping the peace through blood-feud. People, and the injuries that might be done to them, were given a value, generally in shillings or 'sceattas', the

From the calendar page for September in the 'Tiberius Miscellany' (c.1025–1050) this scene shows woodland with huntsmen and foraging hogs.

payment of which was required if injury was done and feud and bloodshed were to be avoided. While this would suggest that 'flashpoints' might frequently occur, it does not of itself indicate an inherently unstable or overtly violent society; these were the means by which instability and uncontrolled violence might be avoided. But the practice of private vengeance would give cause for concern by the tenth century. Expressing his distress at 'the illegal and manifold conflicts which take place among us', King Edmund attempted to outlaw the feud but failed, so integral was it to society.

Family, Kin and Class

Implicit within these arrangements was the importance of family and kin as the basic social unit, and the system of 'wergeld' itself was based on a deeply hierarchical society. Lordship is explicit, as are the free and the unfree, but these in turn might be further 'ranked'. In the Kentish laws there were at least two ranks among the free, three among the 'half-free' (laets, found only in Kent), and three among female slaves, while in seventh-century Wessex the free were also divided into several ranks; blood-worth, and the levels of compensation due,

varied accordingly. In King Ine's laws, the nobleman, described as a gesith (companion), forerunners to thegns, had a wergeld of 1200 shillings, six times that of the ceorl or ordinary freeman, but they also provided for men of gesith rank with twenty, ten or three hides of land, reflecting ranks within the nobility. By the eleventh century it was generally held that men of thegnly status should possess a minimum of five hides of land.

Such arrangements were not restricted to the English alone. In Wessex provision was made for Britons, again ranked according to their land-holding, but with a lower tariff than among the English, indicating social and economic integration but not equality. Similar arrangements for the English and British populations of Mercia undoubtedly existed but it is not possible to determine details or the legal relationship between the populations as expressed in terms of wergeld. However, although lacking a Mercian law code, there survives from the early eleventh century a private document known as A Compilation on Status, which includes a short section on 'Mircna laga' or Mercian law, which also stated that a ceorl's wergeld was valued at 200 shillings and that of a

"Implicit was the importance of family and kin as the basic social unit, and the system of 'wergeld' itself was based on a deeply hierarchical society."

thegn at 1200 shillings. Early society therefore comprised the free and the unfree, the English and the British, and each category was divisible into several classes.

Early Rural Settlements

What did early Mercian settlements look like? The archaeological identification of early settlement sites is difficult and there are few excavated examples from within Mercia, but what is known is consistent with elsewhere in England, indicating an early settlement pattern of dispersed farmsteads, as at Yarnton and Worton in Oxfordshire, or in Northamptonshire parishes like Raunds and Brixworth, the latter with at least eight small occupation sites scattered around the parish before *c.*850.

Characteristic of many early settlements were 'sunken featured buildings' (SFB), or *Grubenhäuser*, a German term that conveys their method of construction, 'pit-houses' dug out of the earth, but a term which unfortunately gave rise to the notion of Anglo-Saxon farmers living in hovels. Such buildings occur widely and have been identified on sites across Mercia, as at Yarnton and most recently on a site between Rugby and Daventry, where two sub-square enclosures, a possible SFB and a truncated post-built timber structure have been excavated (EN 15). But the generally poor stratigraphy and paucity of finds often hinder a detailed understanding of their role. Some have been interpreted as the 'cellars' to more substantial 'huts' and in many cases an industrial purpose has been supposed, their frequent association with

spindle-whorls and loomweights linking them with weaving and textile production. The SFB recently excavated in Lichfield was a subsidiary building, probably used for the storage of unprocessed cereal crops. Many SFBs were probably habitations, but they were not the only form of building found on early occupation sites. Even settlements like New Wintles, Eynsham (Oxfordshire), dominated between the sixth and early eighth centuries by widely scattered SFBs, had a small number of post-built structures.

Archaeologists have sometimes attempted to use the plans of early settlement sites to understand the nature of the social and economic organisation, but this is rarely straightforward, not least because many are only partially excavated. At West Stow, for instance, an important early site in Suffolk that was excavated in the mid-twentieth century, the settlement area uncovered was found to comprise clusters of buildings of three basic types, one of which was referred to as a hall, and the others as huts and *Grubenhäuser*. However, does this reflect a settlement based upon a lord's hall, or one organised on an extended kindred with the hall as a place of assembly, or a combination of the two? What might be true of one place cannot be assumed of another, but it has been suggested that many fifth- and sixth-century settlements probably had populations numbering between thirty and fifty people, which if so makes kindred-based communities seem very credible in the early Anglo-Saxon period.

The earliest settlements were dispersed, lacking obvious indications of planning or managed layout, but were not necessarily disorganised; the lack of

Above: A reconstruction of an early
Anglo-Saxon settlement at West Stow
in Suffolk with a 'sunken featured
building' (*Grubenhäus*) in the foreground and (inset) a similar
structure under excavation at Yarnton in Oxfordshire.

Main image: St Edmundsbury Heritage Services/West Stow Anglo-Saxon Village Trust
Inset: Courtesy of Oxford Archaeology

clear hierarchy in early settlement may suggest a relative weakness of elites. However, from about the late sixth and early seventh centuries the range of settlement forms started to become more diverse, often associated with various kinds of enclosure.

Catholme

Catholme in the Trent Valley is the only rural Anglo-Saxon settlement site so far substantially excavated in the Mercian heartland. Long-lived and stable, the settlement had Anglo-Saxon phases running from the early seventh to the late ninth centuries. Although it has not been possible to date the phases and development of Catholme very closely, some sixty-five buildings were excavated, together with trackways and ditched or fenced enclosures, probably associated with the management of livestock, in a layout suggestive of

orderly planning and monitoring. Shallow features such as fence lines might easily be lost through ploughing but fences seem likely on most sites, the late seventh-century laws of Ine of Wessex stating that 'a ceorl's homestead must be fenced winter and summer', noting too that they might have meadow or other land divided into shares and fenced or hedged. Industrial activity, such as metalworking, was carried out near the boundaries at Catholme, but there were no industrial or other functional zones as such.

Catholme had eighteen *Grubenhäuser*, all of two-post type, usually reconstructed as tent-like with a gable entrance, but most of the buildings were 'wall-post' structures, generally rectangular and built using posts set in post-pits, or less frequently, in trenches, several at least with opposing entrances in their long walls. Internal

"From the later seventh and eighth centuries, and lasting into the ninth century and beyond, a gradual transformation began to take shape in the landscape, changing how settlements looked, and their relationship with the countryside."

partitions were identified in some buildings, and in four instances the main building had an attached 'annexe'. Only some of these were habitations, others being barns and workshops.

The individual farmsteads, ancillary buildings and enclosures that made up Catholme were ancestral properties over several generations; no obvious centre or focal point was seen within the excavated area but it is possible that less than half of the total settlement area was excavated.

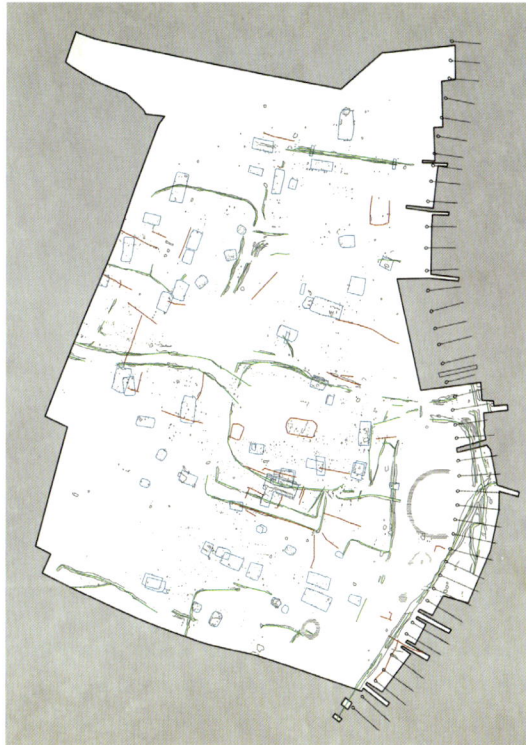

Courtesy Trent and Peak Archaeology

Catholme: an Anglo-Saxon settlement at the heart of Mercia.

Mid-Saxon Changes

From the later seventh and eighth centuries, and lasting into the ninth century and beyond, a gradual transformation began to take shape in the landscape, changing how settlements looked, and their relationship with the countryside. These changes were intimately linked with the developing social and economic structure of rural communities and an intensification of agricultural production, perhaps initially in response to increased 'consumer' demand from minsters, towns and major centres, but later also through the restructuring of Anglo-Saxon estates.

Lord and Peasant

The 'free peasant', holding a hide of land, has been traditionally imagined as the backbone of an early English society that was agrarian and essentially rural in character, but the implicit assumptions of freedom and equality that underpin this perception, if ever true, were rapidly eroded. The seventh-century laws already demonstrated the exercise of lordship over freemen as well as the unfree, and a

society that was characterised by inequalities of wealth and resources, distinctions that became increasingly emphatic over time. In King Alfred's laws of the ninth century we can detect a powerful and wealthy aristocracy dominating a subordinate peasantry that was required to render labour services; one clause, for instance, guaranteed certain holidays during the year to freemen, among them 'in harvest time the whole week before the feast of St Mary', but not to slaves or unfree labourers.

There is no reason to think that Mercia was any different, in either the ninth century or earlier. In

Courtesy Trent and Peak Archaeology

Sunken featured buildings often contain evidence of industrial or weaving activities, as here at Catholme where AS20 contained several clay loomweights.

fact, Mercia provides some clear evidence of the extent to which men and their families had become tied to lords and to the estates on which they lived. When in 887 Ealdorman Æthelred granted land in Oxfordshire to the bishopric of Worcester, it included six men with their descendants and their children from the royal estate at Bensington, who passed to the minster at Pyrton 'in eternal possession'. These *geburs* were serfs, servile tenants, who were tied to the estate over generations. Similarly, a grant of Elmstone Hardwicke in Gloucestershire by Bishop Waerfrith of Worcester in *c*.900 also referred to *ceorls* transferred with the estate.

What may be a 'tightening' of social order, or the strengthening of seigneurial rights and controls that these examples suggest, is seemingly reflected in the working of estates and the physical arrangements of some settlements and their landscapes. Some

settlements from the eighth century and later are characterised by complex systems of ditched enclosures that were maintained over several generations. Their continuity and regularity suggest co-ordination and direction from somewhere and that properties were maintained by some measure of legal sanction and control.

Yarnton

At Yarnton, for example, the character of the settlement had begun to change by the eighth century, being more ordered and less dispersed, with paddocks, a droveway and buildings within enclosures, among them a granary and a fowl-house. While SFBs were still present, at least one hall was built, to which was added another in the ninth century within a new enclosure; there was also a small cemetery on the site. These changes were accompanied by an intensification of arable

"The seventh century laws already demonstrated the exercise of lordship over freemen as well as the unfree, and a society that was characterised by inequalities of wealth and resources, distinctions that became increasingly emphatic over time."

farming, particularly from the second half of the ninth century, with increased cereal production (wheat and barley), new crops such as rye and legumes, and flax production. The area under cultivation was expanded to take in heavier clay soils and there was a hay meadow on the Thames floodplain.

The level of finds recovery from Yarnton was very low, but the impression is of a relatively modest community. Few pieces of jewellery, dress fittings or ornaments were found, but those that were, such as an equal-armed brooch and decorated strap-ends, were most probably traded items, as were pottery and some bone objects such as hair combs. There was also local bone-working, probably making the implements needed for weaving and textile production. Parts of a padlock suggest that some had possessions worthy of additional security. The population consumed a diet that included bread, porridge, soup and griddle-cakes; peas, beans and plum; beer, domestic fowl, beef, pork and mutton, with some evidence for smaller joints of meat being consumed in the middle Saxon period than was the case earlier.

Elsewhere in the Thames valley similar agricultural intensification and specialisation were underway, with cattle farming at Lechlade (Gloucestershire), possible sheep-farming at New Wintles, and pig-farming at Shakenoak (Oxfordshire). Such changes were occurring across the Mercian landscape by the late eighth century.

In the tenth century Yarnton was again reorganised with the formation of seven enclosures,

sharing in a wider phenomenon of settlements characterised by systems of ditched enclosures of varying sizes. Changing farming practices seem probable, with livestock closer to settlements, as well as new attitudes towards property which involved controlled and co-ordinated activity. Such developments heralded the most significant transformation in the English landscape, the emergence of villages.

Villages in the Mercian Landscape

England has often been thought of as a country of villages, but there has been much debate about how and when this type of settlement was established. This process, often referred to as 'nucleation', was a gradual one that reshaped the rural settlement pattern in many areas between the ninth and thirteenth centuries, but for which there is neither a universal model nor a precise chronology. While many dispersed settlements gave way to villages, this was not the case everywhere, and even where it did happen, as in the Vale of Evesham, isolated farms and hamlets continued to be a part of the landscape.

At Raunds in Northamptonshire a major landscape research project concluded that from the later ninth and tenth centuries there was a phase of imposed landscape and settlement reorganisation, with the focus for new settlements taking the form of high-status complexes focused on a hall and its associated buildings – changes which probably reflected the hand of lordship at work. But elsewhere in the midlands this concept of rapidly

> *"The settlement pattern laid out across the Mercian countryside was therefore a varied one, fashioned in response to the environment and influenced by political and social factors such as the fragmentation of large estates into smaller manors."*

imposed change and 'social engineering' has been challenged in favour of a slower, more evolutionary process driven by factors such as population increase, forcing some communities and farmsteads into closer associations and greater co-operation in their management of the land. In some cases soil type and land use seems critical, the urgencies of the agricultural cycle demanding a concentration and co-operation of labour that was most readily met by living in villages; the presence of meadowland, vital for livestock, also encouraged nucleation. The settlement pattern laid out across the Mercian countryside was therefore a varied one, fashioned in response to the environment and influenced by political and social factors such as the fragmentation of large estates into smaller manors.

Villages and Fields

Central to understanding how farming worked and what the countryside looked like has been the question of the origins of 'open' and 'common' fields. The relationship between village and field has been seen as so interdependent that it has generally been assumed that the two shared a common history and origin. Open fields were found across most of England but common fields were more restricted to central and southern England, being a specialised form of open field characterised by the presence of furlongs and strips in two or three fields of similar size, the intermingling of holdings, and a strong communal regulation of cropping.

While the general probability of a link between common field farming and settlement nucleation remains strong, their extent in Mercia cannot yet be demonstrated, despite recent arguments for their origin here between 670 and 840 as part of far-reaching landscape reorganisation (EN 16). What the charter evidence suggests are open fields, generally in those areas most intensively developed in the Roman period, like the Feldon of Warwickshire and the Vale of Evesham, present in places by the late ninth to mid-tenth century, but that beyond these lay 'irregular' field systems, smaller and more scattered, enclosed by hedgerows, with varying distributions and densities of woodland.

While debate continues, it is clear that the Mercian landscape was neither static nor empty. Rich in resources, these were actively exploited within a managed countryside that was widely settled. As increasing agricultural specialisation and intensification of activity shows, it was home to an expanding population, the rural estates on which they lived providing the bedrock of wealth and power in Mercia.

Anglo-Saxon Manorial Society

By the late Anglo-Saxon period the nature of rural society is conveyed in accounts such as that found in the celebrated *Rectitudines Singularum Personarum*, or, *Rights and Ranks of People*. Dating to the time of Edward the Confessor, it describes the conditions of those men who might be found

Little Oxendon in Northamptonshire typifies change in the English landscape with the development of common fields and of nucleated settlements.

on a great estate, quite probably somewhere in the western midlands, and reflects the emergence of a manorial society and economy that would become very familiar from *Domesday Book* and later. Together with other documents of a similar date, such as the survey of an estate at Tidenham in Gloucestershire, we can detect land reserved for the use of the lord (demesne), land for tenants, the presence of free and servile peasants, and the imposition of various labour obligations.

A visual impression of late Anglo-Saxon rural society, and of the livelihoods that sustained it, may be gained from the illustrations that accompany the calendars of the first half of the eleventh century with their focus on labour and on the productivity of the land as they assigned labours to the month concerned. January depicted ploughing, February pruning vines, March digging, and so on. While the key tasks in the agrarian cycle were presented from sowing to harvest, tending sheep in late spring and feeding hogs in woodland in the autumn, winter preparations were marked by stacking firewood in November, and lords were shown benefiting from these labours, feasting in April and hunting with falcons in October. Here was depicted the reassurance of the harmonious world, a productive landscape and the ordained social order.

English society of this period was divided into four main groups. The lord of the estate was the *thegn*, who held his land by title of a charter, granted or purchased, and in return for certain services to the king, mostly military-related. There followed the *geneat*, a term which originally meant a 'companion' and implied a man of some status, perhaps typically holding around thirty acres of land. He might act as a messenger, man-at-arms or bailiff, and had to undertake a range of services, such as provide food for his lord, cut deer-hedges and maintain snares, and build and fence the lord's house, although his agricultural work was limited, mostly restricted to reaping and mowing at harvest time.

The next class described in the *Rectitudines* were the *cottars*, whose position varied according to the custom of the estate; 'custom' represented some constraint on what the lord might expect and the peasants of the estate also enjoyed various common rights, such as a 'drinking feast' for ploughing and a 'harvest feast' for reaping corn. The *cottar* generally held at least five acres of land, and although he did not pay rent he was required to perform labour services and other duties as the lord required. The fourth class described were the *boors* or *geburs*, who look very much like later medieval 'villeins' and whose circumstances varied from estate to estate. They paid rents and renders and had to meet a range of obligations which often included extensive labour services, calling no doubt for strong sons or co-operative neighbours to assist.

The *gebur* and his family were involved in every aspect of cultivation and stock-rearing in the agricultural year, receiving from his lord livestock, seed and equipment, but all of which the lord took back when his tenant died, making them very dependent upon their lord. They owed rents and renders, performed ploughing and carrying services, tended the lord's sheep and supported his hunting dogs.

In addition to these main classes of society, the author of the *Rectitudines* also discussed what might be described as 'agrarian specialists', chief among whom was the bee-keeper and the swineherd, but also included the likes of cow-herds, shepherds, cheese-makers and haywards. For slaves, there was no mention of limits to their obligations, only to the amounts of food that they might expect, but they too lived and worked within the customs of the manor.

The Tidenham survey, having described the estate and its fisheries on the Severn and the Wye, similarly described the rights of the lord and the obligations of its population. The lord, for instance, was entitled to a proportion of the fish caught, and to 'rare fish' such as sturgeon, porpoise, herring and sea fish. The labour services required were demanding. *Geneats* provided labour, riding and transportation services, among others such as driving herds, while *geburs* undertook ploughing, reaping and mowing services, had to supply some seed and materials, and performed other tasks such as fencing and hedging.

While these surveys present the prevalent view of Anglo-Saxon rural society as essentially manorialised by the eleventh century, it has also been argued by some that to generalise and extend these to the population as a whole may be misleading. Rather, they suggest that such surveys reflected only the specific needs and organisation of the demesne land on an estate; and that these documents represented a process of putting in place such expectations rather than simply reflecting the norm. ✠

Manorial Sites – New Directions

© Crown copyright. Historic England

The Anglo-Saxon church at Earl's Barton, with its stone tower and earthwork defences, had its origins as a high-status aristocratic residence.

Near the north-eastern edge of Mercia, south of the Humber and overlooking the floodplain of the River Trent, excavations at Flixborough in Lincolnshire have revealed a remarkable settlement site. Some forty buildings, with ovens, pathways and fences were uncovered, occupied from the seventh into the eleventh century. A privileged lifestyle in the eighth century saw the consumption of pigs, sheep, large quantities of cattle, and wild animals, notably dolphin, crane and wild fowl. This associated with imported pottery and glass drinking vessels from Europe, suggesting an ostentatious aristocratic lifestyle in which feasting was a part.

In the late eighth and early ninth centuries the character of the settlement changed completely. It was re-planned with smaller buildings and included specialist craft activities and sheep-farming. The conspicuous consumption and social display of the earlier period had gone, possibly because of a period of management by a monastic landowner; but this too ended with demolition in the late ninth century and by the early tenth century it had been again re-planned. The conspicuous consumption of cattle and wild species resumed but without the overtones of luxury feasting, with artisanal activity focused on iron-working and domestic textile manufacture. Exotic items were now more generally associated with the towns, but emerging here in the countryside was a secular elite lifestyle, exploiting the resources of the estate. The same may be seen elsewhere in the tenth and eleventh centuries at sites such as Goltho (Lincolnshire) and Raunds (Northamptonshire).

At Goltho, emerging from a modest early farmstead was an enclosed fortified site, best interpreted as a thegnly residence. By the turn of the ninth-tenth century an earthwork enclosed a hall and other buildings, one of which may have been a weaving shed; in the second half of the tenth century the hall was rebuilt as a quasi-aisled structure. By the early eleventh century, at the time of King Cnut, the site comprised a series of timber buildings that included a rebuilt hall, bower and a kitchen, behind a substantial defensive rampart and ditch, whose artefacts were consistent with its role as a residence and estate centre.

At Raunds, on the West Cotton site, the principal buildings were partially enclosed by a timber palisade and

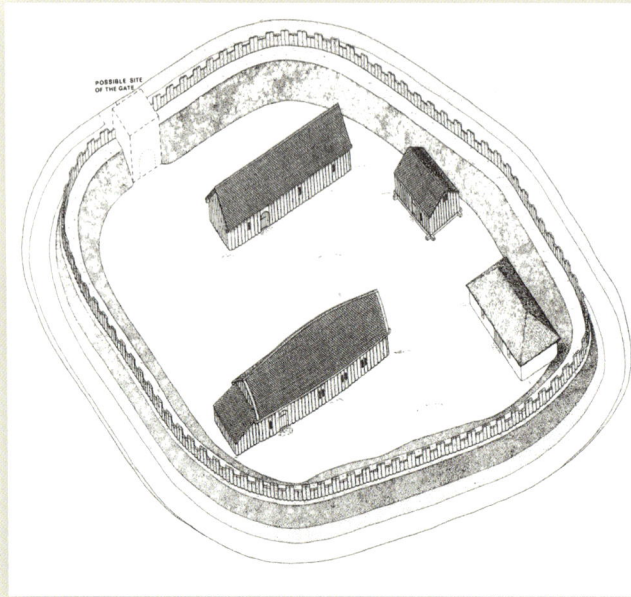

From Fig. 32, Beresford, 1987. Courtesy Historic England

POSSIBLE SITE OF THE GATE

Reconstruction of a defended thegnly residence of c.850 at Goltho in Lincolnshire.

substantial ditch, abandoned in favour of a more open courtyard setting at the end of the tenth century. At the Furnells site there was an aisled hall set within a rectilinear enclosure where, in the late ninth or early tenth century, a small single-celled church was built outside the east entrance to the manorial enclosure. From the mid-tenth century the church was itself enclosed by boundary ditches, as a chancel was added and burial began on the site. The re-planning undertaken to accommodate such small estate churches, or *tunkirkan*, signalled not only a changing 'religious geography' as the devotional practices of communities began to change and minsters gave way to local churches, but also the

importance to lords of such prestigious possessions in demonstrating their status.

Aristocratic residences were not only estate centres; they were intended to display status, their defensive character contributing to their distinction. There is no better site to illustrate this than the stone tower of Earl's Barton church, which had its origins as a thegnly tower. Belonging to a group of at least thirty-five such examples associated with seigneurial residences or major monasteries of the tenth and eleventh centuries, the site stands at the heart of a nucleated settlement, protected by a ditch and earthwork which may pre-date the tower. The ground floor functioned as a private chapel, with residential provision on the floor above entered by a separate door, presumably with a timber structure to the south. The striking use of pilaster strips to enhance the external walls, particularly on its upper stage, projected status through display. ✠

Magnates, Earls and Earldom

A TALE OF TWO FAMILIES

In the early eleventh century Mercia was one of the great earldoms of the Old English kingdom, which at the start of Cnut's reign stood alongside Wessex, East Anglia and Northumbria. Within a little over fifty years they were all swept away in the wake of the Norman Conquest. What follows explores this dramatic period and its consequences for regional society through the eyes of two Mercian magnate families.

The fabric of English political life before the Conquest was recast when Cnut replaced the traditional system of ealdormen with earls and earldoms, and appointed sheriffs in the localities. New earldoms were created within Mercia for Danish lords, but during the turbulent reign of Edward the Confessor (1042–1066) the tenure and boundaries of the earldoms fluctuated with the fortunes of the magnate dynasties that dominated them and English affairs.

The earls of Mercia, distinguished by their Old English ancestry in a political environment dominated by newcomers, faced the challenge of retaining authority in their earldom and their position within the polity of England where the ascendant power was that of Earl Godwin of Wessex and his sons. By the 1050s the Godwinssons were the most prominent comital family in England, whose ambitions threatened the Mercian earls and eroded their territory as the earldoms of the Confessor were frequently reshaped.

Wulfric Spott and his Family

In 996, King Æthelred confirmed to Wulfric Spott the gift of an estate at Abbots Bromley (Staffordshire) made by the thegn's mother, who bade her son to 'abandon his frivolous ways'. She was the lady Wulfrun, a noblewoman associated today with Wolverhampton, whose importance was sufficient to see her capture by the Danes at Tamworth in 943 being recorded in the *Anglo-Saxon Chronicle*. His father may have been a thegn, also named Wulfric, who was witnessing charters between *c*.946 and 958 and held land in Warwickshire.

That Wulfric Spott was a man of considerable importance and wealth is revealed in his will of about 1004, drawn up in association with his refoundation of Burton Abbey. He bequeathed land in some seventy to eighty named places and held an unspecified number of estates in South Lancashire and the Wirral. The majority of his holdings were in Staffordshire, Warwickshire and Derbyshire, but he also held lands in Shropshire, Leicestershire, Yorkshire, Gloucestershire, Worcestershire and Lincolnshire. This considerable landed wealth generated cash, Wulfric leaving over 200 gold coins to various beneficiaries. It was also the wealth of an aristocratic military elite, Wulfric leaving to the king, his lord, swords, horses and weapons, presumably as 'heriot' – the return of the gift of weapons from lord to man which created one of the bonds in noble society. A powerful member of a powerful kin, it is not certain when he died but the *Chronica Abbatum* reports that Wulfric was buried under a stone arch in the cloister of Burton Abbey, as had been his wife, Ealhswith, some years earlier.

Previous page: King Cnut and Queen Emma, celebrated as religious benefactors, presenting a cross to New Minster, Winchester; from the New Minster '*Liber Vitae*', c.1031.

The charter of King Æthelred II that confirmed the bequests made by his thegn, Wulfric Spott, in his will of c.1004.

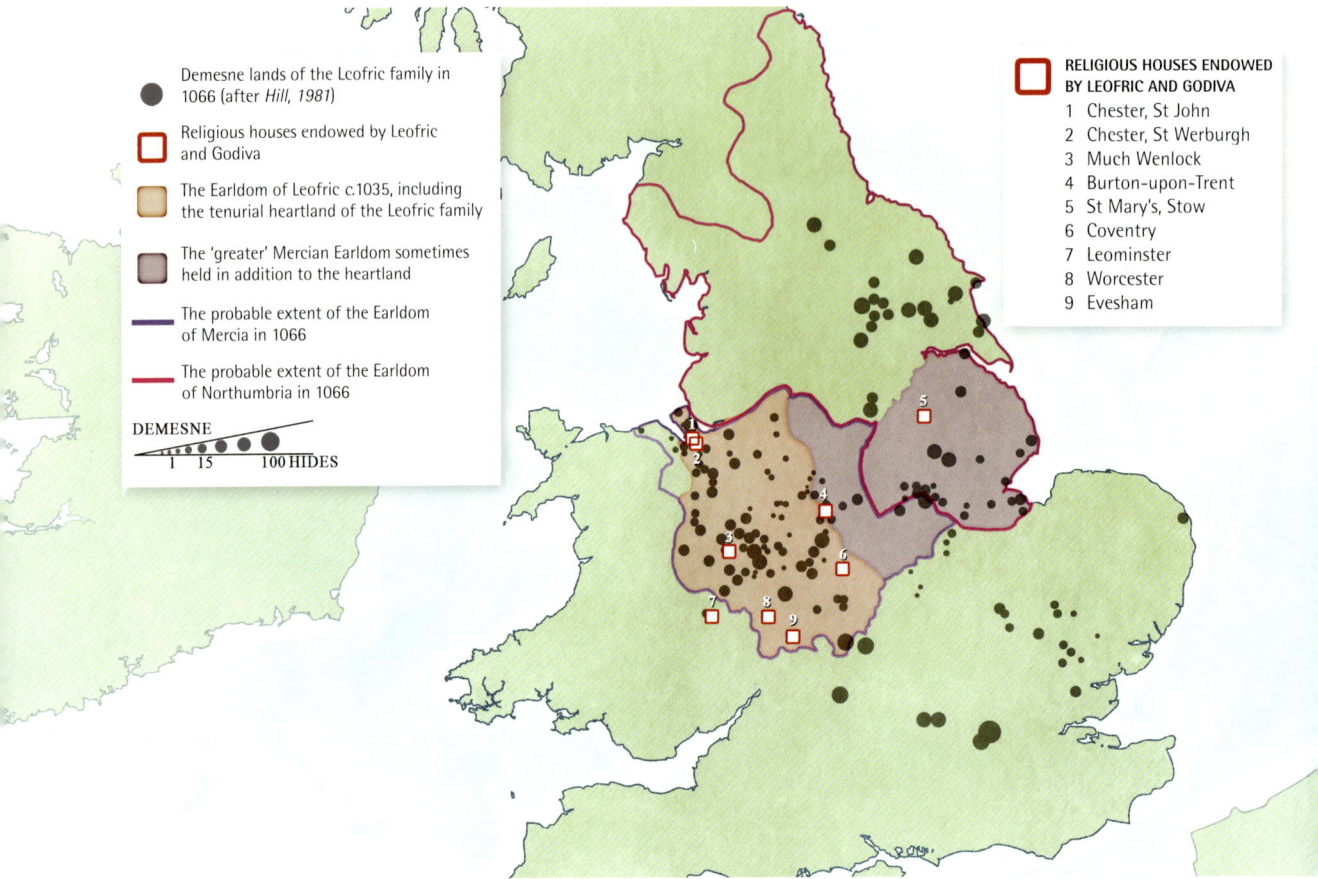

The dynamics of power: land tenure and religious patronage in the Mercian Earldom on the eve of the Norman Conquest.

The Making of a Magnate Family

How did Wulfric's family reach such heights? The answer lies in the charters, starting with Abbots Bromley where we find that the estate had previously been held by three generations of his family, among them Wulfsige the Black, or Wulfsige 'Maur', the probable father of Wulfrun. From here we can look back to an earlier charter, of 942, by which this estate and others came into the possession of the family, when King Edmund granted Wulfsige 'Maur' a significant block of land on both sides of the upper Trent. These lands were conferred upon him to reward his military service,

probably on Edmund's campaign and conquest in 942 of northern Mercia. By this and other charters, Wulfsige acquired a considerable land holding of some forty hides forming a strategic block of territory in a vulnerable area.

This was a kind of 'marcher' lordship countering the Danish threat to the north and north-east, which the Danish raid on Tamworth in 943 demonstrated were not idle fears. This kind of grant was a familiar one in Mercia as the West Saxon kings encouraged the infiltration of loyal thegns into politically marginal or sensitive regions, by grant or through the purchase of estates, in an effort to undermine

Danish influence and strengthen military capacity. Wulfsige 'Maur' and his family, whose origins were Mercian rather than West Saxon, had attached their fortunes to the ascendancy of the southern kings, playing a key role in the consolidation of West Saxon control over the north midlands, and benefiting as a result.

However, such grants were made in the expectation of future service, particularly of military service, and men like Wulfsige had to ensure that they could meet these expectations. They did this by nurturing a community of retainers, men like Æscbyrht, whom Wulfsige appears to have placed in Abbots Bromley as his tenant, providing for his support and livelihood while in his service.

Aristocratic Society and Landscape

Retainers expected to attract the active support of their lords, and there is much evidence from Mercia in the early eleventh century to show how their lords made such provision. Earl Leofric of Mercia (d.1057) supported his thegns by seizing and reusing church estates, as when the Danish thegn, Sigmundr, described as a soldier of Leofric, took land in Crowle (Worcestershire) that belonged to the church of Worcester, or as at Hampton Lovett (Worcestershire) where Erngeat, son of Grim, successfully resisted Bishop Wulfstan because of the support he received from Leofric. Such arrangements were being put in place within local society by the mid-tenth century, part of a 'shift' that was then starting to gather pace within English society.

By the late ninth century, large and often ancient estates began to break down or fragment and the lands granted in 942 were a part of this process. This led to the creation of large numbers of smaller estates, and with it, the emergence of small-scale landowners and numerous smaller lordships. A tenurial pattern was emerging that readily allowed the likes of Wulfsige and his successors to find the estates needed to maintain dependent thegns, alongside other small independent lords.

Although the chronology is controversial and debated among historians, English society and landscape were witnessing change. The creation of smaller estates often encouraged lords to make their presence felt through monumental and memorial building, notably proprietary churches; local churches for their estates as communities' devotional attitudes themselves became more localised. Furthermore, the collection and payment of church tithes were enforced to support such local churches. Together with the growing prominence of manorialism, the appearance of nucleated settlements, and the presence of open field agriculture, Anglo-Saxon society was taking the shape familiar from *Domesday Book*.

From the mid-tenth century until the opening years of the eleventh, the family of Wulfsige the Black and Wulfric Spott were a dominant force in the affairs of northern Mercia, although not ealdormen. But the reign of Æthelred II could be a dangerous time for the nobility, and in 1006,

"By the late ninth century, large and often ancient estates began to break down or fragment. This led to the creation of large numbers of smaller estates, and with it, the emergence of small-scale landowners and numerous smaller lordships."

Coln Rogers church in Gloucestershire may have originated among those local churches ('*tunkirkan*') that Anglo-Saxon thegns built on their estates.

Wulfric's prominent brother, the ealdorman Ælfhelm, was murdered and his sons blinded at the king's command. Royal confidence in the family had clearly been lost. However, these shifts in the early eleventh century did not push the family of Wulfric Spott into obscurity. With their extensive hereditary lands, the family remained essential to the control of the north midlands. Cnut recognised this and sought their support, marrying Wulfric's niece, Ælfgifu of Northampton.

The House of Leofwine, Earls of Mercia

The earls of Mercia also valued Wulfric's family, formalised through the probable marriage of Wulfric's great-niece to Ælfgar, the son of Earl Leofric and Godiva. In 1017 Eadric Streona was followed in Mercia by Leofwine, ealdorman of the Hwicce, who was succeeded by his son, Leofric, at some point between 1023 and 1032. By 1035 Leofric was supporting Harold Harefoot in his claims on the English throne, this immersion in dynastic politics arising at least in part from his links with the family of Wulfric Spott; Harold Harefoot was the son of Cnut and Ælfgifu of Northampton and therefore kin to Leofric's daughter-in-law.

When Leofwine became earl of Mercia, he was not alone. Cnut also appointed a number of Danes to earldoms – Hrani in Herefordshire, Hakon Ericson in Worcestershire, and Eilaf Thorgilson in Gloucestershire. It is not clear to what extent, if at all, these men were subservient to Leofwine and his son, but there can be little doubt that their presence represented a constraint on the earls of Mercia.

The House of Leofwine, Earls of Mercia

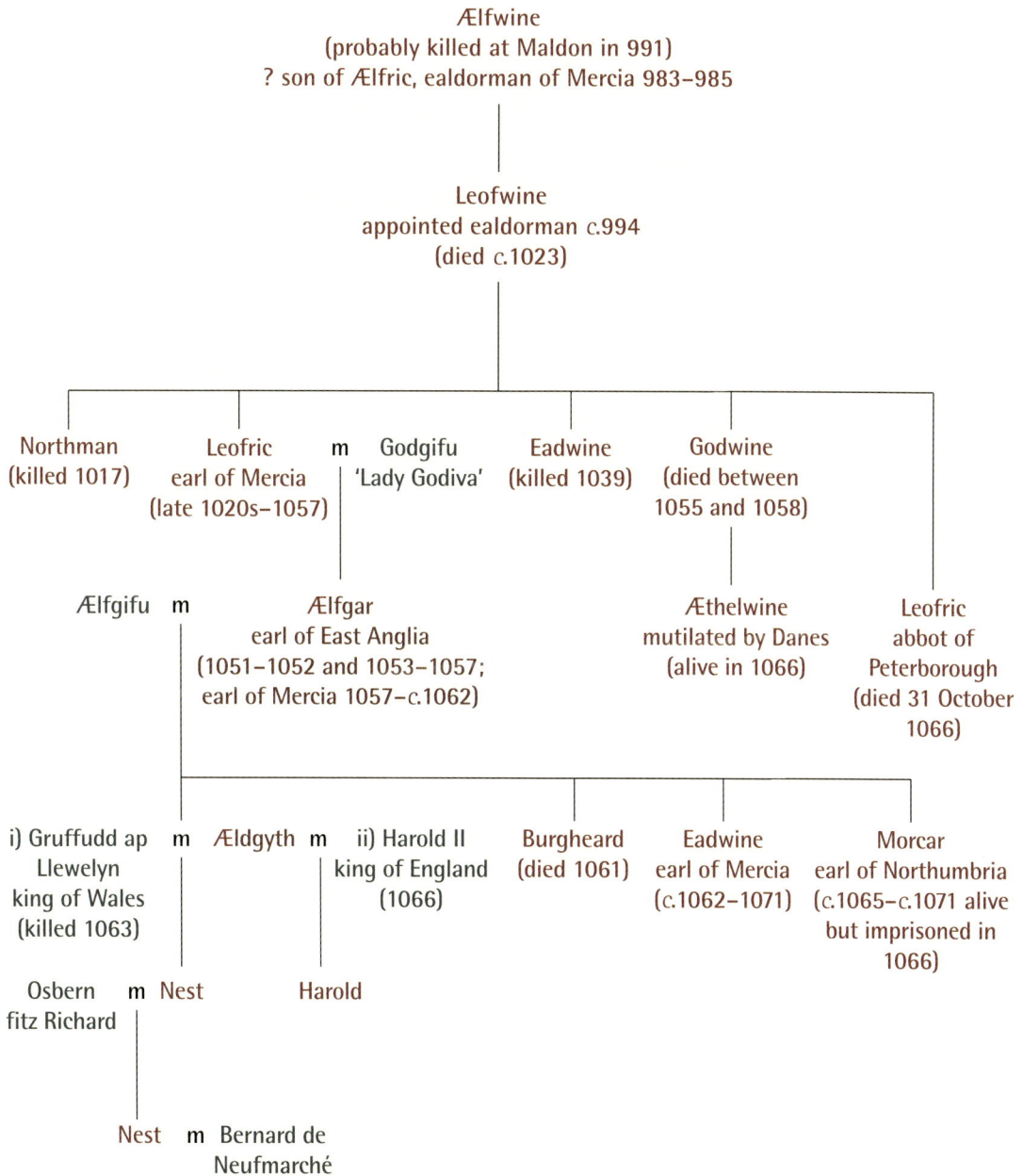

Ælfwine
(probably killed at Maldon in 991)
? son of Ælfric, ealdorman of Mercia 983–985

Leofwine
appointed ealdorman c.994
(died c.1023)

Northman
(killed 1017)

Leofric   m   Godgifu
earl of Mercia   'Lady Godiva'
(late 1020s–1057)

Eadwine
(killed 1039)

Godwine
(died between
1055 and 1058)

Ælfgifu   m   Ælfgar
earl of East Anglia
(1051–1052 and 1053–1057;
earl of Mercia 1057–c.1062)

Æthelwine
mutilated by Danes
(alive in 1066)

Leofric
abbot of
Peterborough
(died 31 October
1066)

i) Gruffudd ap   m   Ældgyth   m   ii) Harold II
Llewelyn   king of England
king of Wales   (1066)
(killed 1063)

Burgheard
(died 1061)

Eadwine
earl of Mercia
(c.1062–1071)

Morcar
earl of Northumbria
(c.1065–c.1071 alive
but imprisoned in
1066)

Osbern   m   Nest
fitz Richard

Harold

Nest   m   Bernard de
Neufmarché

After Baxter, 2007

"Together with the growing prominence of manorialism, the appearance of nucleated settlements, and the presence of open field agriculture, Anglo-Saxon society was taking the shape familiar from Domesday Book."

The Sinews of Power

Leofwine and his sons could not simply assume their authority and right of political patronage as there were now credible alternatives. They had to defend, maintain and further enhance their lordship in those areas that were less directly under their control, even if still under their authority. They had the immense advantage of their lineage in maintaining their authority across the Mercian earldom, and their standing beyond it. Power was made real by authority over people, but these people, the thegns and leaders of local society, had to be 'courted' and retained. A family whose ancestry and associations with Mercia reached back into the tenth century had a natural advantage in their traditional and accepted prominence, but tradition and sentiment was also reinforced by land, wealth, patronage and assertive lordship.

The marriage of Ælfgar to Wulfric's great-niece was perhaps formulated against this background but the family pursued other strategies as well to recruit and provide for retainers and project the interests of their family. *Domesday Book* shows that the family dominated landholding in much of the midlands, with estates valued in excess of £2,800 and this was very probably an under-assessment. They were most secure within the north-west midlands, particularly in Cheshire, Shropshire and Staffordshire, the focus and traditional heartland of their authority but even here there was no room for complacency, and further afield the family had to take steps to compete for loyalty and service.

Their tenurial pre-eminence was reinforced by political, social and religious patronage, the latter principally within the dioceses of Lichfield and Worcester, but reaching also into those of Hereford and Dorchester. Among these endowments was their refoundation of the house at Coventry (later known as the Priory of St Mary) which was to become a family mausoleum, both Leofric and Godiva being buried there; their *Eigenkirche* in the same way as that at Burton served Wulfric Spott and his family.

The patronage of the earls was focused within the Mercian earldom itself, and for good reason. Their support of religious houses promoted the family's position, countering the influence of other lords and fostering communities of interest closely tied to them. It offered an entrée into areas where they felt a need to consolidate their position and influence.

Patrons or Despoilers?

Why then was it that Hemming, a monk of Worcester writing later, looked upon Leofric and his kin as despoilers of his church? Simply, it arose from the earls' needs to use church lands to maintain their resources and support their retainers. By the second quarter of the eleventh century opportunities for breaking up large estates were more difficult to come by. Therefore, exploiting the large landed resources of the churches over which a family had either a perceived legitimate control, or else which it was powerful enough to intimidate, was an inevitable response.

The tangle that might result may be seen in the *Domesday Book* entry for Alveston in Warwickshire. Before 1066, Brictwin had held the manor, but as far as his two sons and four others were concerned, they did not know whether he held the land from the church of Worcester or 'from Earl Leofric, whom he served'. As far as the sons themselves were concerned, however, they had held the land from Leofric. Such confusion was inevitable after a period of time, and it worked to the benefit of the comital family and their thegns.

Mercia and the Normans

Earl Leofric was survived by his wife, Godiva, who died after the Conquest, most probably in 1086. Her son Ælfgar was succeeded as earl by his son, Edwin, in 1065. It has been suggested that had Ælfgar lived, Harold Godwinsson's succession to Edward the Confessor in January 1066 would not have gone unchallenged, but whatever the truth of this, Edwin was in no position to do so. However, Harold's reign proved short-lived as his accession prompted the challenge of various rivals, among them Duke William of Normandy, whose victory at Hastings in October left Harold II dead on the battlefield.

In 1066 Godiva's grandsons Edwin and Morcar were, respectively, earls of Mercia and Northumbria. The kinship between the two earls mirrored that of the thegnly families within their lordships, so when the Norwegian king Harald Hadrada landed in Yorkshire, the brothers joined forces to resist him. It is a moot point as to whether it was the mauling that they received at the hands of Hadrada, or their enmity towards the Godwinssons, which led to their non-appearance at Hastings. Whichever, this fact, and their subsequent submission to William, left them in possession of their estates and status after 1066.

Although it did not preclude all Norman influence, the fact that the midlands was still in the lordship of an Englishman hindered Norman incursion into much of the region. In the years immediately following the Conquest William seems to have left Earl Edwin in place and did not reinforce his own authority either with an extended demesne or with French tenants. However, William needed to make provision for those French lords who had supported his campaign, and the most certain way of controlling a region was to settle his men across it; but he could not risk offending those English lords who had sworn their obedience to him. Edwin had professed his loyalty, and the two leading churchmen in the region, Æthelwig of Evesham and Bishop Wulfstan of Worcester, both loyal to the new order, were well-placed to influence the young earl of Mercia.

Royal lands and the forfeit estates of Harold Godwinsson provided some mitigation, but the restraint which Edwin's survival necessitated remained a factor until the early 1070s. However, perhaps concerned by his declining importance and certainly influenced by ties of kinship, he was drawn

"A family whose ancestry and associations with Mercia reached back into the tenth century had a natural advantage in their traditional and accepted prominence, but tradition and sentiment was also reinforced by land, wealth, patronage and assertive lordship."

© Historic England. Licensor canmore.org.uk

Warwick Castle was built in response to Earl Edwin's support for the failed rebellion of 1068.

first into a rebellion in 1068 which was readily put down, not least by the construction of Warwick Castle, and then in 1069-70 into the much more serious rebellion whose epicentre lay in Yorkshire. It was this rebellion that gave rise to the infamous 'Harrying of the North', refugees from which reputedly sought alms as far south as Evesham Abbey, although the same campaign also devastated Staffordshire and led to the construction of a royal castle in Stafford.

Although Edwin seems not to have been a protagonist, it is unlikely that he could have stood aloof of the involvement of his thegns, and it is difficult to believe that he had any credit left with the Normans. According to John of Worcester, Edwin escaped from William's court in 1071, but was murdered by his own men while fleeing to Scotland. With his death, the earldom of Mercia ceased to exist.

"Whether the people of the medieval midlands realised it or not, their Mercian past had shaped their daily lives and the world in which they lived."

Aftermath: Norman Land-taking in Mercia

Most probably by 1070, when the rebellion was put down, and certainly from 1071 with the death of Edwin, the way was clear for substantial Norman aristocratic colonisation across the region. Orderic Vitalis commented that William now 'divided up the chief provinces of England amongst his followers, and made the humblest of the Normans men of wealth, with civil and military authority', while by the 1090s, the Worcester monk, Hemming, was bemoaning the usurpation of the inheritance of Englishmen. A few Englishmen, like Turchil of Warwick (or Arden), whose family had been prominent in Anglo-Saxon Mercia and was closely associated with the earls, survived the Conquest as men of substance. But this was not generally the case, and *Domesday Book* illustrates the formation of new lordships and restructured estates held by new men across the former earldom.

The Norman honors and estates that took shape between 1071 and 1086 were created by a combination of mechanisms. Some lands were transferred from Englishman to Frenchman through rules of inheritance and succession, whereby the new Norman lords moved into the lands formerly held by specific and known Anglo-Saxon predecessors, emphasising a legalistic framework for land transfer and a sense of continuity; other lands came as territorial grants from the king but around half were transferred in a context of 'land rush'. One of the purposes of *Domesday Book* was to clarify and end this rather disorderly and confused state of affairs.

The estates of the former earls of Mercia, and the associations that they had, influenced what followed as new lordships were built around them. As for their men, it was frequently the case that the English thegns were not entirely dispossessed, but rather that they suffered partial dispossession or rearrangement of their tenure, which for most brought a reduction in status and wealth. But exploring how midlands society and landscape changed in the wake of the Norman Conquest is the subject for another book.

The Mercian kingdom had ceased to exist nearly two-hundred years before the demise of the earldom. Families recalled their heritage but memory of that Mercian past and of the traditions associated with it had largely passed into the guardianship of the region's monastic houses, through their muniments and their chroniclers, just as Mercian benefactors had always anticipated.

But whether the people of the medieval midlands realised it or not, their Mercian past had shaped their daily lives and the world in which they lived. The social structure and the dynamic of lord and peasant, free and unfree, and the regime of the manor; a landscape that contained nucleated villages and common fields; high-status residences associated with lordship, and a transformation of devotional attitude that saw the eclipse of minsters in favour of local parish churches; monasteries, dioceses and parishes; shires and a network of major towns, many of which had emerged from Mercian religious, royal and military centres; language and culture. These were all features that were a part of the region's Anglo-Saxon and Mercian legacy. ✠

End Notes

1. Dr Margaret Gelling's work was central to this revision; cf. Margaret Gelling, 'The Evidence of Place-Names', in P.H. Sawyer (ed), *Medieval Settlement*, London, 1976.

2. This suggestion was made by Dr Steven Bassett; cf. Steven Bassett, 'How the West was Won: the Anglo-Saxon Takeover of the West Midlands', in David Griffiths (ed), *Anglo-Saxon Studies in Archaeology and History*, 11, Oxford, 2000.

3. I owe this phrase to Professor Nicholas Brooks; cf. Nicholas Brooks, 'The Formation of the Mercian Kingdom', in Steven Bassett (ed), *The Origins of Anglo-Saxon Kingdoms*, Leicester, 1989.

4. Saint Wilfrid, a Northumbrian of noble birth, was a towering figure in the affairs of the seventh-century church. His career and influence is outlined in the '*Life of Wilfrid*', written by his companion, the priest Eddius Stephanus, between 710 and 720. King Wulfhere had previously attempted to entice Wilfrid into the bishopric of Lichfield and gave him land there to establish the bishopric.

5. Ismere or *Husmerae* is an old provincial name; the land granted was 'by the river called Stour', *æt Sture* being the original name of Kidderminster before the founding of the monastery.

6. This interpretation was offered by Dr David Kirby; cf. D.P. Kirby, *The Earliest English Kings*, London, 1991, Chapter 8.

7. This work is discussed by Dr Steven Bassett in his article, 'Divide and rule? The military infrastructure of eighth- and ninth-century Mercia', in *Early Medieval Europe*, 15 (1), 2007.

8. Offa's Dyke has attracted several scholars since the early twentieth century. Key contributions have been made by Dr Cyril Fox, *Offa's Dyke*, London, 1955 (8a); Patrick Wormald in 'The age of Offa and Alcuin', in J.Campbell (ed), *The Anglo-Saxons*, Oxford, 1982 (8b); Dr David Hill (8c); David Hill and Margaret Worthington, *Offa's Dyke: history and guide*, Stroud, 2003 (8d); a recent reappraisal of the Dyke and its interpretation has been offered by Dr Damien Tyler in D.J. Tyler, 'Offa's Dyke: a historiographical appraisal' in the *Journal of Medieval History*, 37, 2011 (8e).

9. This case has been argued by Dr John Maddicott in J.R. Maddicott, 'London and Droitwich, c.650-750: trade, industry and the rise of Mercia', in *Anglo-Saxon England*, 34, 2005.

10. This quotation is taken from Richard Jewell's discussion of the Mercian sculpture at Breedon-on-the-Hill and its associated pieces at Castor and Fletton in his 'Classicism of Southumbrian Sculpture' in Michelle P. Brown and Carol A. Farr (eds), *Mercia. An Anglo-Saxon Kingdom in Europe*, Leicester, 2001.

11. Professor Michelle Brown. See her, *The Book of Cerne. Prayer, Patronage and Power in Ninth-Century England*, London, 1996.

12. The argument with regard to metalwork has primarily been made by Leslie Webster; cf. 'Metalwork of the Mercian Supremacy' in Michelle P. Brown and Carol A. Farr (eds), *Mercia. An Anglo-Saxon Kingdom in Europe*, Leicester, 2001.

13. This observation was made by Professor Sir David M. Wilson in his *Anglo-Saxon Art. From the Seventh Century to the Norman Conquest*, London, 1984.

14. Sir Frank Stenton, *Anglo-Saxon England*, Oxford, 1971, page 231.

15. Thanks are due to Andy Boucher and Jake Streatfeild-James of Headland Archaeology for information regarding this site.

16. These arguments were put forward by Dr Susan Oosthuizen, 'The Anglo-Saxon Kingdom of Mercia and the Origins and Distribution of Common Fields', in *The Agricultural History Review*, 55, No 2, 2007; they have not been received uncritically.

Glossary

British **British** refers to the post-Roman population of Roman Britain, the people among whom the Anglo-Saxons settled. See also 'Celtic'.

Byzantine In his attempts to bring stability to the Roman Empire, Emperor Diocletian's (284–305) reforms effectively divided the empire into eastern and western halves, each with an emperor (Augusti) supported by a lieutenant and successor with the rank of Caesar. Rome was the natural capital of the Western Empire, but it was not until the Emperor Constantine (272–337; proclaimed emperor in 306) that the eastern capital was established at **Byzantium**, a wealthy commercial centre on the Bosphorus, initially founded as a Greek colony in the seventh century BC. The new capital was dedicated in May 330, to be known as 'New Rome' although from the beginning it was popularly referred to as the 'City of Constantine', that is 'Constantinople'. The Eastern Empire and its rulers are referred to as **Byzantine**, after the original name of the city. The city was also known as 'Miklegarde' to the Scandinavians, and is now known as Istanbul, uniquely situated on the continents of both Europe and Asia. The eastern Roman Empire survived the fall of that in the west.

Caliphate The word **Caliph** has the literal meaning of 'successor', referring to the successors of Muhammed, and the Caliphate refers to the area that they ruled. From the eighth century the **Caliphate** was gradually transformed from an Arab kingdom to an Islamic Empire. The **Abbasid** dynasty ruled the Caliphate from the mid-eighth to the mid-thirteenth century, having overthrown the Umayyad dynasty. The second Abbasid caliph established Baghdad as the capital of the caliphate.

Carolingian In the mid-eighth century the Merovingian rulers of Frankia were displaced by a new dynasty known as the **Carolingians**, a name derived from '*Carolus*', the Latinised name of Charles Martel, from whom the dynasty descended. The dynasty was at its peak during the reign of Charles the Great (742–814), also known as **Charlemagne**, who in 800 was crowned Emperor by Pope Leo III in Rome. The extensive territories that Charlemagne ruled are generally referred to as the **Carolingian** Empire, and the term is widely used as a period reference in Frankish history, and to the cultural, artistic and intellectual activity of Charlemagne's court and kingdom.

Celts Classical writers referred to the prehistoric peoples of Spain, Gaul and central Europe as **Celts**, a term that has been extended to encompass the inhabitants of the British Isles before the Roman period. While they did not represent a coherent or unified cultural or political entity, the Celts did share dialects of a common language and common art forms.

Celtic When used in the context of the **Celtic Church**, this refers to the Church that was established in the British Isles prior to the mission of Saint Augustine. Celtic Christian communities were established in Roman Britain, and they survived in Wales, Scotland, Ireland and Cornwall. Thus terms such as the 'British Church' or the 'Irish Church' may also be used. Encouraged by shared linguistic traits, the term Celtic may also be used in other contexts, making reference to the population of pre-Roman Britain, or as an alternative to terms such as 'British' and 'Welsh' for the population that interacted with the Anglo-Saxon settlers. Finally, the term is also commonly applied in artistic and cultural contexts, referring to particular artistic forms and motifs used by the Celts, and often to Celtic manuscript illumination that draws on this repertoire, although here the term 'Hiberno-Saxon' or 'Insular' is generally to be preferred.

Glossary

Conversion 'The Conversion' is the term that in the history of Anglo-Saxon England traditionally refers to the evangelising missions of the Roman Church that brought the Anglo-Saxon kingdoms into the Church of Rome, initiated by the mission of St Augustine and his companions who arrived at Thanet in 597. However, the transition from paganism to Christianity, and the establishment of Christian kingdoms also owed much, especially in Mercia, to the British Church and its congregation. The term may also be applied in a wider European context, referring to the various missions by which the people of Europe were over time persuaded from paganism to Christianity, such as the Anglo-Saxon missions to the Frisians.

Danelaw The area of England that was from the ninth century to fall under Scandinavian settlement and authority was known as the '**Danelaw**', the area where Danish law and customs pertained, as distinct from the laws of Wessex and Mercia mentioned in the later 'Laws of Henry I'. The resurgence of Viking attacks by the late tenth century led to the English government paying tribute to their attackers in order to buy them off. This became known as the payment of '**Danegeld**' or Dane tribute / payment, developing in England into a system of national taxation. Generally referred to as a 'geld', the term 'Danegeld' was not used until the early twelfth century.

Debasement of Coinage The practice of mixing more common metal with the precious metals that gave the coin its worth. This generally arose at times when there were difficulties in obtaining sufficient supplies of the precious metal, and to enable the production of more coin. Confidence could easily be lost in **debased coinages**, undermining their value for trade, so kings frequently took steps to maintain standards.

Deira The Anglo-Saxon kingdom of Northumbria was a fusion of several smaller kingdoms. **Deira**, a British name, was one of these that comprised the land between the rivers Humber and Tees, but whose main focus lay in the area around York, Malton and the Wolds. The other main kingdom of Northumbria was **Bernicia**, located further north and based on the coastal stronghold of Bamburgh. The neighbouring British kingdoms of **Elmet**, south-west of York, **Gododdin** in the north on the Firth of Forth, and **Rheged** in the north-west were all absorbed into the Northumbrian kingdom.

Eigenkirchen This German word encapsulates the sense of 'family churches', essentially private proprietary foundations over which the founding kin retained rights and interests. The singular is '**Eigenkirche**', and the term 'Eigenkloster' may also be used in reference to monasteries.

Emirate The literal meaning of the word **Emir** is 'Commander', a title that was given to Arab caliphs and generals. Between 711 and 718 all but the mountainous northwest of the Iberian peninsula was conquered by Islamic forces. The rulers of Islamic Spain took the title of emir, and an Umayyad refugee, Abd-al-Rahman I (756–788), successfully overcame rivals to establish the **emirate** of Cordoba.

Entrepôt The growth of long-distance trade developed around a European network of **entrepôts**, major ports and trading communities that were generally international in character, importing and exporting goods and engaged in trade and manufacture. The term '**emporia**' or '**emporium**' may also be used to refer to such major trading communities and marketplaces, serving as nodal points in long-distance trade networks.

Germanic Roman writers never fully defined the area that they referred to as *Germania*, but it was the area dominated by the North German Plain, drained by the rivers Weser, Elbe, Oder and Vistula; beyond the frontiers of the Roman Empire, it was that part of Europe that stretched from the Rhine and Danube valleys to the North Sea and the Baltic. The term 'German' was applied by the Romans rather than by the people who lived in this area, but the word '**Germanic**' is generally used to refer collectively to these peoples, defined philologically and also archaeologically by their material cultures, thereby also adding southern Scandinavia to the Germanic territories. The people who Bede tells us came to Britain, the Angles, Saxons, Jutes and Frisians, all originated in this area. The **Angles** may be associated with southern Scandinavia, as may the **Jutes** with the northern part of the Danish peninsula; the **Saxons** may be placed particularly in the area between the rivers Elbe and Weser, and the **Frisians** with the Dutch coastal plain.

Genomes   Genomes are an organism's complete set of DNA, including all of its genes. DNA, or deoxyribonucleic acid, is a molecule that carries the genetic characteristics of living organisms. Genome-wide association studies investigate common genetic variants.

Grubenhäuser A German term that refers to buildings whose construction included digging out the interior floor area to below ground level, creating literally 'pit-houses' dug out of the earth. The sunken nature of these interiors has given rise to an alternative term for buildings of this type, '**sunken featured buildings**' or '**SFBs**', a term often considered to be less nuanced than the German word *Grubenhäuser*.

Insular   Deriving from the Latin '*insula*' meaning 'island', the term **insular** is regularly applied to denote Great Britain and Ireland in the post-Roman period. The term is often used in association with Insular Celtic languages, and most commonly in the context of Insular Art, another term for Hiberno-Saxon art (see 'Celtic').

Lindsey   The name **Lindsey** is now found as a modern district-name, applied to the northern and eastern parts of Lincolnshire (with Kesteven and Holland) but it has its historical and linguistic origins in the Anglo-Saxon kingdom name, *Lindissi*, which in turn is thought to derive from a British word; although the name Lindsey is commonly used of the Anglo-Saxon kingdom, *Lindissi* was originally larger than its modern descendant.

Open Fields The terms 'open field' and 'common field' have sometimes been treated as interchangeable as both were 'open' in the sense that neither were internally divided by physical barriers, but important distinctions can be made based on layout and organisation. **Open Fields**, occurring across most of England, might be found in a wide range of layouts, often but not necessarily further divided into furlongs, and usually into strips (selions). In open field systems the distribution of holdings was uneven, sometimes in blocks rather than intermingled, and in which the lord's arable was often held in a block outside of the open fields. **Common Fields** were geographically more restricted to central and southern England, being a specialised form of open field; they were characterised by the presence of furlongs and strips in two or three fields of similar size, the intermingling of holdings, so that the lord's and tenants' strips were fairly equally distributed across the fields, and a strong communal regulation of cropping.

Viking   From the late eighth century the people of Scandinavia poured out from their homelands and expanded in all directions in the pursuit of trade, plunder and land to settle. Characterised by their ships that allowed them to penetrate deep into the lands that they raided, they struck fear across Christian Europe and beyond. The word '**viking**' has become a term of convenience, associated with the Old Norse noun *viking* meaning piracy or a pirate raid, and *vikingr* meaning a pirate or raider. Contemporaries frequently referred to them as Northmen or pagans, or by the countries from which they came. Those who raided and then settled England were predominantly Danes, with Norwegians in the far north and west of Britain.

Further Reading

Abbreviations

ASE	*Anglo-Saxon England*
ASSAH	*Anglo-Saxon Studies in Archaeology and History*
BWAS	*Birmingham and Warwickshire Archaeological Society*
EHR	*English Historical Review*
HWM	*History West Midlands*
SAHS	*Staffordshire Archaeological and Historical Society*

General

References with reading relevant to several chapters in this book.

Michael Alexander, *Beowulf* (Harmondsworth, 1973).

Steven Bassett (ed), *The Origins of Anglo-Saxon Kingdoms* (LUP, 1989).

M.P. Brown and C.A. Farr (eds), *Mercia. An Anglo-Saxon Kingdom in Europe* (LUP, 2001).

James Campbell (ed), *The Anglo-Saxons* (Phaidon, 1982).

Ann Dornier (ed), *Mercian Studies* (LUP, 1977).

G. Garmonsway, *The Anglo-Saxon Chronicle* (Dent, 1972 repr.).

Margaret Gelling, *The West Midlands in the Early Middle Ages* (LUP, 1992).

Nicholas Higham and Martin Ryan, *The Anglo-Saxon World* (YUP, 2013).

John Hunt, 'The Rise and Fall of the Kingdom of Mercia' (*HWM*, Autumn 2014).

D.P. Kirby, *The Earliest English Kings* (Unwin Hyman, 1991).

R.E. Latham, *Bede. A History of the English Church and Peoples* (Harmondsworth, 1979).

Ann Williams, *Kingship and Government in Pre-Conquest England, c.500–1066* (Macmillan, 1999).

Barbara Yorke, *Kings and Kingdoms of Early Anglo-Saxon England* (Seaby, 1990).

Chapter 1

Margaret Gelling, *Signposts to the Past* (Dent, 1978).

Margaret Gelling, *Place-Names in the Landscape* (Dent, 1984).

Della Hooke, 'Locating Another Age. Place-Names in the West Midlands' (*HWM*, Autumn 2014).

Chapter 2

Martin Carver *et al*, *Wasperton. A Roman, British and Anglo-Saxon Community in Central England* (Boydell, 2009).

Vera Evison and Prue Hill, *Two Anglo-Saxon Cemeteries at Beckford, Hereford and Worcester.* (CBA Research Report 103, CBA, 1996).

William Ford, 'Anglo-Saxon Cemeteries along the Avon Valley' (*BWAS*, 100, 1996).

William Ford, 'The Romano-British and Anglo-Saxon Settlement and Cemeteries at Stretton-on-Fosse, Warwickshire' (*BWAS*, 106, 2002).

Della Hooke, 'The Post-Roman and the Early Medieval Periods in the West Midlands: a Potential Archaeological Agenda', in Sarah Watt (ed), *The Archaeology of the West Midlands. A Framework for Research* (Oxbow, 2011).

Chapter 3

Nicholas Brooks 'The Formation of the Mercian Kingdom' in Bassett (ed) (1989).

Damian Tyler 'An Early Mercian Hegemony: Penda and Overkingship in the Seventh Century' (*Midland History*, 30, 2005).

Chapter 4

Bertram Colgrave, *Felix's Life of Saint Guthlac* (CUP, 1956 pbk. 1985).

D.H. Farmer (ed), *The Age of Bede* (Harmondsworth, 1983).

Warwick Rodwell, Jane Hawkes, Emily Howe and Rosemary Cramp, 'The Lichfield Angel: a Spectacular Anglo-Saxon Sculpture' (*Antiquaries Journal*, 88, 2008).

David Rollason, *Saints and Relics in Anglo-Saxon England* (Blackwell, 1989).

Andrew Sargent, 'Religion and Politics in the Kingdom of Mercia. The Lands of Saint Chad' (*HWM*, Autumn 2014).

Alan Thacker, 'Kings, Saints and Monasteries in Pre-Viking Mercia' (*Midland History*, 10, 1985).

Barbara Yorke, *The Conversion of Britain. Religion, Politics and Society in Britain c.600–800* (Harlow, 2006).

Chapter 5

Richard Hodges, *The Anglo-Saxon Achievement. Archaeology and the Beginnings of English Society* (York, 1974).

Chapter 6

Stephen Allott, *Alcuin of York – his Life and Letters* (York, 1974).

Steven Bassett, 'Divide and rule? The Military Infrastructure of Eighth- and Ninth-century Mercia' (*Early Medieval Europe*, 15, 2007).

Steven Bassett, 'Anglo-Saxon Fortifications in Western Mercia' (*Midland History*, 36, i, 2011).

Simon Keynes and Michael Lapidge, *Alfred the Great. Asser's Life of King Alfred and other Contemporary Sources* (Harmondsworth, 1983).

Damien Tyler, 'Offa's Dyke: a Historiographical Appraisal' (*Journal of Medieval History*, 37, 2011).

Damien Tyler, 'Offa's Dyke. A Symbol of Kingship?' (*HWM*, Autumn 2014).

John Williams, Michael Shaw and Varian Denham, *Middle Saxon Palaces at Northampton* (Northampton, 1985).

Chapter 7

Julian Ayre and Robin Wroe-Brown, 'The Post-Roman Foreshore and the Origins of the Late Anglo-Saxon Waterfront and Dock of Æthelred's Hithe: Excavations at Bull Wharf, City of London' (*Archaeological Journal*, 172, 2015).

Robert Cowie, 'Mercian London' in M.P. Brown and C.A. Farr (eds), *Mercia. An Anglo-Saxon Kingdom in Europe* (LUP, 2001).

Jeremy Haslam, 'King Alfred, Mercia and London, 874–86: A Reassessment (*ASSAH*, 17, 2011).

J.R. Maddicott, 'London and Droitwich, *c.* 650–750: Trade, Industry and the Rise of Mercia (*ASE*, 34, 2005).

Janet L. Nelson, 'Carolingian Contacts' in M.P. Brown and C.A. Farr (eds), *Mercia. An Anglo-Saxon Kingdom in Europe* (LUP, 2001).

Martin Welch, 'The Archaeology of Mercia' in M.P. Brown and C.A. Farr (eds), *Mercia. An Anglo-Saxon Kingdom in Europe* (LUP, 2001).

Chapter 8

Steve Bagshaw, Richard Bryant and Michael Hare, 'The Discovery of an Anglo-Saxon Painted Figure at St Mary's Church, Deerhurst, Gloucestershire' (*The Antiquaries Journal*, 86, 2006).

Michelle P. Brown, 'Mercian Manuscripts? The Tiberius Group and Its Historical Context' in M.P. Brown and C.A. Farr (eds) *Mercia. An Anglo-Saxon Kingdom in Europe* (LUP, 2001).

Further Reading

Michelle P. Brown, *The Book of Cerne. Prayer, Patronage and Power in Ninth-Century England* (British Library, 1996).

Michelle P. Brown, *Manuscripts from the Anglo-Saxon Age* (British Library, 2007).

Ann Dornier 'The Anglo-Saxon monastery at Breedon-on-the-Hill, Leicestershire', in Ann Dornier (ed), *Mercian Studies* (LUP, 1977).

Richard Gem, Emily Howe and Richard Bryant, 'The Ninth-Century Polychrome Decoration at St Mary's Church, Deerhurst', (*The Antiquaries Journal* 88, 2008).

Jane Hawkes, 'Constructing Iconographies: Questions of Identity in Mercian Sculpture' in M.P. Brown and C.A. Farr (eds), *Mercia. An Anglo-Saxon Kingdom in Europe* (LUP, 2001).

Richard Jewell, 'Classicism of Southumbrian Sculpture' in M.P. Brown and C.A. Farr (eds), *Mercia. An Anglo-Saxon Kingdom in Europe* (LUP, 2001).

Catherine E. Karkov, *The Art of Anglo-Saxon England* (Boydell, 2011).

Warwick Rodwell, Jane Hawkes, Emily Howe and Rosemary Cramp, 'The Lichfield Angel: a Spectacular Anglo-Saxon Painted Sculpture' (*The Antiquaries Journal*, 88, 2008).

Leslie Webster, 'Metalwork of the Mercian Supremacy' in M.P. Brown and C.A. Farr (eds), *Mercia. An Anglo-Saxon Kingdom in Europe* (LUP, 2001).

Leslie Webster, *Anglo-Saxon Art. A New History* (British Museum, 2012).

Chapter 9

Stephen Allott, *Alcuin of York – his Life and Letters* (York, 1974).

Martin Biddle and Birthe Kjølbye-Biddle, 'Repton and the Vikings' (*Antiquity* 66, No 250, March 1992).

Martin Biddle and Birthe Kjølbye-Biddle, 'Repton and the 'great heathen army', 873–4', in James Graham-Campbell, Richard Hall, Judith Jesch & David N Parsons (eds), *Vikings and the Danelaw: Papers from the Proceedings of the Thirteenth Viking Congress, Nottingham and York, 21–30 August 1997: Select Papers from the Proceedings of the Thirteenth Viking Congress* (Oxbow 2001).

Chapter 10

Kenneth Cameron, *Place-name Evidence for the Anglo-Saxon Invasion and Scandinavian Settlements. Eight studies collected by Kenneth Cameron* (Nottingham, 1977).

Nicola Cumberledge, 'Reading Between the Lines: the Place of Mercia within an Expanding Wessex' (*Midland History*, XXVII, 2002).

R. H. C. Davis, 'Alfred and Guthrum's Frontier' (*EHR*, 1982).

Anne Dodd *et al*, 'Excavations at Tipping Street, Stafford, 2009-10' (*SAHS Transactions*, XLVII, 2014).

Simon Keynes, 'King Alfred and the Mercians', in Mark Blackburn and David Dumville (eds), *Kings, Currency and Alliances. History and Coinage of Southern England in the Ninth Century* (Woodbridge 1998).

Pauline Stafford, *The East Midlands in the Early Middle Ages* (LUP, 1985).

Pauline Stafford, *Unification and Conquest. A Political and Social History of England in the Tenth and Eleventh Centuries* (Arnold, 1989).

Pauline Stafford, 'The Annals of Æthelflaed: Annals, History and Politics in Early Tenth-Century England', in J. Barrow and A. Wareham (eds), *Myth, Rulership, Church and Charters. Essays in Honour of Nicholas Brooks* (Ashgate, 2008).

Sheila Waddington, 'The Anglo-Saxon Origins of the West Midlands Shires' (*HWM*, Autumn 2014).

Ann Williams, '*Princeps Merciorum gentis*: the Family, Career and Connections of Ælfhere, Ealdorman of Mercia, 956–83' (*ASE*, 10, 1981).

Chapter 11

Guy Beresford, *Goltho. The Development of an Early Medieval Manor c.850–1150* (English Heritage, 1987).

Andy Boddington, *Raunds Furnells. The Anglo-Saxon Church and Churchyard* (English Heritage, 1996).

Andy Chapman, *West Cotton, Raunds. A Study of Medieval Settlement Dynamics, AD 450–1450. Excavation of a Deserted Medieval Hamlet in Northamptonshire 1985-89* (Oxbow, 2010).

Helena Hamerow, 'The Development of Anglo-Saxon Rural Settlement Forms' (*Landscape History*, 31, i, 2010).

Gill Hey, *Yarnton. Saxon and Medieval Settlement and Landscape* (Oxford, 2004).

Della Hooke, *England's Landscape. The West Midlands* (English Heritage, 2006).

Stuart Losco-Bradley and Gavin Kinsley, *Catholme. An Anglo-Saxon Settlement on the Trent Gravels in Staffordshire* (Nottingham, 2002).

David Parsons and D.S.Sutherland, *The Anglo-Saxon Church of All Saints Brixworth, Northamptonshire. Survey, Excavation and Analysis 1972–2010* (Oxbow, 2013).

Chapter 12

Stephen Baxter, *The Earls of Mercia. Lordship and Power in Late Anglo-Saxon England* (OUP, 2007).

John Hunt, 'Land Tenure and Lordship in Tenth and Eleventh Century Staffordshire' (*Staffordshire Studies*, Volume 4, 1991-2).

John Hunt, 'Piety, Prestige or Politics? The House of Leofric and the Foundation and Patronage of Coventry Priory', in G. Demidowicz (ed), *Coventry's First Cathedral. The Cathedral and Priory of St Mary* (Stamford, 1994).

Pauline Stafford, *The East Midlands in the Early Middle Ages* (LUP, 1985).

Websites

The Electronic Sawyer. Online catalogue of Anglo-Saxon Charters
http://www.esawyer.org.uk/charter/96.html

Early English Laws
http://www.earlyenglishlaws.ac.uk/laws/texts

St Chad Gospels, Lichfield
https://lichfield.as.uky.edu/st-chad-gospels/gallery

Index

Note: italics denote images.

Abbots Bromley, Staffordshire 142, 144–5

Abingdon, Berkshire 101

Abingdon Abbey, Oxfordshire *116*

'*Adventus Saxonum*' 19

Ælfflaed, Queen of Mercia *30*, 107

Ælfhere, ealdorman 124

Ælfwald, King of East Anglia 58

Æthelbald, King of Mercia 10, *30*, 48, 49, *49*, 50–1, 53, *54*, 55, 56, *56*, 57–62, *59*, 67, 69, 70, 71–2, 77, 87, 101–2, 115

Æthelberht, King of East Anglia 63, 64, 65

Æthelberht, King of Kent 43, 47, 62

Æthelflæd, Lady of the Mercians *116*, 118, 120–1, *126*, 126–7

Æthelheard, Archbishop of Canterbury 109, 110

Æthelhere, King of East Anglia 33, 35

Æthelred, King of Northumbria 64

Æthelred, Lord of the Mercians 118, 120, 123, 124, 134

Æthelred, Saint, King of Mercia *30*, 36–7, 41, 48, 49, 51, 56, 107, 112

Æthelred II, King of England ('Æthelred the Unready') 125, 142, *143*, 145–6

Æthelred Mucil, ealdorman 112

Æthelric 48, 58, 99

agriculture 11–12, *12*, *128*, 129, 135–8, *137*

Alban, Saint *63*, *70*, 71

Alcester, Warwickshire *5*

Alcuin, scholar 65, *68*, 69, 70, 72, 74, 82, 83, 85, 105

Alfred, King of Wessex 10, 72, 75, 89, 112, 113, 117, *118*, 126, *126*, 133

All Saints Church, Brixworth *47*, *95*, 96

Alveston, Warwickshire 21, *21*, 23, 149

Anglo-Saxon Chronicle 18–19, 108–9, 113, 117, 125, *126*, 126–7, *127*

Anna, King of East Anglia 31, 33

Annals of Æthelflæd 126, 127

archdiocese 55, 64–5, 110–11

architecture 93, 94–5, *95*

aristocracy 11, 48, 50–1, 88, 124, 133, 145–6

art 13, 93–102, *94*, *95*, *96*, *97*, *98*, *100*

Ashdown, Berkshire 112

Ashingdon, Essex, battle 125

Asser, scholar 69, 79

Atcham, Shropshire *74*, 76

Athelstan, King of England 122, 127

Avon valley 17, 20, 22, 24

'B dynasty' 107, 108

Baginton, Warwickshire 21, *21*, 22, *22*

Baldred, King of Kent 109

Bamberg Bible 68

Barberini Gospels 97, 100

barrows 20–1, *21*, 101

Basing, Hampshire 112

Basingwerk, Cheshire 110

Bassett, Steven 77

Beckford, Worcestershire 20, *20*, 21, *21*, 24

Bede 19, 27, 29, 31, 34, 35, 36–7, 43, 44, 45, 52–3, 60, 67, 74, 90

Benty Grange helmet 101

Beonna, King of East Anglia 67

Beorhtfrith 107, 108

Beorhtwulf, King of Mercia 107, 109

Beornred, King of Mercia 62

Beornwulf, King of Mercia 107, 108, 109, 110, 111

Beowulf 7, 12, 38–9, 75

Berhtwald 107

Berkshire 64, 109

Bibles *28*, *46*, 70–1, *71*, 72, 94

Bidford-on-Avon, Warwickshire 20, *21*, 23, 88

Boethius 72

Boniface, Saint 13, 56–7, *59*, 60–1, 69, 75

Book of Cerne 98, 99, 100

Book of Nunnaminster 100

books *92*, 98, 99–100

bracteates (pendants) 22

Brandon, Suffolk *92*, 100, 101

Bredon, Worcestershire *45*, 49

Breedon-on-the-Hill, Leicestershire *45*, 48, 59, 83, 97, *97*

'bretwaldas' (kings) 29

Bristol *76*

Brixworth, Northamptonshire *45*, *47*, *95*, 96, 131

brooches *16*, 20, 21–2, *22*, 23, *23*, 101, 102

Brooks, Nicholas 31

Burghal Hidage 89

Burghred, King of Mercia 87, 107, 112, 113

burhs 13, 89–91, *90*, 120–3

burial sites 13, *20*, 20–5, *21*, *22*, *23*, 129, 134

Burton Abbey, Staffordshire 142, 148

Byzantine era 41, 53, 73, 77, 97, 98–9, 100

'C dynasty' 107

Cadwallon, warlord 31

Canterbury, Kent 43, 51, 58, 59, 64, 65, 67, 72, 105, 112; Archbishops 37, 44, 45, 59, 73, 109, 110

Caradog, King of Gwynedd 110

Carolingian Empire 65, *71*, 72, 73, 81, 83–5, 88, 93, 96, 97, 99, 102

Castor, Peterborough, carvings *13*, 97

Catholme, Staffordshire 24, 132–3, *133*, *134*

Cearl 29

cemeteries 13, *20*, 20–5, *21*, *22*, *23*, 129, 134

Cenwealh, King of Wessex 33, 105

Ceolfrith, abbot 49, 94

Ceolfrith Bibles 94

Ceolred, King of Mercia *30*, 56–7

Ceolwald *30*, 57

Ceolwulf I, King of Mercia *30*, 105–7, 110, 117

Ceolwulf II, King of Mercia *30*, 107, 113

ceramics 21; *see also* pottery

Chad, Saint 8, 45, 52–3, 64, 65, 99; *Gospels of St Chad* 103, *103*

Charlemagne (Charles I), Emperor and King of the Franks 69–70, *81*, 81–6

Charles II the Bald, King of the Franks *71*, 72

Chelsea, Middlesex 64, 75, 99, 101, 110

Chertsey Abbey, Surrey 36, 87

Chester, Cheshire 51, *76*, 77, 120

Christianity 7, 11, 13, 25, 27, 34, 35, 40, 43–8, *45*, 51, *55*, 69–72, 81, 93, 101

Church 7, 43–51, *45*, *46*, 57, *59*, 60–2, 69–72, 75, 94–7, *95*, 96, 99, 140, 145, *146*; *see also* Roman Church

Cirencester, Gloucestershire 19, 31, 43, 96

class, social 130–1, 138

Cnebba *30*

Cnut (Canute), King of Denmark and England 108, 125, 140, *141*, 142, 146

Codex Bigotianus 100

Coenred, King of Mercia *30*, 56, 108

Coenwulf, King of Mercia 10, *30*, 69, 72, 75, 79, 105–7, 108, 109, 110–11

coins 12, 59, 66, 66–7, 70, 83, 87, 88, 89, 109, 112, 113, 122, *123*, 142

Coln Rogers church, Gloucestershire *146*

'common' fields 136, *137*

Cookham, Berkshire 64

Coppergate helmet, York 101

court and courtiers 69–75, *71*, *73*, *74*

Creoda 29, *30*

Crowland, Lincolnshire 50, 51, 70

Cuthbert 59

Cuthred, King of Kent 59, 109

Cwenthryth, Abbess of Minster-in-Thanet 105

Cyneberht, ealdorman 49, 58

Cynewald *30*

Cynewulf, King of Wessex 64, 72

Danegeld 95

Danelaw 117–20, *119*, 125

Danes 10, 14–15, *104*, 112–13, 115, 117, *118*, *119*, 120, 121, 122, 123, 125, 126–7, 142, 144–5, 146–7

'Dark Ages' 17

Deerhurst, Gloucestershire *45*, 96–7, 98

Degannwy, Gwynedd 110

Derby, Derbyshire *76*, 118, 121, 122, 123

dioceses 7, 43, 44, *45*, 45–7, 51, 55, 151

Diuma, priest 44

Dobunni, tribe 17

Domesday Book 87, 89, 137, 148, 149, 151

Drayton, Oxfordshire 76

dress adornments 93, *94*, 101, 102; *see also* brooches

Droitwich, Worcestershire 12, 58, 87, 88, 129

Dyfed 110

Eadberht Praen, King of Kent 84, 109

Eadric Streona 124, 125, 146

Eadwald, King of East Anglia 109

ealdormen 75, 105, 124, 142

Ealdred, King of Hwicce 58

Ealhhelm, ealdorman 124

Ealhswith 112, 142

Eanulf *30*, 49, 57

Eardwulf, King of Northumbria 84

earls 11, 124, 142, *144*, 146, 148–9, 151

Earls Barton, Northamptonshire *139*, 140

East Anglia 9, *9*, 19–20, 24, 31, 33, 34, 35, 36, 41, 43, *55*, 58–9, 60, 62, 64, 65, 67, 107, 108, 109, 112, 113, 121, 125, 142

Ecgberht, King of Kent 62, 64, 84, 108, 109

Ecgfrith, King of Mercia 27, *30*, 65, 70, 85, 105

economy 12, 88, 129–31, 137; *see also* trade

Edmund, Saint, King of East Anglia *104*, *108*, 112, 122, 124, 130, 144

Edward the Confessor, King of England 136–7, 142, 149

Edward the Elder, King of Wessex 10, 121–2, 127

Edwin, Earl of Mercia 149–51

Edwin, King of Northumbria 29, 31, 43

Eigenkirchen ('family churches') 48–50

Einhard, scholar 81–2

Ellendun, battle 108, 109

Emma of Normandy *141*

Eowa 29, *30*, 33, 57

estates 11, 12, 75–7, 87, 129, 133–4, 136–40, *139*, *140*, 145–6, 148, 149–51

Evesham, Worcestershire *45*, 48, 94, 108, 124, 136, 149, 150

farming *see* agriculture

Fetter Lane, London, sword hilt *100*, 101

fields, 'open' and 'common' 136, *137*

fisheries 138

'Five Boroughs', fortified centres 117–18, 122

Fladbury, Worcestershire *45*, 48

Flixborough, Lincolnshire 139

Flores Historiarum 19–20

fonts 97

fortifications 14, *14*, *76*, 77, 89, 120–3, 140, *140*

Frankish Empire 60, 61, 67, 69–70, *71*, 77, 81–3, *82*, *83*, 85–6, 105

Gandersheim Casket, Peterborough 102

Gervold, Abbot of Saint-Wandrille 83, 85

Gildas, scholar 19

Gloucester, Gloucestershire 43, *76*, 77, 89, 113, 118, 123; St Oswald's church *8*, 120, *121*

Godiva (Godgifu), Countess of Mercia *144*, 146, *147*, 148

Godwin, Earl of Wessex 142

Goltho, Lincolnshire 140, *140*

Gospels of Saint Willibrord 103

Gospels of Saint Chad (Lichfield Gospels) 103, *103*

Graveney boat *83*

Gregory I, Pope 43, 44, 47, 48, 110

Grubenhäuser ('pit-houses') 131, *132*, *134*

Gumley, Leicestershire 71–2

Guthlac, Saint 13, *38*, 39, 50, *50*, *54*, 56, *56*, 57, 58, 70, 102

Guthrum 113, 117, 118

Gwynedd, Wales 31, 34, 35, 37, 110

Hadrian, Pope 72

Halfdan 113

Hanbury, Staffordshire 51

Hanbury, Worcestershire *14*, 15

Harold I 'Harefoot', King of England 146

Harold II, Godwinsson, King of England 142, 149–50

Hatfield Chase, battle 31, *32*

Heahberht, King of Kent 62

Heardberht 57

Heavenfield, battle 31, 32

helmets 40, 101

Hemming, monk 94–5, 148, 151

Henry of Huntingdon, scholar 19–20

Hereford, Herefordshire 15, 33, 45, 59, 62, 64, 76, 77, 89, 123, 148

Hinton St Mary, Dorset 43

Historia Anglorum 19–20

Hwicce 17, 31, 33, 35, 37, 45, 48, 58, 65, 113, 124

Icel 27, 29, *30*

Iclingas, royal kin 27, 29, *30*

Ine, King of Wessex 57, 130, 132

Inkberrow, Worcestershire *45*, 49

Ismere 49, *49*, 58, 152

Jaenberht, Archbishop of Canterbury 64, 67, 72, 110

Jewell, Richard 97

John, Eric 108

Kent 37, 41, 47, *55*, 57, 58, 59, 60, 62–5, 72, 84, 105, 108, 109, 110, 129–30

Keynes, Simon 120

Kidderminster, Worcestershire *45*, 49, 152

kin 11, 27, 29, *30*, 33, 37, 47, 48–9, 51, 56, 72, 77, 105, 130–1

kingdoms 11, 17, 27, 28–34, *32*, 36, 37, 43, 127

King's Men 72–5

kingship 10, 11, 33–5, 47, 55, 69–70, 72, 75, 77, 81, 107, 108

Kirby, David 110

landscape 7, 129, 135–6, *137*

language 14–15

laws 75, 83, 129–31, 132, 133

learning 74–5, 100

Leicester, Leicestershire 64, *76*, 77, 95, 97, *102*, 117–18, 121, 122

Leo III, Pope 81, 110, 153

Leofric, Earl of Mercia *144*, 145, 146, *147*, 148, 149

Leofwine, House of, Earls of Mercia, 146–9, *147*

Liber Vitae 141

Lichfield, Staffordshire 8, 43, 45, 53, *55*, 57, 64–5, 72, 95, 98, 99, 100, 110, 131

Lichfield Gospels 103, *103*

Life of Saint Alban 63

Life of Wilfrid 36, 152

Lincoln, Lincolnshire *76*, 77, 95, 118, 123

Lindisfarne, Northumbria 44, 103

Lindsey 34, 37, 44, 45, 58, 64, 65, 123

Little Oxendon, Northamptonshire *137*

Londinium 90, 90–1

London 36, 58–9, 65, 67, *76*, 77, 86, 86–91, *90*, *100*, 101, 110, 112, 121

Longbridge Park, Warwickshire *16*, 22

Ludeca, King of Mercia 107, 109

Lundenwic 90, 90–1

Magonsæte 33, 37, 43, 45, 51, 58, 65, 122, 125

Maldon, battle 7

Malmesbury, Wiltshire *45*, 48

Mannig, Abbot of Evesham 94

manorial sites and society 11, 129, 136–40, *137, 139, 140*, 145, 151

manufacturing 12, 86, 87–9, 91, 139

manuscripts 8, 25, *26*, *38*, 41, *50*, *56*, *63*, 74, 93, 94, *98*, 99–100, 102, 103, *103, 104, 108, 116, 118, 126*, 126–7, *127, 128*

Mercian Register 118, *121*, 126–7, *127*

Merewalh, King of the Magonsæte 33, 43, 51, 58

metalwork 8, 12, 23, 40–1, 88, 91, 93, 99, 100, 102, 132

Middle Angles 33, 44–7, 58, 65

Middlesex 56, 59, 109

migration 17, 19, 25, 41

millstones *84*, 85

Minster-in-Thanet, Kent 59, 105, 110

minsters *45*, 48, 50, 51, 57, 61, 70, 71, 89, 129, 133, 140, 151 missionaries 44, 47–8, 60, 82

monasteries 13, 35–6, 43, 48, 57, 61, 71, 87, 88, 94–5, 110, 124, 140, 151

monks 48, 61, 94–5, 148, 151

Much Wenlock, Shropshire 35, 51, 56, 95, 118

Norman Conquest 11, 15, 142, *144*, 149–51

Northampton, Northamptonshire *73, 76, 76*, 77, 89, 93, 118, 121, 146

Northumbria *9, 9*, 29, 31, 33, 34, 36, 44, 60, 67, 73, 112–13, 122

Nothelm, priest 59

Nottingham, Nottinghamshire *76*, 77, 89, 112, 118, 121, 123

Ofa (Oba) 57

Offa, King of Mercia 10, *30*, 49, 55, 56, 58, 60, 62–5, *63, 64, 66*, 67, 69–71, 72, 74–5, 77, 81, 83–5, 94–5, 96, 105, 108–9, 110

Offa's Dyke *61, 62, 78, 79*

Olaf Guthfrithsson 122, *123*, 124

Old Oswestry, Shropshire, battle *32*, 33

'open' fields 136, *137*

Oswald, King of Northumbria 27, 31, 33

Oswald, Saint 120

Oswiu, King of Northumbria 27, 35, 44

Oswulf, ealdorman 108

paganism 13, 19, 20, *21*, 34, 41, 48, 105, 112

Paschal I, Pope 110

patronage 94–5, 96

Peada, King of Mercia *30*, 35, 37, 44, 57

Peak District 20, 21, *21*

peasants 133–4

Penda, King of Mercia 29, *30*, 31–5, 37, 41, 51, 56, 105, 107, 108

Peter, Saint 70

Peterborough, Northamptonshire *13*, 36, 97, 100, 102

Peterborough Chronicle 62

pit-houses (*Grubenhäuser*) 131, *132, 134*

place-names 14–15, 43

Pope Gregory I 43, 44, 47, 48, 110

Pope Hadrian 72

Pope Leo III 81, 110, 153

Pope Paschal I 110

Pope Vitalian 45

pottery 89, 91, 135, 139

Powys 33, 34, 37, 79, 110, 112

priests 44, 48, 59, 61, 69, 72–3

Pybba, father of Penda 29, *30*

Raunds, Northamptonshire 131, 135, 140

Reculver, Kent 110

reeves 73, 75

relics *52, 52*–3

Repton, Derbyshire 8, *38*, 50–1, *52, 53, 54*, 101, 108, *111*, 113, *114*, 114–15

Rights and Ranks of People 136–7

Rochester, Kent 59, 62, 67

Roman Britain 6, 8, 14, 17–19, *21*, 22, 23, 43, 77, 83, *90*, 90–1, 95, 108, 136

Roman Church 11, 12–13, 34, 37, 43–5, *45*, 47, 51, 81, 83, 96; *see also* Church

Runcorn, Cheshire *76*, 121

St Alban's, Hertfordshire *70*, 71

St Brice's Day Massacre *124*, 125

St Frideswide, Oxford 125

St John's College, Oxford *124*, 125

St Oswald's, Gloucester 8, 120, *121*

St Peter's, Bredon 49

St Peter's, Gloucester 121

St Peter's, Lichfield 53

saints 13, 29, 36–7, 43, *45, 50*, 50–3, *51, 52*, 99

salt 12, 58, 86, 87, 88, 129

Sandbach, Cheshire *96*, 99

scriptoria 60, 72, 99–100

sculpture 8, 53, *81*, 83, 96–9, *97*, 100, 102

settlements 131–40, *132, 133, 134, 139, 140*

Severn valley 118

sheep farming 87, 129, 135, 137, 138, 139

shires 7, 10, 58, 89, 122–3, 151

Shrewsbury, Shropshire 76, 89, 123

slavery 39, 86, 130, 133, 138

South Saxons 36, *55*, 64

Stafford, Pauline 123

Stafford, Staffordshire 76, 89, 121, 123, 150

Staffordshire Hoard 12, 13, *40*, 40–1, *42*, 94, 101

Stamford, Lincolnshire 118, 123

stone carving 8, *8*, 53, *81*, 97, *97*, 100, 101, 102

Stretton-on-Fosse, Warwickshire 23–4

sub-kings 36, 58

sunken featured buildings (SFBs) 131, *132*, *134*

Sutton Hoo, Suffolk *36*, 39, 40, 101

swords 100, *100*

Synod of Chelsea 99

Synod of Whitby 43–4, 51

Tamworth, Staffordshire 8, *9*, 62, 75, *76*, 77, *84*, 89, 117, 121, 123

tanning industry 86, 91

Tatwine, priest 59

'T' (tau) cross head, Alcester *5*

taxation 85, 87, 89

textiles 24, 86, 91, 129, 131, *134*, 135, 140

Theodore of Tarsus, Archbishop of Canterbury 37, 45, *45*

Tiberius Miscellany 100, *128*, *130*

trade 66–7, 81, *82*, *83*, *84*, 85–9, 91

Trent valley 7, 8, 20, *21*, 24, 115, 132

Tribal Hidage 25–7, *26*, 33

Tyler, Damian 34

Vikings 10, 88–9, 105, *106*, *108*, *111*, 112–15, *114*, 117, *119*, 120, 122, 125

villages *132*, 135–6, 151

vills 75, 129

Vitalian, Pope 45

Vortigern, warlord 17, 19

Wales 50, 60, 62, 79, 103, 109, 122

warriors 33, *38*, 38–9, *63*, 101

Warwick, Warwickshire *16*, 22, 89, 121, 123, 150, *150*

Wasperton, Warwickshire 20, 21, *21*, 23, *23*, 24

Watlington, Oxfordshire 113

Wat's Dyke *76*, 79

weaving *see* textiles

'*wergeld*' ('blood-price'), value system 129–31

Wessex 9, *9*, 10, 27, 29, 31, 34, 36, 37, *55*, 56, 57, 59, 62, 64, 73, 89, 107, 108–9, 112, 113, 117, 120, 122, 124, 126, 127, 130, 144, 145

West Stow, Suffolk 131, *132*

Wiglaf, King of Mercia 51, 53, 107, 108, 109

Wigmund *30*, 107

Wigstan, Saint *30*, 51, 53, 107–8

Wihtred, King of Kent 57

Wilfrid, Saint 36, 45, 82, 152

William of Malmesbury, scholar 69

Winchcombe, Gloucestershire 51, 76, 77, 105, 108, 109, 123

Wing, Buckinghamshire 97

Winwaed, battle *32*, 35, 37

Witham River, Lincolnshire, dress-pin set 93, *94*, 102

Withington, Gloucestershire *45*, 49

Wolverhampton, historic Staffordshire 15, 102, 142

wool 67, 129

Wootton Wawen, Warwickshire *45*, 48

Worcester, Worcestershire 18, 43, 45, *45*, 57, 60, 71, 89, 100, 113, 118–20, 123

Wormald, Patrick 39

Worton, Oxfordshire 131

Wroxeter, Shropshire 18, *18*, 43, 98

Wulfhere, King of Mercia 27, *30*, 35–6, 37, 41, 51, 87, 91, 152

Wulfred, Archbishop of Canterbury 85, 110, 111

Wulfric Spott 142, *143*, 144–6

Wulfrun 15, 142, 144

Wulfsige Maur 144–5

Yarnton, Oxfordshire 131, *132*, 134–5

York 86, 101, 110, 112, 122, *123*, 127

Yorke, Barbara 57, 107

zoomorphic decoration 22, 23, *23*, 93, 102, 103, *103*

The author

Dr John Hunt is an Honorary Research Fellow in the Department of History at the University of Birmingham and a member of the Centre for West Midlands History. His specialisms are medieval lordship and community, landscape and medieval cultural history in England and France, with a focus on the pre- and post-Conquest history of the West Midlands region. He is the author of numerous books and articles on medieval history and archaeology.